Underdogs

ANIMAL VOICES
ANIMAL WORLDS

Robert W. Mitchell, series editor

Underdogs

PETS, PEOPLE, AND POVERTY

Arnold Arluke
Andrew Rowan

The University of Georgia Press
ATHENS

© 2020 by the University of Georgia Press
Athens, Georgia 30602
www.ugapress.org
All rights reserved
Set in 10/13 Kepler Std Regular
by Kaelin Chappell Broaddus

Most University of Georgia Press titles are
available from popular e-book vendors.

Printed digitally

Library of Congress Cataloging-in-Publication Data

Names: Arluke, Arnold, author. | Rowan, Andrew N., author.
Title: Underdogs : pets, people, and poverty / Arnold Arluke,
    Andrew Rowan.
Description: Athens : The University of Georgia Press, [2020] |
    Series: Animal voices : animal worlds | Includes bibliographical
    references and index.
Identifiers: LCCN 2020024756 | ISBN 9780820358239 (hardback) |
    ISBN 9780820358222 (paperback) | ISBN 9780820358246 (ebook)
Subjects: LCSH: Pets—Social aspects—United States. | Pet owners—
    Economic aspects—United States. | Veterinary services—Costs—
    United States. | Animal welfare—United States.
Classification: LCC SF411.43.U6 A75 2020 | DDC 636.088/7—dc23
LC record available at https://lccn.loc.gov/2020024756

CONTENTS

ACKNOWLEDGMENTS   ix

INTRODUCTION Pets, Poverty, and the
Problem of Access to Veterinary Care   1

San Rafael, Costa Rica

ONE Liminal Pets and Their People
*Living With Street Animals in
Traditional Costa Rican Culture*   23

TWO Who Speaks for the Underserved?
*Cooperation and Conflict Among
Welfare and Veterinary Groups*   46

THREE Sterilization as an Agent of Social Change
Changing How Communities Think About Pets   70

West Charlotte, North Carolina

FOUR Underdogs and Their People
Living With Pets in Racially Concentrated Poverty   91

FIVE The "Costs" of Care
*Nonfinancial Barriers to Using Free or
Low-cost Veterinary Services*   115

SIX "Perfect Is the Enemy of Good"
Thinking Differently About Low-income Pet Owners　142

SEVEN Forms of Veterinary Capital
The Unintended Consequences of Increased Access　166

CONCLUSION Increasing Access to Veterinary Care
Problems, Partnerships, and Paradoxes　185

NOTES　209

BIBLIOGRAPHY　217

INDEX　239

ACKNOWLEDGMENTS

Many individuals and organizations helped us to understand how people in or near poverty interact with pets and street dogs and why sometimes it can be difficult to provide them with veterinary care. The shelter workers, volunteers, and veterinarians at the humane societies in West Charlotte, North Carolina, and San Rafael, Costa Rica, shared their experiences working with pet owners or those caring for street animals in disadvantaged communities and allowed us to accompany them when making home visits or when operating mobile sterilization clinics in distant and poor villages. In particular, Bennett Simon and Suzanne D'Alonzo at the Humane Society of Charlotte and Lillian Schnog at El Refugio were always willing to provide know-how for negotiating the local customs, facilitate the many visits to their shelters, and offer helpful insights about the problems people have keeping or caring for dogs and cats when they often have trouble feeding and getting health care for themselves and their families.

Several organizations enabled the first author's fieldwork in Costa Rica and North Carolina. The generous help of the Humane Society of the United States made possible many long-distance field trips to Costa Rica and North Carolina and gave us complete freedom to report our analysis as we called it. Sabbatical support from Northeastern University and funding from the UCLA Animal Law and Policy Small Grants Program also expedited our field research in both locations. The Massachusetts Society for the Prevention of Cruelty to Animals and the Food and Nutrition Resources Foundation made it possible for the first author to study the problems of feeding pets among the poor and how they coped with pet food insecurity.

Several individuals played vital roles at various stages of the research and writing. Jack Levin served as scholarly mentor throughout the project; Kate Atema offered invaluable insights into the community problems of managing street dogs; Hal Herzog pointed out the forest and not just the trees in our first draft; Gary Patronek helped us to unpack the debate about sterilizing pets; Carter Luke and Virginia Aronson encouraged our research on pet food insecurity; Linda Bronfman provided generous funding and inspiration; and Phyllis Langton, as always, served as a beacon of fine scholarship and writing. At the University of Georgia Press, thanks to Beth Snead for providing a perfect mix of structure, flexibility, and guidance throughout the review and revision process and to Joseph Dahm for his careful editing. Finally, Lauren Rolfe's unflagging support for every phase of the project and in every location, whether in Costa Rica, North Carolina, Massachusetts, or Florida, made it possible to write *Underdogs*.

Underdogs

Pets, Poverty, and the Problem of Access to Veterinary Care

Until recently, unwanted animals were the biggest problem facing the humane community in the United States and abroad. Before the 1970s, "intact" dogs and cats were the norm, and it was common to see strays on the street and shelters swamped with unowned dogs and cats. In the early 1970s, a flurry of newspaper reports and academic papers (e.g., Djerassi et al., 1973; Feldman, 1974) called attention to the large number of dogs and cats entering animal shelters every day and then being euthanized because they were not being adopted. For example, in 1973 shelters euthanized an estimated 13.5 million dogs and cats, when their total population was 65 million (Rowan & Williams, 1987).

Following this flurry of media attention, the main humane and veterinary stakeholders in the United States organized conferences in the mid-1970s to discuss what might be done about the crisis of pet overpopulation. Many attendees argued that sterilization or the spaying and neutering of puppies and kittens—surgical procedures that remove ovaries or testicles—could not address the issue because there were just too many unwanted pets and too few sterilizations being performed on these animals. Indeed, in 1970 the rate was very low (only 10% of registered dogs in Los Angeles were sterilized that year), but dissenters at the conferences proposed that it could deal with the problem, through legislation and education, if the rate of sterilization of pet dogs and cats were increased.

By the end of the 1970s, sterilization became an important element of a national campaign, led by the humane movement and some veterinarians, to reduce dog and cat overpopulation. American organizations across the country established sterilization programs to manage the large number of dogs and cats on the street who ended up being euthanized in shelters. Today sterilization has become movement dogma: most dogs and cats are sterilized. Shelters typically require sterilization of all adopted animals before they are taken home, and many states legally mandate it (AVMA, n.d.-a). Those who own a sterilized pet are now dubbed "responsible owners" (Nolo, 2019) who have done their "part" to reduce the number of unwanted animals that are euthanized (AVMA, n.d.-b).

Indeed, the overall problem of unwanted healthy animals being euthanized in shelters is close to nonexistent. In 1973, shelters euthanized 13.5 million animals, representing 20% of the dog and cat population, but by 2016 "only" an estimated 1.8 million animals were euthanized, representing about 1.4% of the pet dog and cat population. Most analysts credit sterilization (whether carried out by individual veterinary practices or nonprofit programs) for the enormous drop in the number of dogs and cats annually euthanized in U.S. shelters (and the decline in the euthanasia of healthy and adoptable animals is even larger). Overall, it is estimated that sterilization is saving over 10 million healthy dogs and cats from an early death every year.

From the Unwanted to the Underserved

With the success of sterilization, public education, and flexible adoption programs in reducing shelter euthanasia in the United States, animal welfare advocates and some veterinarians have started to set their sights on a new problem:[1] the millions of pets receiving little if any veterinary care who live in underserved areas plagued by high rates of unemployment, low educational attainment, and poverty.[2] The estimated 19 million pets living in these communities (HSUS, 2018) are less likely to be sterilized or to be provided with basic veterinary care, such as essential vaccinations and basic checkups. Estimates are that 88% of these pets are unsterilized and 69% have never been seen by a veterinarian (HSUS, 2018). In fact, there is some evidence that the proportion of owned pets in the United States that receive no health care from a veterinary practice has steadily increased in recent years (Stull et al., 2018).

Some veterinarians see this lack of access as the profession's foremost crisis today (Access to Veterinary Care Coalition, 2018), while animal advocates consider it to be a "new frontier" (Arrington & Markarian, 2017) or a "national crisis" causing "hardship and heartache for many pet owners" and a "social justice issue in its own right" (HSUS, n.d.-b). Unsterilized animals reproduce, worsening the overpopulation problem, which puts more animals on the streets in poorer health. Unvaccinated animals are at risk of developing life-threatening or fatal illnesses and of putting humans, if bitten, in danger. And untreated animals suffer from an endless array of medical problems that could be effectively managed, running from fleas to mange.

Providing community outreach and support for pet owners in these communities seem like obvious remedies, but they are still underemphasized and challenging components of "companion animal welfare."[3] Most discussions about accessing or improving companion animal welfare make no mention of getting basic care to dogs and cats in disadvantaged communities and instead concentrate on issues such as prohibiting feline declawing, caring for assistance animals, stopping puppy mills, helping renters with pets, opposing breed-specific legislation, monitoring the showing of pets, promoting "no-kill" shelters, and outlawing the human consumption of dogs. Recent years have seen slow growth in programs, often attached to animal shelters, that provide low- or no-cost basic veterinary services to disadvantaged pet owners, including sterilization but also vaccinations, wellness exams, basic treatments, pet food, and even fences to allow for the unchaining of dogs.

Sterilization remains the driving force in these programs, even though critics of the surgery have surfaced. Publications in the twenty-first century have begun to challenge routine sterilization, arguing that this surgery produces adverse physiological and behavioral changes in dogs and cats. One article (Torres de la Riva et al., 2013) garnered particular attention even though it was not the first to raise questions about the appropriateness of routine sterilization (Nolen, 2013). The authors reported that sterilized golden retrievers experienced an increased incidence of joint disorders and certain cancers. Other studies followed on Labrador retrievers (Hart et al., 2014) and German shepherds (Hart et al., 2016) that also reported increases in joint disorders and cancers in sterilized dogs versus intact ones. A more recent study of golden retrievers found that those spayed or neutered were more likely to be overweight or obese (Simpson et al., 2019).

Results from studies like these have fueled a national debate over the propriety of sterilizing dogs (similar studies have not been made of cats). National newspapers like the *Washington Post* have featured stories about dog owners not sterilizing their pets, even though they had no intention of breeding them, because they felt it to be a healthier option (Brulliard, 2019). These new conversations about the necessity and risk of spaying and neutering pets have led some owners, veterinarians, and critics of the procedure to question whether responsible ownership must include sterilization and whether Americans should not be such casual owners compared with those in Europe, where the surgery is far less common (Horowitz, 2019).

However, the people raising concerns about the adverse impact of sterilization on individual animals have not made a compelling case for its widespread cessation in the United States or abroad. While they have identified some adverse health consequences (some breeds have higher rates of bone cancers), there are countervailing benefits (lower incidence of mammary cancer and uterine infections). And the negative outcomes may well be outweighed by the positive, most notably the fact that sterilization has reduced the euthanasia of unwanted animals in shelters from 13.5 million annually to around 1.7 to 2 million. In the end, while it is entirely appropriate for veterinary researchers to look at disease incidence and to report trends that should be addressed, it is also hoped that the final cost-benefit assessment will include a longevity number (if sterilized dogs live longer they will have an increased risk of cancer) as well as an accounting of the millions of dogs every year not dying in shelters because sterilization has cut the oversupply of puppies.

Despite the concerns of some for the welfare of sterilized animals, the procedure is very likely to be continued, especially in underserved communities and developing countries that face serious overpopulation and stray issues and where animal ill health and lack of preventive care are the norm. Here, sterilization is often coupled with free or low-cost vaccinations and basic treatment not just to combat overpopulation but to increase access to veterinary care more generally. One recent study indicates that street dogs in cities that have a sterilization program are healthier and in better shape than those that have not been sterilized (Yoak et al., 2014).

Underlife of Affordable Care Policy

While critics of routine sterilization have focused on its impact on animal health and biology, which is understandable given their veterinary background, this intervention—and other basic care often coupled with sterilization—can affect people too. People must agree to have animals operated on, vaccinated, examined, and treated for basic health problems, a behavior that may be novel for those who have never taken an animal for veterinary care of any sort. When visiting shelters or veterinary offices, they interact with animal advocates whose comments and actions can change their thinking and feeling about dogs and cats. Once animals are sterilized and treated for problems like worms or mange, owners may regard them differently as they tend to their postoperative recovery and see a different, healthier animal that might be touched more than in the past. Nor are pet owners the only people affected by basic veterinary care. Those providing this care might also be affected by these services if they have to convince pet owners to use this care or lower their expectations for how much underserved owners might change.

Policy makers advocating for affordable veterinary care have a narrower view of their efforts' impact on people. They assume pet owners, or those bringing street animals for veterinary care, behave rationally when offered these services and will use them when cost or access barriers are removed. In other words, their animals need basic veterinary services, so people who cannot afford such care will choose to use it when provided at little or no cost. But the assumption of rationality does not explain why some people fail or are slow to take advantage of these services; an estimated 20% of the underserved population of pet owners want nothing to do with free or low-cost veterinary care. Nor does the assumption of rationality help us understand the decision-making process of those who finally use these services if they are reluctant to do so, perhaps delaying animals' care or not taking advantage of all the available free or low-cost care.

Organizational bureaucrats and policy makers make an assumption of rationality because they understand problems like homelessness or welfare reform—or in our case underserved pets—in terms that do not strongly resonate with the actual lived experiences and understandings of those for whom policies and programs are made (Irvine, 2003; Loseke, 2001). Pet owners can have subjective experiences dealing with institutions, such as the local animal shelter, that create a disjuncture with how organizations and policy makers expect them to behave. What is deemed necessary to solve alleged problems, such as providing only free or low-cost basic veterinary care, may then not always be enough. *Underdogs* explores this disjunction, or what Freidson (1975) calls the underlife of social policy, by examining whether pet owners always think and act the way policy makers assume.

By exploring this disjuncture, or the underlife of affordable care programs, *Underdogs* differs from most social policy evaluations that focus on the outcomes of social programs to determine how effectively they achieve their goals. Epidemiologists and veterinarians studying these programs usually focus on the impact of sterilization on improving animal welfare, reducing dog population numbers, and lowering rates of rabies and other zoonotic diseases, with an occasional study examining their impact on community attitudes toward dogs. By contrast, *Underdogs* takes a broader look at the implementation of affordable care programs by focusing on the process of delivering these services and their impact on people rather than animals. By taking this approach, we are not advocating for these programs in general or for sterilization in particular but are trying to understand and describe how basic veterinary services, including but not limited to sterilization, are disseminated in underserved communities; what it means to keep pets in low-income or poverty-ridden communities; how low-income pet owners view and experience affordable care options; and how those who provide these services interact with pet owners and coordinate (or do not coordinate) their efforts with other humane organizations and animal advocates.

Studying the process of programs providing free or low-cost veterinary services means examining two perspectives—those of providers of affordable basic care and of the clients who might use these services—because each group's perspective affects the other. How people think about pets or street animals and whether to get them affordable veterinary care will be shaped by the thinking and acting of those providing this care, and vice versa. For providers, we need to understand how they actually deliver these services and what they think about people in underserved communities who have pets or deal with street animals. And we need to understand how pet owners and those who live in neighborhoods with dogs and cats on the street customarily behave with these animals, how their everyday lives intersect with the lives of pets and street animals, and what they experience when interacting with shelter workers, neighbors, friends, and others before, during, and after using services.

Focusing on process also means we must consider factors other than cost and assess that could impede equal access to veterinary services. While cost and access can be formidable barriers to seeking this care, living in or near poverty has a major impact on the everyday lives of people and animals.[4] We strongly suspected that living in a disadvantaged community would have a profound effect on the use of affordable veterinary care because researchers have documented how poverty, along with systemic and institutional bias, affects the use of human health care services. These studies have shown that low income and lack of health insurance are not the only reasons why people living in poverty are less likely to seek medical care. Feeling alienated due to their marginal position in a class-stratified, highly individuated society results in lower utilization of human health care services such as vaccinations and prenatal care (Heller et al., 1979).

Conversely, efforts to reduce the poor's sense of alienation and marginality have been found to increase their use of health services. As such, intervening cultural, racial, and class factors need to be addressed to make palatable the offer of affordable veterinary care to people who might be apprehensive about using a shelter's services. In the end, it may be that programs providing free or low-cost services for animals are effective not only because they remove cost and access barriers per se but also because they address larger issues faced by people living in or near poverty.

We believe that through its focus on process *Underdogs* will be useful to policy makers, service providers, and scholars of human-animal relations, or what has become known as anthrozoology. Designers, administrators, and advocates of programs that provide these services will be able to understand the factors that limit their success or increase their effectiveness, to tailor and customize their operations to reach a wider audience of underserved pet owners or those caring for street animals, and to advocate for changing legal policies that impact the diffusion of their services to those in need. Scholars will be able to clarify and add to the existing anthrozoology literature on how class and race shape pet keeping and caring since there are few studies of how these demographic factors influence human-animal relations; the findings have sometimes been contradictory and the methods often woefully inadequate to investigate the questions we raise.

Class, Race, and Pet Keeping

Cost and access can be formidable barriers to using affordable care, but we also need to explore, more generally, how the use of these services might be influenced by the nature of pet keeping and human-animal relations in underserved communities and the surrounding culture. Unfortunately, few researchers have studied what dogs and cats mean to people and how they interact with them in underserved communities, whether in developing countries or in the United States.

While the study of human perceptions of animals is receiving increasing attention, by the end of the twentieth century scholars had not yet studied human-pet interactions in a developing country (Barba, 1995). Only a handful of studies have done so in subsequent years (see, for example, Coppinger & Coppinger, 2016), apart from reports on the impact of sterilization or anti-rabies vaccinations that occasionally include a measure of pet owners' attitudes. In fact, most scholarly discussions about the meaning and importance to people of dogs and cats, whether modern pets or befriended street animals, are blind to social class because researchers either did not set out to study class differences or perhaps failed to report what they found (see Saunders et al., 2017, for a recent exception). While classic studies written decades ago about the meaning of pets make no mention of how social class might affect pet ownership (e.g., Veevers, 1985), more recent anthrozoological scholarship also omits such discussion. Despite purporting to survey the field, researchers have made no mention, even in a speculative way, of social class's influence on relationships with dogs and cats in developed or developing nations (e.g., Bradshaw, 2017; DeMello, 2012; Hosey & Melfi, 2019; McCardle et al., 2011; Pręgowski, 2016).

When the connection between social class, race, and pet ownership has been studied in modern societies, researchers have mainly focused on the prevalence of pet ownership, pointing to somewhat higher rates in white, affluent households.[5] Pet ownership appears to be common across all income levels (Lian & Mathis, 2016), although there is some evidence that higher income individuals are slightly more likely to own dogs or pets in general (AVMA,

2012; Marx et al., 1988).[6] And although whites purportedly are more likely to own pets than any other racial or ethnic group (AVMA, 2007; Brown, 2002; Burns, 2008; Saunders et al., 2017; Sheikh et al., 2016; Westgarth et al., 2010; Westgarth et al., 2013), these studies may skew racial differences because some nonwhite groups are more likely to live in rental housing whose owners do not permit pets or restrict their number or kind.

Fewer studies have examined the impact of class and race on pet owners' responsibility for and attachment to their animals, and when they have, their authors have often concluded that lower-income black or Hispanic pet owners are less attached, find their pets less important, and are less responsible for their animals than are middle- and upper-income white pet owners. We should be cautious about accepting this conclusion. Studies of how race and social class impact emotions suggest that lower-income African Americans are often attached to their children (Hill, 2001; Sherry et al., 2013; Tudge et al., 2000) and may similarly regard their pets as family members. They are also found to have greater empathy and to be more likely to help others in distress than more affluent test takers (Manstead, 2018), which might transfer to concern for the welfare of pets.

In some cases, this conclusion is based on reputed cultural differences. Some studies claim that pets are less important to African Americans, Hispanics, and lower-income people than to middle- and upper-income whites (Brown, 2002; Siegel, 1995). This finding may result from pet owners having more utilitarian views toward animals than do whites (Kellert & Berry, 1980), especially southern blacks who, according to Kellert (1994), are comparatively less concerned for and interested in animals. If viewed for their utilitarian value, dogs in black and Hispanic communities are more likely to be viewed as a source of protection than as pets, so they will be tied up outside to guard the backyard and prevent trespassers (Anderson, 1990; Risley-Curtiss et al., 2006).

In other cases, this conclusion is drawn from studies of spending for pets and veterinary care. Such spending is lower for people who are minorities, have less income and education, live alone, and do not own their residence (Wolf et al., 2008). African Americans or low-income pet owners may spend less on their pets because of cultural differences in the human-animal bond or variation in norms relating to ownership and its responsibilities. But it would be wrong to conclude that spending less on pets than their more affluent, white counterparts means that low-income black or Hispanic owners do not want to be responsible for their charges or fail to see the benefit of providing them with veterinary care. Although they may spend less on veterinary services, low-income pet owners may still think sterilization is a good idea. For example, most study participants in one poor Hispanic town on the Texas border would have liked to sterilize both their male and female dogs and cats, but only 11% of their dogs and 27% of their cats had been sterilized (Poss & Bader, 2007). When cost and transport barriers are removed, low-income black and Hispanic pet owners behave no differently than do white owners (Sparks et al., 2018), indicating that they do care for and will be responsible for their pets.

Findings from studies of homeless people also suggest that lower-income and minority pet owners can be attached to and responsible for their animals. Estimates are that about 10% of the homeless population has pets, with this percentage increasing to almost 25% in some areas (Rhoades et al., 2015). Many homeless pet owners are reportedly strongly attached to and have empathy for their animals (Singer et al., 1995; Taylor et al., 2004) but often struggle to provide food and veterinary care for them (Kidd & Kidd, 1994), find it difficult to secure housing (Baker, 2001), and face criticism from the public as unsuitable pet owners (Irvine, 2013). Donations of food from some of the public enable homeless pet owners to keep their animals healthy and to resist this stigma by forming an identity as responsible pet owners, despite their lack of resources (Irvine et al., 2012). Indeed, they ultimately see themselves as better pet owners than most others not only because their animals are not starving but also because they are in constant contact with their pets and allow them much freedom (Irvine, 2013).

It is likely that studies of homeless pet owners have produced contrary results about attachment to and responsibility for animals because the researchers used a qualitative rather than survey-based approach. This approach gave the researchers access to the culture behind pet keeping and caring and hence to what the experience of owning a pet among the disadvantaged is really like. For example, in one qualitative study African Americans did not always see pets in utilitarian or anthropocentric ways. Wolch and Lassiter (2000, pp. 84–87) found that African American women expressed considerable "animal rights commentary," a finding not discovered in survey studies.

In other words, to better understand what it means for a low-income pet owner to have a pet and try to be responsible for its welfare, we need to comprehend that person's everyday life as it is tempered by his or her social class and racial or ethnic membership. Such tempering results from continued participation in a particular social context that shapes a person's culture-specific self and pattern of thinking, feeling, and acting (Grossmann & Huynh, 2013; Stephens et al., 2014).

The Shelters

Underdogs looks at how two shelters diffuse basic veterinary services to low-income pet owners or those living in poverty, identifying the barriers that make some owners hesitant to use these services as well as the bridges that encourage and enable them to do so. We chose to study these two programs precisely because many regard them as among the most successful animal advocacy programs for reaching underserved pet owners. In their own countries if not globally, these shelter-based programs are at the forefront of helping underserved pet owners obtain veterinary care. If they have problems increasing these pet owners' access to veterinary care, other programs will likely too. Of course, the programs we studied have more resources and funding to reach underserved pet owners and deliver veterinary care, along with having an established mission or ideology, than do many smaller or newer programs. Nevertheless, if the shelters have managed these problems, learning about how they have done so may help emerging or developing advocacy programs better reach their disadvantaged communities of interest.

We also chose to study these two programs because they are different from each other. While their goals are very similar—to help people get their pets sterilized, vaccinated, examined, and treated for basic problems—how they go about providing this help, the context surrounding their efforts, and the response of pet owners to this help are very different. Each setting presents its own set of cultural, organizational, and structural factors that can complicate access to basic veterinary care and require novel strategies to overcome these complications in disadvantaged communities. In one case the population served is largely rural and indigenous, often at great distance from the shelter, while the other is urban poor, in the same neighborhood as the shelter. In one case the delivery of affordable care takes place among a myriad of groups and organizations competing for clients and often sharply conflicting in their approaches to helping underserved communities, while the delivery of care in the other setting takes place in a more benign organizational environment. And in one case there is a class "issue" for pet owners whose low incomes and lack of education distinctly separate them from more affluent pet owners, whether natives or tourists, while in the other there are both class and race "issues" for pet owners who struggle with gentrification and institutional racism. While our two cases cannot highlight every barrier and bridge to using low- or no-cost veterinary care that will be faced by other programs trying to deliver these services around the globe, we believe that the differences between the shelters enable our research to uncover many of the most common and sometimes intractable sources of resistance to using low-cost veterinary services, while suggesting many potential solutions to increasing access.

The first case we examine is El Refugio, or the Asociacion Humanitaria Protecione Para Animales, based in the city of San Rafael de Heredia on the outskirts of Costa Rica's capital of San Jose. El Refugio is the largest animal shelter in the country, whose operation and function compare to conventional American shelters with a large facility for adopting out sterilized dogs and cats and an animal hospital. The shelter provides these services in a country where around 50% of households own 1.6 dogs on average, which translates to approximately 200 dogs per 1,000 people. About 10% of households have cats. In addition to adopting out animals to these pet owners and providing veterinary care, the shelter also wants to reduce the number of animals on the streets, particularly in rural and coastal areas. Its approach to managing the country's large stray population is quite different, and far more humane, than the customary way of dealing with this problem. Until the end of the last century, Costa Rica's approach to animal overpopulation was to poison the animals in the streets (Kartal & Rowan, 2018). Dogs and cats lucky enough to have a home were seen as working animals. When the animals were no longer useful or wanted by their owners, they would be thrown out on the street. Since many of the abandoned animals were females, overpopulation of stray animals was a huge problem. In 1991 El Refugio's new director had to convince officials to bring strays to the shelter (rather than simply killing them) where they could be sterilized and potentially adopted into homes.

Locally, the shelter provides dogs and cats for adoption and offers veterinary services to pet owners. Remotely, it operates a mobile outreach program that provides low-cost sterilization in underserved villages, such as Limon, Playa del Coco, and Aquas Zarcas, where there are no local veterinarians or clinics and where poverty and unemployment are common. Poverty rates are even higher in these locations than nationally, where about 30% of rural Costa Ricans live in poverty, 7% in extreme poverty. Minimum wage is about $500 per month for those with full-time employment, but resources and jobs are scarce in rural areas.

Since the late 1990s, El Refugio and private veterinary services have grown, assuming a greater presence as providers of animal health care. The shelter's budget for veterinary services grew from $140,000 in 1999 to $400,000 in 2016. Since 2000, there also has been an explosion in the number of private veterinary clinics in Costa Rica, with approximately 600 clinics in operation in 2018, mostly focusing on companion animals. Although the growth of Costa Rica's private veterinary market may be partially due to the example set by El Refugio, two other forces may have fueled this growth. One is the collective efforts of many different groups offering low-cost sterilization, ranging from organizations that no longer operate physical shelters for adoption to small, informal spay/neuter rescue groups that exist throughout the country. Another is Costa Rica's modernization combined with growing tourism and immigration by middle- and upper-class Americans and Europeans who bring their own pets or adopt them in Costa Rica, thereby increasing demand for private-practice veterinary services.

Evidence suggests that this modernization is increasingly leading Costa

Ricans to have pets (about 50% of households own dogs), to adopt West-ern pet-keeping practices, and to value the human-pet relationship (Drews, 2003). For example, anecdotal reports after Hurricane Otto in November 2016 claimed that storm-damaged cities received more food donations for cats and dogs than for farm animals, the first time that had been the case in Costa Rican history. Surveys claim that pet owners increasingly allow their dogs to sleep inside the house; prevent their dogs from being on the street unsuper-vised; play weekly with their dogs; have taken their dogs to veterinarians in the past year; groom them; own dogs that live longer than six years, which sug-gests improved pet care; provide fresh, clean water once a day, although it is still a minority; view their dogs as companions rather than as guard dogs; and know that there are laws to protect animals and prevent abuse (WSPA, 2012). There are also informal reports that some Costa Ricans are interacting differ-ently with street dogs, allegedly now more likely to look at, engage, pet, and feed strays or village dogs, although not necessarily street cats. However, these reports may not reflect pet-keeping norms in the locations that the shelter's outreach teams visit to provide low-cost sterilization or where the shelter it-self is located because they are less urban and more rural, with less modern and less dense housing.

By contrast, the Humane Society of Charlotte (HSC), founded in 1978, op-erates a no-kill animal shelter for pet adoptions and an animal hospital pri-marily for sterilization and basic veterinary treatments. Although it serves all pet owners in the Charlotte area, it offers free or low-cost veterinary services to underserved owners. In 2016 the shelter provided these services to approx-imately 500 new people and 1,000 new pets. Over the last decade or two it has partnered with the Pets for Life program, a national effort to provide vet-erinary services to pet owners living in or near poverty in ways that respect their presumed alienation and marginality from animal health care services. Through the Pets for Life program HSC has managed to sterilize and vaccinate many animals in the local community, with estimates ranging from 80% to as high as 90% of the pets in West Charlotte, a rate higher than those of other programs offering low-cost services.

The Pets for Life program at the shelter provides free veterinary services to owners from the most poverty-stricken zip codes of West Charlotte.[6] In these targeted neighborhoods (such as Enderly Park, Camp Green, or Thomasboro), the vast majority of residents are African American. Because West Charlotte still has racially concentrated poverty (Nichol & Hunt, 2016), many of these residents live below or near the poverty line, are on fixed incomes, are un-employed (approximately 34%), or work in temporary, low-paying jobs.[7] And upward mobility is rare; Charlotte ranked last on economic mobility among America's 50 largest cities (Chetty et al., 2014). Poor residents struggle to save relatively small amounts of money by not turning on lights, heating, or air conditioning and often do not have the funds to pay for additional expenses for family members, let alone pets.

Residents in this "bad part of town" (Lacour, 2015) own pets but at a lower rate than those in more affluent, white communities. In studies of similar metro areas, about 26.2% of residents own a dog, 21.5% own a cat, and 8.5% own both a cat and a dog (Saunders et al., 2017). In the past, pets in West Charlotte were rarely sterilized, vaccinated, treated for basic veterinary problems like worms, prevented from roaming, or provided with proper diet, shelter, and veterinary care. Maintaining a pet or pets—providing them with food, vaccinations, veterinary examinations, sterilization, medications, and other treatments—can easily become a financial strain or burden; certainly, fees charged by private-practice veterinarians that are set for middle- and upper-income pet owners deter the vast majority of pet owners in West Charlotte from going to their offices for this care.

Indeed, it is a novel idea for West Charlotte pet owners to provide basic veterinary care to their animals. Most have never taken their animals to a veterinarian or used veterinary services at a shelter. Just as food deserts prevent some residents of underserved communities from accessing affordable healthy food, pet resource deserts prevent people in these communities from accessing affordable veterinary services and supplies for their companion animals. Although there are approximately 60 private-practice veterinarians in the area, they are not close enough to most of West Charlotte for residents to carry or walk their pets, even if they could afford the cost.[9] Prior to using Pets for Life services, 87% never contacted or used any animal services, including those from humane societies and animal control, while 77% of animals seen through Pets for Life have not previously seen a veterinarian.[10] The majority of those who had seen a veterinarian did so only for an emergency, such as a dog being hit by a car, but usually did not receive services because they were too expensive. In many cities the owner loses the injured pet because the veterinarian may pair it with a local shelter or rescue group that can afford to "fix" the animal but will subsequently put it into its own program for readoption to a new owner or the original owner relinquishes the pet to a city shelter or animal control department that either euthanizes it or treats the problem and puts it up for adoption.[11] Even if West Charlotte pet owners could afford to pay a veterinarian, the neighborhood is a pet food dessert. High-quality pet food is not an option because it is expensive or unavailable in area stores, and large markets or pet supply stores that offer quality pet food at lower prices are also far away. This inconvenience forces pet owners who do not have access to cars or public transportation to buy inferior and more expensive pet food at local convenience stores.

The Study

From the beginning we were aware of special problems posed by being outsiders studying insiders (Kauffman, 1994). We were affluent white males from another culture in one setting, observing and talking with people about how they interacted with pets and with those providing them with affordable care. This gap required us to be particularly sensitive to the methodological problems of doing class, race, and gender analyses (Cuadraz & Uttal, 1999; Masse, 2015). So we drew on feminist research approaches that privilege those being studied by giving them a voice in the research process (Brooks & Hesse-Biber, 2007).

To include the voices of pet owners, shelter staff members, veterinarians, and rescue workers, we encouraged people to raise research questions for us to explore, suggest where, when, what, and whom to observe, explain how they view their circumstances, define issues in their own terms, identify processes leading to different outcomes, and interpret the meaning of their lives to the research. Rather than using survey questionnaires, we followed a qualitative approach that considered the subjectivity and experience of the people we studied. We wanted to hear from them so they could guide our observations and interviews in any direction they saw as relevant and important. Doing this allowed us to explore whatever issues pet owners in or near poverty had caring for their animals and using free or low-cost veterinary services as well as whatever issues shelter workers and other stakeholders had about delivering affordable care.

This approach called for immersion in the situations faced by pet owners and shelter workers as well as their surrounding cultures, such that similarities and differences would emerge in shelters' active and long-standing veterinary programs for underserved pet owners. To this end, the senior author spent approximately 18 months performing fieldwork in greater San Rafael, Costa Rica, and Charlotte, North Carolina, while based at El Refugio and HSC. The location and geographical range of the research differed in the two settings because the shelters' strategies for diffusing veterinary services differed. In Charlotte the fieldwork was local, focusing on West Charlotte pet owners visiting the shelter or living in their homes or apartments with pets, while in Costa Rica it was sometimes far from the shelter because its veterinarians drove hundreds of miles to provide low-cost sterilization in poor, remote villages having unique microcultures, such as a heavy Jamaican influence that might affect Costa Ricans' attitudes and behaviors toward dogs and cats or NGO practices. Fieldwork was carried out in the central valley, including San Jose, Ipis, Heredia, San Ramon, Cartago, and San Rafael, and down toward the Caribbean and Pacific coasts, including Puerto Viejo, Manuel Antonio, Puntarenas, and Nosara. This strategy made it possible to collect data in demographically and culturally varied neighborhoods, whether urban, rural, native, tourist, poor, or middle class.

Establishing rapport with respondents is vital to obtaining reliable information (Rojas, 1979), so we sought their cooperation and support at every stage of our fieldwork in both locations. Pet owners in Costa Rica and West Charlotte allowed observations of their pet keeping at home and at the shelters and welcomed questions about their dogs or cats and their experiences at the shelters or outreach clinics. They were forthcoming about why they were hesitant to use these services when that was the case. Shelter workers, volunteers, and others involved in providing free or low-cost services were also eager to be observed and to share their experiences and opinions, perhaps due to their strong commitment and passion for their work. In addition, shelter staff members helped the senior author gain access to and rapport with pet owners at the shelters, outreach clinics, and pet owners' homes, where he was introduced as "someone helping the shelter understand the pet owner's experience with its services." When anyone wanted to hear more about the author's presence, the individual was given a brief verbal description of this study as well as his university affiliation and expertise in human-animal relationships.

Over 250 hours of observations were made of human-animal interactions on the streets of Costa Rica and Charlotte, in the homes of pet owners in both locations, and at the shelters and outreach clinics we visited that sterilized, vaccinated, examined, and sometimes treated pets in or near poverty. During these observations, interactions were noted between people on the street and stray animals, household members and their pets, and veterinarians, shelter workers, volunteers, and rescue workers with each other and underserved pet owners coming to the shelters or clinics. At all times, there were no restrictions placed on what, where, or when observations could be made. These observations included but were not limited to listening to informal discussions among shelter workers and volunteers about the pet owners they served, consultations with pet owners over the cost or fear of preoperative, surgical, and postoperative care, and casual conversations among pet owners waiting at the shelter or outreach clinic for their animals to be sterilized, vaccinated, or otherwise examined and treated. During all observations the investigator was visible to anyone in the area as notes were taken, while not impeding the movement of pet owners as they registered and waited for veterinary services.

In addition, approximately 200 semistructured, in-depth interviews were conducted with humane NGO staff members, shelter workers, volunteers, animal control workers, veterinarians, government employees, animal advocates, rescue group members, and both underserved and more affluent pet owners.[12] However, underserved owners and shelter workers represent the bulk of interviews because they were at the center of our focus on barriers and bridges to using affordable veterinary care and could therefore yield the most insight. Pet owners were usually interviewed while waiting for free or low-cost services, while a few were interviewed inside their homes. Most were spoken with privately and individually, except when a translator's assistance was needed in Costa Rica or when an outreach worker was present when interviewing West Charlotte pet owners in their homes. Interviews with other stakeholders were usually conducted privately, in person, and on the job, although a few were done by phone with Pets for Life staff members around the country and in Costa Rica with shelter staff, rescue workers, and veterinarians in parts of the country that were too remote to be reached.

Because pet owners in racially concentrated poverty or low-income neighborhoods were the center of our analysis, we took advantage of serendipitous occurrences to have a comparison group of more affluent owners. While this is not an ideal comparison group, there were always some people in both locations who slipped in to the shelters or clinics to use the low-cost services intended for those from underserved neighborhoods or villages. These interlopers were often white middle- or even upper-income pet owners but were usually not refused services, so we were able to watch them as they waited for services and interview them about their own experiences of caring for pets and using veterinary services.

Interviews were designed as recorded conversations led by a semistructured topic list, focusing on a few general issues to explore with respondents, with follow-up questions for each topic to flesh out meaning and detail. The senior author started by introducing himself and talking briefly about his academic background and research and why he was studying the delivery of affordable veterinary care, which softened the atmosphere before beginning the interview (Legard et al., 2003). Respondents could talk as long as they wished but were sometimes interrupted to clarify points. Most interviews lasted from 30 minutes to two hours, although some people were repeatedly interviewed over weeks or even months, which enabled the discovery of crucial topics not considered at first, such as how pet owners in West Charlotte kept their animals after being evicted from apartments. Respondents sometimes asked questions in return, often directed at the senior author's own perceptions of their communities and the kind of animal care he witnessed. Pet owners were curious as to whether he worked for the shelter, which they were reassured was not the case, and how his research might help programs trying to provide affordable veterinary care.

Interviews relied on the critical incident technique (Flanagan, 1954), where respondents described both positive and negative experiences as well as fulfilled and unmet expectations when seeking and receiving veterinary services, whether through private practice or through the shelters. These interactions, after all, are one type of consumer relationship (Ackerman, 2013). Since this technique has been successfully used to examine the relationship between customers and various service industries and why dissatisfactions arise (Edvardsson & Roos, 2001), it promised to be equally useful in studying the interactions between veterinary patients and those people providing these services.

There were also many informal conversations when the senior author was hanging around the shelter or calling contacts at the shelters to talk about the progress of the research. Informal conversations on the phone or by email enabled the senior author to keep regular contact with respondents and to make them feel involved in the research process. Such talks also helped to confirm or refine certain observations, suggest new lines of thinking, and recommend additional stakeholders to meet. Even when little or no new information was shared, these informal contacts further cemented rapport.

Key informants also played a valuable role in gaining access and information. These informants have more detailed and specialized knowledge than do ordinary people in the shelters and settings we studied. Some pet owners became key informants in their neighborhoods and spoke with the investigator about neighbors who were pet owners but did not want to use veterinary services. Since these informants lived in the neighborhoods of interest and were friends with their neighbors, their reports were very trustworthy. Shelter workers and veterinarians also served as key informants, providing firsthand, personal information about the beliefs and behaviors of pet owners as well as other professionals providing animal care to underserved communities and arranging access into the operation of the shelter, its clinics, and the homes of pet owners. Access to these key informants enabled the senior investigator to draw upon organizational records and data, such as on HSC's dog population census, which provides information about the number of animals served, their concentration in certain areas, and the behavior and attitudes of citizens toward them. Once fieldwork ended in both Costa Rica and North Carolina, contact continued with a few key informants out of friendship more than research, but still offered the opportunity to reject, modify, or confirm conclusions.

Although *Underdogs* provides a more nuanced picture of the process and problems of delivering no- or low-cost veterinary services to underserved pet owners than will surveys tallying the outcomes of such programs, doubts can be raised about the validity of our findings. For one, the question we studied— why some people hesitate to use or do not use low- or no-cost veterinary services—ideally calls for direct interviews with pet owners who reject the shelter's veterinary services, but our study primarily focused on observing and interviewing pet owners who decided to use at least some of the shelter's free or low-cost services. Nevertheless, relevant and valid data about pet owners who decline veterinary services can be gathered without going into the community and approaching pet owners independently of any shelter outreach into these neighborhoods. Some pet owners who did use the services talked about their own initial reluctance to accept them and speculated about why some neighbors might refuse. The researcher's status as independent of the shelters likely made it easier for pet owners to express their reservations about using free or low-cost services, especially if they were at all critical of veterinarians or the shelter. The investigator also shadowed veterinarians as they went from village to village in Costa Rica to offer sterilization to pet owners and shelter outreach workers as they went door-to-door in West Charlotte to ask residents if they had any pets and whether they wanted any veterinary services.[13] When they came to the sterilization clinics or answered the door and said they had pets, some hesitated to accept or declined services but said why. Moreover, shelter outreach workers with established rapport in West Charlotte neighborhoods gathered firsthand information about why some pet owners refused services and shared it with the investigator; some staff members had worked at the shelters for years and had considerable experience with pet owners, recalling in considerable detail why some owners decided to use or refuse services.

A question can also be raised about the generalizability of our findings, given our reliance on data from two locations. The value of ethnography is to provide richly detailed case studies that highlight a problem, a set of behaviors, or a group's beliefs. Because of this case study approach, caution should be exercised before generalizing our results to other shelters and programs trying to provide free or low-cost veterinary services because they have fewer resources than the shelters and programs we studied and they may be working with underserved communities whose local cultures, social structure, and historical experiences are very different from those in greater San Juan or West Charlotte.

That being said, the Costa Rican and West Charlotte cases are not unique in a more general sense. Any effort to diffuse veterinary services will be influenced, in varying ways and degrees, by the social context surrounding these services. In any disadvantaged community, the decision to use low- or no-cost sterilization, vaccinations, or basic treatments will be informed by local cultural norms for how pet owners think about and treat dogs and cats along with how they view and experience the personnel and social policies of humane organizations that provide these programs. In all disadvantaged communities, large-scale social characteristics, such as race, class, ethnicity, and gender, will color everyday life for humans as well as animals and impinge on the application of social policies, like providing low-cost veterinary care to low-income pet owners or those in poverty. And in every disadvantaged community the application of these policies, whether for animal or for human welfare, will not be a top-down, linear, or rational process but a complex one having complications and unexpected consequences. We hope that our description of the issues of delivering low-cost veterinary care and how humane staff deal with these difficulties will resonate, at least to some degree, with animal advocates and policy makers in any community rife with the problems of poverty.

The Plan

Underdogs is divided into two sections, each devoted to understanding pet keeping and the delivery of affordable care in a different culture, where the operation and scope of programs differed, as did the impact of class, race, and ethnicity. Each section begins with a baseline description of pet keeping and caring by the people targeted for affordable care because we could not fall back on existing research (chapters 1 and 4); most of what is currently known is based on middle- and upper-class pet owners who are, more often than not, white. If pet keeping varies across classes, how is it different for the underserved? And given our initial question about barriers to accessing basic treatments for pets, in what ways might these differences affect accessing free or low-cost veterinary care?

The first section, drawing on our research in Costa Rica, looks at how diffusing any innovation—in this case affordable care—does not take place in a social vacuum but is shaped by interactions between groups and individuals. Getting underserved pet owners to adopt new behaviors can become a political process at an intergroup or face-to-face level, as actors try to change the behavior of others, through words or actions, in ways actors desire and that favor their own interests or goals. Chapter 2 shows how the shelter had to deal with many individuals, small groups, and organizations that each had a stake in providing basic veterinary care to pet owners but did not always have compatible approaches, leading to tensions and conflicts that the shelter had to manage. But delivering affordable care can also become a political process at the interpersonal level. Chapter 3 captures how the shelter and its workers tried to influence pet owners to change their thinking and behavior when it came to interacting with and caring for their animals.

Underdog's second section, on pet keeping and affordable care in North Carolina, focuses on how the delivery of affordable care affects people as well animals. Chapter 5 looks at how low-income pet owners experience their use of affordable care at the shelter and why, when this experience is negative, they are reluctant to use low- or no-cost basic services. The shelter is aware that some West Charlotte pet owners can have this experience and wants to address this reluctance, so chapter 6 explores how its workers sometimes modify their thinking and acting to convince pet owners to use free or low-cost veterinary services. Since technological innovations can impact people beyond their narrow intent—and getting the underserved to sterilize and vaccinate their animals is such an innovation—chapter 7 examines how using affordable care can affect low-income pet owners' identities and behaviors.

Answers to these questions revealed richer and more complicated themes about how social class and culture shape human-animal relations and create reluctance to use affordable veterinary care in low-income communities. We examine these themes in the final chapter, starting with the parallels between human-animal relations and parent-child relations in disadvantaged communities. Seeing these parallels not only helps us better understand the nuances and challenges of having pets in or near poverty but also clarifies the problems of providing affordable veterinary care as well as their possible solutions. These problems and solutions are shot through with paradoxes, as are human-animal relations in general (Herzog, 2010), the final theme we explore.

San Rafael, Costa Rica

CHAPTER ONE

Liminal Pets and Their People

LIVING WITH STREET ANIMALS IN
TRADITIONAL COSTA RICAN CULTURE

In the modern Western human-pet relationship dogs and cats are uniquely owned by a person or family who accepts responsibility for providing them with food, shelter, and veterinary care as well as having them sterilized. Certainly for dogs but less so for cats, they also have their movement restricted to a house or yard when not being walked on a leash. In the United States 60 to 70% of pet cats are indoor-only pets. In other parts of the world cats are freer to roam. Dogs in particular are very dependent on their human owners who have, in recent decades, exercised ever greater control over what have become canine good citizens (Grimm, 2014; Uddin, 2003) who are expected to further rather than disrupt neighborhood bonds (Perin, 1990).

By comparison dogs and cats in underdeveloped or developing countries are less controlled, with estimates of about 500 million "private" dogs (pets/controlled dogs) and somewhere between 300 and 500 million street dogs. While cats can and do live as truly feral animals, dogs are only rarely feral and "independent" of people, who provide them with the bulk of their food whether they are inside or outside the home. Nearly all street dogs are "owned" in that a household will claim some association with a particular dog and will provide some food and possibly shelter. But these dogs are not owned in the sense that pets are "owned" in high-income countries. Most of the literature on street dogs refers to them by terms such as "village" dogs (e.g., Ruiz-Izaguirre et al., 2015), "community" dogs (Kwok et al., 2016), "semiferals" (e.g., Boyko et al., 2009), or strays (e.g., Beck, 2002), but these terms are imprecise and do not reflect the complex relationships between humans and dogs, whether pets or street animals.[1]

Individual residents often tolerate or even appreciate the presence of street dogs, but local governments have sometimes been more intolerant, viewing them as municipal dirt, quite separate from and foreign to the human community because they are regarded as disorderly, dirty, dangerous, and not part of a fixed social relationship (Jenner, 1997; Thomas, 1983). Once viewed as a form of dirt, street dogs can become outcasts to avoid and control or perhaps even kill. Such distancing from street dogs can be built into some cultures, although even then there still will be people who live comfortably with and accept their presence. For example, in some Muslim communities in India, the view of street dogs as separate from and unwanted in the human community is embedded in the country's political and legal history. There, street dogs have long been considered as outcasts and a source of pollution, such that some, but certainly not all, residents are intolerant of them, while elsewhere in India street dogs have been given caste names (Agoramoorthy, 2007) that label them as pariahs, a view that some claim almost led to a dog "genocide" by the Bangalore Municipal Corporation (Srinivasan & Nagaraj, 2007).

The appearance and fear of rabies cases can exacerbate strained relationships between local governments and street dogs. Despite occasional protests, this fear has led to the killing of street dogs in, for example, nineteenth-century New York (McNeur, 2014) and Poland between World War I and World War II (Plach, 2013). In the second half of the twentieth century, hysteria over rabies led to mass killings of dogs in places like Lima, Peru, and Maoist China (Pearson, 2016). And in the first decades of the twenty-first century mass killing or calls for it have continued in places like Bali, India, northern Canada, and Russia because of fear of rabies, bites, maulings, or declines in tourism (Clifton, 2010; Gronskaya & Makarychev, 2014; Reese, 2005). But culling has consistently failed to control or eliminate street dogs, and the World Health Organization has pronounced culling to be an ineffective means of controlling rabies.

Population Control as an Innovation

Today international animal protection groups, humane societies, animal control officers, and local governments advocate for more humane and effective methods of controlling the overpopulation of street animals. These groups promote the control of street dogs because they can cause social, economic, and public health problems, whether as nuisances, carriers of disease, biters, or tourism detractors. People who own pets that are allowed to roam are labeled as "irresponsible" by these groups (Perin, 1990, p. 109) because they have not vaccinated them to prevent serious veterinary problems, sterilized them to control their population, given them basic treatments for problems like worms or mange let alone treated them for serious injuries, or fed and watered them regularly.

In the modern West efforts toward sterilization and more responsible pet ownership have dramatically reduced the number of street dogs, except in some dense urban, very rural, or Native American areas (Clancy & Rowan, 2003). However, dog population control has fared less well in many underdeveloped or developing nations, although there have been a few locally effective spay, neuter, and release programs (Jackman & Rowan, 2007). Indeed, some researchers claim the street dog population has increased because of urbanization and the popularity of acquiring pet dogs that are later abandoned on the streets, as in Taiwan (Hsu, 2007b), although we should be suspicious of such claims because they are often not based on systematically collected data; it appears as though relative dog populations change relatively little. To help residents in these countries control the number of street dogs and improve their health, humane organizations, shelters, and rescue groups have tried to provide basic veterinary services, such as sterilization, at little or no cost and to encourage more responsible pet ownership in general.

But getting people in these places to use basic veterinary services or to adopt modern Western pet-keeping practices is a social innovation, and innovations are rarely if ever adopted immediately by most of those exposed to the potential change (Rogers, 2010). In the early stages of an innovation's diffusion into any given population, only about 20% of those targeted—the "elite adopters"—will change their behavior. After that, the diffusion process hits a sociological wall, with laggards and nonadopters not changing their behavior accordingly. Why is there usually this cap on initial diffusion? Macrosocial processes promote the adoption of innovations, like modernization, but these processes often do not uniformly impact a country; less modernized areas are slower to see behavior changes. To wit, attempts in the 1990s to diffuse birth control behavior in Costa Rica succeeded in penetrating only segments of the country that were more modernized (Rosero-Bixby & Casterline, 1994).

In Costa Rica the diffusion of modern pet-keeping norms, such as vaccinating and sterilizing pets, will also not be uniform. Parts of the country have modernized, with better education, higher incomes, greater internet access, and more plentiful job opportunities. Here, urban, educated Costa Ricans are elite adopters who have embraced modern Western attitudes toward pet care, including but not limited to preventing pets from roaming the streets, having them sterilized and vaccinated, and giving them veterinary care. But elsewhere in the country—in the shantytowns, coastal villages, and distressed urban neighborhoods—there has been less modernization, and in some cases people continue a traditional Costa Rican way of life. Much of this population is poor and does not customarily provide any veterinary care for animals or control their roaming. These Costa Ricans are the laggards or resistors, to use Rogers's terms, who have not adopted modern pet-keeping norms and may hesitate to use low-cost veterinary services.

El Refugio, as well as some international animal protection groups, would like to change the behavior of these laggards so they would sterilize dogs and cats and perhaps provide other basic treatments, but veterinary innovations will be resisted if they seem to be disadvantageous over the ideas or practices they supersede, conflict with existing values, beliefs, and experiences, or are hard to comprehend or see value in (Rogers, 2010). That is, behavior change is less likely when there is a clash of customs and norms, and traditional Costa Rican norms remain regarding how to interact with the country's estimated 1 to 2 million street dogs and countless cats.[2] These norms can create barriers to using veterinary care because they are permeated by a view of street animals that is very different from how animal welfare organizations view them. Instead of seeing them as problems or as out of place, street dogs as well as cats are more accepted and lived with in parts of Costa Rica. They are a social fact—a taken-for-granted aspect of everyday life. El Refugio does not share this view, however, and tries to change how traditional Costa Ricans think about and interact with dogs and cats, while adjusting its own expectations for what it can reasonably expect of these people.

Problematizing Liminality

The notion of liminality was introduced over a century ago (Van Gennep, 1909) to describe the unclear, if not confusing, transitional stage that individuals pass through when leaving a prior status for a new one as part of a rite of passage. During this transition they are betwixt and between their customary roles, making it impossible to classify their emotional states or social positions (Turner, 1969). Pets too, at least in modern Western societies, can be liminal, or have an ambiguous status, by occupying a space between humans and animals (Fox, 2008), and this ambiguity can sometimes be part of their appeal and a catalyst for forming close interspecies relationships, whether in everyday life between pets and owners (Sanders, 2003) or in mental health encounters between therapy animals and youthful patients who allegedly behave differently than they might normally, becoming less aggressive, less anxious, or less withdrawn socially (Arluke, 2010; Katcher, 2002).

Liminality applies to animals other than just modern Western pets. To international animal welfare organizations, street animals in developing countries occupy an ambiguous rather than dichotomous state, lying somewhere in between the extremes of being classified as either good or bad, as part of human families or not, or as tame or wild. These liminal animals or "border species" (Vermilya, 2012) confound the boundary lines between what is regarded as public and private and familiar or out of place. They are pets but not really, they might be owned by someone but not really, and they might be part of the household or neighborhood order but not really. They exist between these cognitive cracks as neither fully domesticated nor entirely independent of humans—relatively free to roam but relying for their survival on occasional handouts from residents, tourists, street vendors, and business owners who might recognize them as neighborhood dogs—and as neither purely emotional or purely instrumental in their perceived value to some local people (Serpell & Hsu, 2016).

Adopting modern dog-keeping practices, such as preventing their roaming or sterilizing them, assumes that those targeted for change will have a dichotomous view of dogs. In the modern view, street animals' liminality is a problem that needs correcting—they should belong to someone who owns them and is willing to take responsibility for providing them with veterinary care. They are disruptive, dirty, diseased nuisances if not dangers that should be rounded up and contained—either back in their homes or in a shelter—so they will not return to the streets, or be deported to become "forest dogs" in "concentration camps" far from people, as in Turkey (Alkan, 2016). In short, those people or organizations having this view believe that owners need to control these animals. Such a view of liminality underlies the efforts of international animal welfare organizations and some shelters and rescue groups in Costa Rica and is common in Western thinking that sees "stray," "street," or "roaming" dogs in opposition to "pet" dogs. Pet dogs have a clear place in the neighborhood social order—they belong to individual households, where good citizens care for and control them (Perin, 1990), while street dogs are "out of place" (Haraway, 2013), are "othered" (Narayanan, 2017), and do not belong anywhere, occupying the space between civilized humans and wild animals (Williams, 2007).

It can be an uphill battle to diffuse modern dog-keeping practices, such as sterilization, vaccination, basic health care, and containment, when people are used to living with street animals or have some fondness for them. At such times, the perspective of domestic and international animal advocacy groups, which see the liminality of street dogs as a problem to be corrected, can clash with the perspective of natives. Caring relationships exist with street dogs in many cultures. In some countries people form loose affiliations with them at the neighborhood level rather than being strongly connected to one family. For example, such "community dog-keeping" (Savvides, 2013) occurs in Bangkok, Thailand. With weak human-canine affiliations, there is tolerance or benign coexistence between residents and dogs on the streets, if not more when people feed these dogs and perhaps name or play with them but not assume further responsibility for their welfare or refer to the dogs as only "theirs." And in yet other countries residents have an even stronger attachment to street dogs they consider as theirs but interact differently with them than do many modern Western pet owners by allowing their dogs to roam the streets.[3] For example, in parts of rural Mexico, 60% to 85% of households admit to owning dogs (Orihuela & Solano, 1995), many of which serve protective roles while also being a source of companionship, but they are allowed to roam.

Of course, accepting the presence of street dogs does not necessarily mean that every resident wants them in their neighborhood or would bother to care for them. People may claim to like them but still prefer to keep their distance. For example, Hasler et al. (2011) found that almost half of their respondents in Colombo City, Sri Lanka, said they "liked dogs very much," that dogs were "valuable possessions," and that "dogs add happiness to people's lives," but almost as many said they "don't like being close to dogs," they "don't like having street dogs around on their street," and "street dogs pose a danger to people." And in Samoa, while 77% of respondents said they "liked" street dogs, few said they would ever care for dogs that were not theirs (Farnworth et al., 2012).

This clash of perspectives occurs in parts of Costa Rica where people do not have a binary view of dogs that sees them as owned or not, pets or not, controlled or not. They do not see street dogs as out of place and unacceptably disruptive, dirty, or even dangerous. Because their presence is normal people coexist with these animals, living comfortably with what to outsiders is a problem in need of correction and embracing what to outsiders is an ambiguous status.[4] This coexistence means that Costa Ricans have complicated and varied relationships with the many different roles played by these animals, relationships that sometimes involve more attachment to and responsibility for them than terms like "stray" would ever suggest to outsiders. And buttressing these relationships are customs and beliefs that justify the very human and animal behaviors that some humane organizations would like to change.

The Social Roles of Street Dogs

For the most part, relationships with street animals in the poorer and more remote villages and towns of Costa Rica do not fit any extreme. Most are not as independent as dump dogs or as dependent as pets in modern countries. Instead, the majority of Costa Rican street dogs are owned, albeit loosely, by an individual or family or shared by a neighborhood with multiple individuals or families who modestly and erratically contribute to their upkeep and care. And in this middle zone between independence and dependence, street animals can occupy many different social roles in terms of how they behave with people and how locals regard them.

Owned dogs that are allowed to roam the streets are hard to tell apart from the few true strays. Most look alike. One rescuer said that if she sees a dog running around on the street in the United States, she grabs it and takes it to a shelter. If it has a collar, she tries to return it to the owner. But in Costa Rica she will not randomly pick up a street dog because it is impossible for her to tell by its appearance if the dog is owned in some way or truly stray. Strays can appear well fed and groomed, while owned dogs can seem not. She elaborated, "In some neighborhoods, you can't tell which dog is a stray and which is someone's in-and-out pet. I used to live in a nice condo and sometimes my Pantheon would get out. There was a similar looking dog to my Pantheon. It was a much larger black and white dog, but they're like, 'Your dog's out again.' And I'd be like, 'it's not my dog.'"

Despite looking alike and sharing the same streets of villages and towns in rural Costa Rica, many street dogs, as well as some cats, are different from true strays because they play a variety of social roles in the community. That they behave differently and have different expectations and norms associated with them is largely due to differing degrees of control over and attachment to them that affect the extent of their daily mobility near a particular location, neighborhood, or entire community. The role ambiguity that results is a major feature of their liminality, which most Costa Ricans do not view as abnormal, confusing, or in any way distressing. People just live with these multiple roles as a social fact.

Being a companion is one common role for some street dogs. The individual or family who consider these companion street dogs as theirs will name and usually provide them with some food and water. The animals may even get veterinary checkups, vaccinations, and treatments for relatively minor problems like worms. However, they are not kept inside homes or behind fencing or chained or tethered in a backyard. They are simply allowed to roam, with varying degrees of freedom. They can leave their owner's property and interact with neighbors who may pat or play with them, call them by name, or even bring them occasional treats or food.

People considering them to be their companions will have some degree of attachment to and responsibility for these animals, although not to the degree usually reported in modern Western pet relationships.[5] Nevertheless, their relations have an affective, emotional component. This finding is contrary to many studies that minimize the affective significance of pets living in or near poverty because they emphasize the utilitarian benefits of pets, such as security, especially in developing countries (Pistorius et al., 1992), and are based on two-dimensional classifications of relationships with dogs as either affective or instrumental (see Serpell, 2004). In reality, these relationships can be more complicated and ambivalent than an either-or classification best suited for surveys. In the lives of the pet owners we studied in rural Costa Rica, pets kept outside for most or all of the day could serve both functions.

On closer inspection, we found that gender had some impact on attachment to these pets in Costa Rica. Male heads of households demonstrated somewhat greater attachment to pets than did females, a finding that is consistent with prior studies of gender differences and attitudes toward pets in developing countries. For example, males in Tanzania (Knobel, Laurenson, Kazwala, & Cleaveland, 2008) and Kuwait (Al-Fayez et al., 2003) are somewhat more attached to dogs than are females. But our observation is contrary to previous studies that either have shown that females generally exhibit a greater degree of attachment to companion animals (Miura et al., 2000; Selby & Rhoades, 1981) or have found relatively small or no gender differences (Herzog, 2007), all of which point to the role that culture plays in shaping attitudes toward animals.

Neighbors acknowledge the association of companion street dogs with a person or family. They are seen as belonging together and having a relationship that sets the two apart from other relationships they have with people or animals in their town. They are a sociological "with" (Sanders, 1999) in that people seeing the two assume some meaningful connection between them and view them as a unit. So a street dog can be owned by someone or family but, despite its roaming, still be regarded by neighbors or others as a social unit even if far from home, where the dog can also have pet-like relations with a number of people.

For example, some Costa Ricans take their pets to work but leave them outside. The dog establishes itself nearby on the street until it is time to drive home, although sometimes wondering a block or two away. For example, every day the owner of Edison takes him to work—a tour information business located on the city's main road used by speeding motorists and buses, just a few feet from Edison's spot outside the door of her owner's store. Edison is known by name by all the local proprietors as well as many customers who frequent these businesses.

Owners trust that their pets on the street will remain close and be smart enough to not be hit by cars, get into dog fights, or run off with packs of dogs in pursuit of risky adventure and scavenging. Indeed, more than one Costa Rican noted the intelligence of these street dogs to recognize and avoid potentially dangerous situations, perhaps justifying the permission given them to explore and roam the general area "with their friends." Owners endorsed this kind of local roaming, especially in groups of other owned dogs, because it was thought to be considerate and humane given the dogs' "nature" to explore the neighborhood.

Other street dogs play ephemeral pet-like roles where the extent of attachment or responsibility for an animal is a fleeting connection lasting but a few hours or at best days. These "vacation pets," as one tourist calls them, are another way that street dogs play the role of companion. Costa Ricans claim that street dogs sometimes adopt strangers and form brief relationships with them. Some tourists respond to the solicitations of street dogs in caring ways and perhaps "adopt" them for a few hours or less commonly for a few days. Tourists may pity them and offer leftovers or scraps. For example, one street dog visited a restaurant in a coastal village and tried to get handouts from a tourist eating outside. The dog sat quietly next to the young man, which led him to start petting and talking to it. Both were soon joined by his sister and mother, who proceeded to give the dog more food, ask a restaurant server for a bowl of water, and discuss how this street dog resembled a former, loved family pet. For the rest of the day, this dog trailed after the family as they toured the town on foot, receiving occasional petting and at one point getting to play fetch with the boy.

Vacation pets can benefit their adopters (Coppinger & Coppinger, 2016). For example, one tourist was vacationing by herself in a small Costa Rican town. A street dog befriended her and followed her all day, allegedly sticking by her side. According to this woman, the dog actually protected her from a man "who was being really creepy. He had a machete and mumbled something that sounded a little threatening to me." In response, the dog immediately jumped at this man and bared his teeth, causing the intruder to run away, although the dog was "nice to everybody else in the city." It followed her into a restaurant and sat under her feet while she had coffee. When she went into a clothing store, the dog knew it could not go inside so it sat outside and waited. On the way back to her hotel, in response to a fight between some rottweilers, this street dog put its side into her, "like it was hip checking me away from the situation. The dog basically adopted me and took care of me the whole day." In return, the street dog briefly received attention, affection, and food.

Street animals can also become more enduring companions, but still not be owned, when they assume the role of mascot to people at work. These human-animal friendships with strangers can sometimes become quite close and involve caring for animals on a regular basis, although falling short of providing basic veterinary care. This kind of relationship can develop when street animals affiliate with a public space where they become mascots that are named, occasionally fed although not daily, and given attention by the humans they encounter. For example, they can become workers' mascots by forming affiliations and developing routine relationships with building or property guards, where they occupy a distinct social space in villages that is neither truly feral nor apart from human connection. While these quasi mascots are usually dogs, occasionally we observed a street cat playing this role. Discussions of stray and village dogs typically ignore the copresence of cats in the same locations where dogs roam because cats are far less visible ("they're always in the bushes and shrubs") than dogs and in underdeveloped and developing nations are rarely regarded as companions. As one Costa Rican said, "I don't want to treat a cat like a pet, it needs to run away."

One such mascot cat lived in the coastal town of Manuel Antonio. Here, at an exclusive ocean-side hotel, a cat named Tigre lives "somewhere in the mountains" at night but provides company for the guards during the day and early evening when they operate a gate into the parking lot. The guards feed Tigre every day (a bag of dry food is kept in the guard station) and let it sleep in front of their guard shed. When guards exit the shed, Tigre sometimes rubs against their legs and the guards might pet the cat, but more often they, somewhat distantly, let the animal mark them. It is highly unlikely that any veterinary care is provided in these kinds of human–street cat relationships.

Other street dogs play a different role—neighbor. With this relationship the emotional investment in these animals and willingness to be responsible for their welfare are diminished. Drifting away from their principal home, these dogs have great independence and stray far, leaving them unprotected from the elements, traffic, and other hazards. Those who own these dogs are less likely to feed, shelter, or provide veterinary care for them and often are unaware of where they go during the day, although the animals are expected to stay in the neighborhood's general vicinity when they leave their owners' homes in the morning. They are mobile fixtures of village streets or blocks where neighbors, shopkeepers, and workers recognize and expect to see them from time to time during the day as fellow residents. Many neighbors may call these dogs by name, even if not the names given by their owners, and think they know which homes claim the dogs as theirs.

Neighborhood dogs are akin to homeless people who have a place at night to sleep or "crash" but consider the street more their "home" (Ravenhill, 2016). For example, one neighborhood dog, after leaving its evening home in Puerto Viejo, routinely stopped at a nearby laundry where employees expected "Pedro" to appear around the premises most days. They had no idea where the dog went at night, nor did the dog's owner know that "Pablo," as he called it, returned to this laundry most days as it explored the neighborhood, also stopping by a sandwich shop, the butcher, the bakery, the post office, and a small department store where it was known by yet other names. Proprietors of these businesses sometimes knowingly leave scraps for Pedro/Pablo, even though it is not regarded as a mascot, or tolerate it rifling through their garbage cans for food.[6] At night he returns to sleep somewhere on his owner's property, whether on the porch, in the driveway, or in the yard.

Other street animals play roles that are even less pet-like, if at all, when they serve more of an instrumental purpose in the community, such as guard dog. These animals do not form bonds with strangers they work with but hang around a particular location, sometimes alone or with a few other animals, where human entry into the setting is restricted, perhaps by a gate, a doorman, a fence, or a ticket booth. Dogs in particular will sometimes linger around a particular place where their presence is viewed by most humans who work there as a form of community security. These street dogs will commonly station themselves near small sheds housing humans who guard properties, such as a condominium complex, zoo, office building, or hospital. Despite their unsolicited help, most do not become mascots. Guards rarely if ever name, play with, or touch them and only occasionally feed them because they do not feel responsible for their welfare or for sterilizing them.

Some street dogs play the role of friendly beggar. They manage to get daily handouts, have shelter from the elements, and are rarely harmed by the people with whom they interact. They are peaceable fixtures living on the fringes of town. Many people feel it is their public duty to help these animals survive, similar to offering money to human beggars. So these animals are tolerated as cohabitants of certain public locations, although more pet-like relationships with them are rare. Rather than roaming throughout the community to acquire resources either alone or in mixed packs of owned and stray dogs, these street dogs might affiliate with or adopt a location where they have shelter, handouts of food, and occasional attention from those who work there or otherwise use or pass through the space.[7] For example, in the shantytown of Ipis on the outskirts of San Jose is a large parking lot covered with a roof that is home to three nameless dogs who are fed scraps, especially raw chicken, from the nearby restaurant. People who routinely use the garage recognize them and think the dogs "live there," but usually neither approach them as pets nor shoo them away. They are seen as familiar and unthreatening habitants of the space they have adopted.

By contrast, other street dogs in their pursuit of food are viewed more as pests than as pets. They do not establish human connections and are sometimes harmed. These neighborhood dogs join opportunistic packs with unowned stray dogs in search of food during the day. When in packs, their social role in the community changes. They are usually not seen or interacted with and seldom behave as pets, appearing to be more wild than domesticated. If seen, they are often ignored, as happens when garbage collectors make their rounds and are trailed through the streets by packs of dogs. Some people at best recognize and tolerate these mixed packs of dogs, but direct contact, such as petting or naming, is rare. These street dogs are more interested in each other than in people, whether to smell, fight, or mate, along with constant scavenging for food. That they keep their distance from people, other than when provided food, is perhaps due to having been abused by strangers who in the past have thrown rocks at them or otherwise tried to harm them. For example, a pack of dogs in Playa Palado, known locally as the Palado Pack (named after the local village), is unaffiliated with a person, family, or neighborhood but hangs out with local fishermen. While volunteer rescuers feed these dogs every day, the fishermen claim little responsibility, rarely offering fish scraps and often throwing bottles at them when drunk.

Whether pest, beggar, guard, neighbor, mascot, vacation pet, or companion, street dogs are ensconced in the community. Ruiz-Izaguirre and Eilers (2012) describe this embeddedness of street animals within their communities as a "social niche," or the transactions of animals with people that insert them into the surrounding community (Gilgun, 1999; Taylor, 1997). As part of a social niche, street animals provide various functions to owners and associate with many others, but they are more sociologically connected to their communities than this term suggests. They occupy a social world where they can perform a mix of roles with different people who come to expect certain behaviors from the animals and from themselves. By playing these customary roles, street animals are part of the community's everyday life and an accepted and essential feature of its social structure. Moreover, these relationships, at least from the animal's perspective, can be more complex than suggested by the term "social niche" because some street animals occupy different roles with different people. The same street animal at night may be someone's semi-pet, in the morning someone's mascot, and in the afternoon a beggar, for example. All of these roles, in turn, are supported by beliefs and values about interacting with street dogs that are handed down from generation to generation and supported by sanctions that ensure that the behaviors of street animals and the people who interact with them remain fairly stable over time.

Limited Responsibility

From the perspective of Costa Ricans, the presence of street dogs is normal. It is accepted and expected that they are somewhat uncontrolled, partially uncivilized, and a natural part of the public landscape of city and village life rather than intruders or spoilers of them, with the exception of elite adopters of sterilization and other veterinary services who may live in higher socioeconomic neighborhoods and share the modern dichotomy of dogs as either controlled pets or truly stray. For those Costa Ricans who live with street dogs as a normal feature of everyday life, expecting them to exert greater control over

these animals, whether supporting efforts to reduce their numbers or restricting their freedom and independence, will be an uphill battle for NGOs trying to
reduce animal overpopulation and change how pet owners interact with their
charges. Responsibility has cultural limits.

From a cultural perspective, in parts of Costa Rica there are customs and
beliefs about dogs and cats that justify Costa Ricans taking limited or no responsibility for their animals' behavior and welfare. Although rural or poor urban residents feed their pets only irregularly, if at all, and let them roam, they
do not perceive themselves to be irresponsible owners. They do not assume
much responsibility because they do not feel attached to or own their pets in
modern Western ways. This view becomes a self-fulfilling prophecy because
it ensures that Costa Ricans will distance themselves from animals and take
less responsibility for their care and welfare when they are on or near their
property. Many dogs and almost all cats are kept outside where their roaming
leaves them covered in dust, dirt, thorns, and bugs, making them "too dirty" to
touch. Costa Ricans then avoid close interactions with dirty animals, making
sure to avoid direct contact with them and to keep them out of the house at all
times. In turn, modern responsibilities for pets, such as washing and grooming and the close contact those entail, become impossible for these Costa Ricans to conceive, as does a view of their animals as pets.

Not feeling responsible for pets is also blamed on the animals themselves.
Many animals find people to "adopt," a term commonly used by Costa Ricans
to describe how they did not intend to acquire an animal but the animal chose
them, allowing the owner to disclaim any responsibility for establishing and
therefore maintaining the relationship. For example, those who decide to have
a dog by adopting or buying it have made a distinct decision and consider it
to be theirs, but if the dog adopts them, they have not made this decision, so
the dog is not considered to be theirs. If Costa Ricans do not choose a dog but
it chooses them, the dog tends to be viewed as more disposable and replace-
able, while also being owed less care, than if a Costa Rican purchased it, was
given to him or her as a gift, or was selected from a litter or at the shelter. In
such adopted-by-animal relationships, dogs and cats become expendable objects that can be easily replaced, if so desired.

Compounding this view, some people have an instrumental view of dogs
and cats that further limits, if not eliminates, their sense of responsibility for
animal welfare. In particular, dogs are often viewed as guards while cats are
valued for their ability to control and eradicate mice, rats, snakes, and other
unwelcomed creatures, especially in rural Costa Rica. These animals are
looked at more as "employees" than as family. Fortunate guard dogs have a
doghouse and access to water, but many do not. They may be named, but if
seen primarily as guards or working animals, they are unlikely to be played

with, groomed, or otherwise interacted with as are pets in modern Western countries. This view of animals also means that sterilization will be avoided when people want to breed cats or dogs to supplement their income.[8] In one town these opportunistic breeders can be seen selling kittens and puppies next to a supermarket.

Animals viewed instrumentally are also seen as more disposable and more easily replaced. If these animals become sick or injured, Costa Ricans accept little if any responsibility for veterinary care and either throw them out on the street and ignore or do nothing as they suffer, until a neighbor reports them, or they will drop off the animal to the shelter themselves. If they do not dispose of the compromised animal, some Costa Ricans simply deny ownership of and therefore responsibility for sick or injured animals if confronted by humane workers.

When limited attachment and responsibility for animals combine with the view of them as street smart as well as natural and happy roamers, many Costa Ricans simply abandon them when they move, lose interest in them, or want to replace them with a new dog. Owners believe their dogs are smart enough to not be hit by cars, get into dog fights, or run off great distances with packs of dogs in pursuit of risky adventure and scavenging. Indeed, more than one Costa Rican noted the intelligence of these street dogs to recognize and avoid potentially dangerous situations, perhaps justifying the permission given them to explore and roam the general area "with their friends." Owners also endorsed this kind of local roaming, especially in groups of other owned dogs, because it was thought to be considerate and humane, given the dog's "nature" to explore the neighborhood, much like strays.

When it comes to taking some responsibility for dogs or cats not on one's own property, it is unsurprising that most rural or urban poor Costa Ricans are usually indifferent to these animals. However, they may take partial and occasional responsibility for a street animal if it is a neighborhood dog they recognize and perhaps know its owner, although it might not have one. Costa Ricans in rural areas claim that they recognize most if not all street dogs in their neighborhoods, often knowing their names and owners if someone claims them, or at least which house or houses they belong to, if they return to one home. In cities, distinguishing strays from neighborhood dogs is more difficult because dogs tend to be kept in homes or yards, so people do not routinely see them. If rural Costa Ricans take limited care of a neighborhood dog, they often do so realizing they are not acting alone, since other nearby families are likely doing the same thing. So, it is understood that this kind of street dog can have multiple caretakers, but not owners, who often provide some minimal level of care in a neighborhood where no one thinks of themselves as the animal's owner.

Despite this weak animal connection, one way that Costa Ricans occasionally care for neighborhood dogs is to feed them, even though they do not own them. For example, if several dogs come and go from a particular home and are fed there, the owner will claim ownership of only one dog, despite feeding the others. If asked why they feed the others, the Costa Rican will typically say, "I felt they needed it, but they're not my dogs." While some people feed these dogs sporadically, there are many cases where they are fed on a regular basis. Ramble is one such neighborhood dog in the town of Nosara. There was a woman who had claimed to own him, but she had a differing name for him and said he never wanted to come home because everyone feeds him. On a typical day, Ramble hangs around a gas station that is near a grocery store and a veterinarian's office. The grocery provides food every morning to the veterinarian, who in turn feeds breakfast to Ramble. Ramble then "sneaks" over to the coffee shop nearby where the people feed him treats. This process is continued until early evening with different daily feeders.

A few neighborhood dogs may even have Costa Ricans pay for some of their veterinary care, yet still not see themselves as their owners. "They go there, they sleep there, they eat there, they were born there, but they're not our cats," as one Costa Rican noted. Some of these community animals occasionally receive veterinary care for everyday problems as well as for more severe issues. For example, Paco is an unowned street dog known by everyone in his village. People have tried to adopt him, but, according to a local Costa Rican, "he'll be happy for like a month (after being adopted). Then he'll start getting out roaming again, and be away for a day, then two days. Finally, people give up (trying to own him). He's just a dog that's never been owned and is happier to just have five owners and come and go as he pleases." Townspeople even opened a Facebook page called "Where's Paco?" to make sure that someone would take care of him if needed. When he was spotted in town they would post something like, "Okay, I saw Paco in town today he's looking really good. Has anybody gotten him a flea collar?" Someone else would comment on the post and say, "No, but if I see him around, I'll put one on him." Community members might also help a street dog in distress, such as picking up stray dogs that are injured and taking them to a veterinarian. For example, Negrita was a little black dog that was hit by a bus. A bystander recalled, "I was like, 'Oh my god.' I ran up to it. Some guy came and helped me take it to a vet, who said he would take care of it. I gave him $20 and said I know it's not enough to take care of this dog and its injuries, but can you please do everything you can. He said 'thanks but I would have helped him anyway.'"

However, even dogs that Costa Ricans consider to be theirs are not always given routine wellness veterinary procedures that are taken for granted in modern Western countries. For example, some Costa Ricans refuse to have their dogs vaccinated. These Costa Ricans believe that "it won't happen to my dog," meaning they are convinced their animal will not get whatever diseases that vaccines prevent, such as distemper. One shelter worker likened this view to Costa Ricans' attitudes toward having HIV. "Ninety percent of Costa Ricans refuse to use a condom because they don't take responsibility, thinking that it won't happen to them. It doesn't happen to me. It doesn't happen to my dog." Compounding this view is the fact that some Costa Ricans believe that strays are less likely to acquire diseases than are pedigree dogs.

When it comes to spaying or neutering animals, Costa Ricans have shown increased willingness to do so with animals they consider to be their own, but not with strays or neighborhood dogs they might feed. These Costa Ricans have come to understand and accept sterilization as a strategy to semi-restrict the movement of their animals to the general area near their homes because they believe that sterilized animals' behavior changes and will be less inclined to roam far from home. In these cases sterilization is seen as a way to protect animals. For example, one man brought two cats to an outreach clinic because he was afraid they would eat poison and die if their roaming continued, so to keep them close to home he had them sterilized, hoping this would change their behavior.

Although these Costa Ricans will sterilize animals, they expect that the surgery will restrict but not stop their roaming. Many keep their dogs on their property at night, behind a fence or chained to a tree, but when they leave for work they open their doors and release them to roam the streets. Owners consider leashes an unnecessary restraint and muzzles a form of cruelty when on the streets.

Indeed, allowing dogs to roam makes sense to many Costa Ricans because they understand it from the dog's psychological perspective. But roaming is a problem to modern Western thinking because it focuses on the street dog's physical health: street animals can suffer malnutrition, encounter animal abuse, and have multiple diseases and disabilities causing them to be unhappy and suffer. Instead, many Costa Ricans believe that it is a dog's nature to be free to roam and that its nature should be respected. Costa Ricans thus see roaming as a positive experience for dogs—they not only find food but also get to experience a "free life" where they can play and have adventures with other dogs, which they could not do if restricted to a house or yard. The result is that dogs on the streets are "happy," claim Costa Ricans, so they do not see the point of getting them off the street.[9] Hence for most rural or poor urban Costa Ricans, allowing their dogs to roam is seen not as an expression of bad citizenship or irresponsibility.

The issue of allowing cats to roam does not arise since virtually all Costa Ricans living in small villages in the countryside or coast, or in poor urban neighborhoods, never restrict these animals to their property. They are free to roam at any time. And cats, unlike dogs, are not usually considered animals one needs to feed because they do their own foraging and hunting while roaming.

Once allowed to roam, dogs commonly get into mischief, perhaps knocking over and spilling garbage cans or threatening people. However, many rural, coastal, and poor urban Costa Rican dog owners consider it to be an optional responsibility to control their animals if they do something that might be considered a nuisance or a threat to the health or safety of others, and at least they will "not shit in my garden." In addition, when "owned" dogs commit untoward acts, they are attributed to the animal's nature and accepted as such. So it is acceptable that dogs are allowed to bark, defecate, run around, and bite whoever and wherever because, as one Costa Rican said, "They are only 'animalitos.' They do not know any better, pobrecitos!"

Taking limited responsibility for street animals along with Costa Ricans' ambiguous view of them are a major part of their "animalito" culture. To succeed, social policies to combat animal overpopulation need to problematize this culture for Costa Ricans or at least question how they have conventionally viewed street animals as something to just be lived with. But changing a culture, or even one aspect thereof, can be a formidable task.

Adjusting to Local Culture

Because they constantly interact with Costa Ricans, their animals, and the surrounding culture, El Refugio's staff members, as well as those from other outreach and rescue groups, understand Costa Ricans' perspective toward dogs and cats. This gives workers and volunteers a realistic view of what is possible to achieve when it comes to diffusing basic veterinary care and modern pet-keeping practices in the most underserved parts of Costa Rica. With this knowledge, staff members and volunteers adjust their expectations for changing Costa Ricans' behavior in ways that are reasonable and practical, given the realities of their lives and their customary ways of dealing with animals.

By adjusting expectations, shelter workers and animal advocates modify or shift their working definition of what constitutes responsible ownership and acceptable pet-keeping behavior to be culturally sensitive. While they believe that responsible ownership of animals should minimally include provision of food and water and freedom from physical abuse and from overly short tethers, their opinions differ as to what can reasonably be expected of Costa Ricans, given local customs and economic realities. So El Refugio's expectations of Costa Ricans are adjusted and lowered from an ideal standard of modern Western pet ownership to match what most Costa Ricans are able and willing to do in terms of being responsible for animals. What it means to have a pet and be responsible for it can then be redefined, so Costa Ricans can embrace these expected behaviors as their own.

One example is the instrumental view of dogs and cats that values them for their labor. Working animals who are "lucky" enough to have a home in rural and coastal towns are primarily kept for protection and pest control rather than for any emotional or relational benefit they might provide. These dogs and cats are usually treated as disposable objects that are easily replaced if lost, not worth the money to treat if injured or sickened, and not given much thought as to their basic welfare. Indeed, the very discomfort of working animals is sometimes justified as making them better at their tasks. For example, some Costa Ricans believe that a hungry cat will catch more mice and a chained dog will be a better guard.

This instrumental view has slowly changed in recent years as more Costa Ricans desire companionship from animals, but it still exists and can sometimes be the main or only motivation to acquire animals at shelters or buy them on the market. Although shelter and rescue workers who handle adoptions may have mixed feelings about adopting out dogs to Costa Ricans who want them as watchdogs, most have taken on a realistic view of Costa Rican culture that allows dogs to be adopted by people who want them for protection rather than companionship. These shelter and rescue workers believe that it is better to get dogs out of shelters than to risk not getting them adopted. They also think that some owners who want watchdogs will learn to treat them compassionately as house pets; with time and education these instrumentally motivated adopters will perhaps discover the pleasures of interacting with their animals in more affective ways. Of course not every worker has become more realistic; some are reluctant to adopt out dogs to serve as guards because they remain convinced that these owners may not treat their dogs humanely.

Many shelter and rescue workers are also realistic about the modern Western practices of keeping pets inside one's home or walking them on a leash. In part, they see roaming as intractable because stopping this practice seems neither practical nor economically feasible. They know that few Costa Ricans can afford proper fencing to keep animals on their property and homes rarely have walls that are escape-proof for dogs, so unless dogs are restrained in the yard, they will escape and roam. In a certain way, Costa Ricans who chain or restrict their dogs with rope or wire are trying to be responsible pet owners. They are probably doing what they think is right in protecting their animals from being poisoned, hit by cars, or impregnated on the street but do not realize that dogs then need to be walked twice a day and that the method of restriction might harm them. Despite a law from SENASA, or the Nacional de Salud Animal, a government organization that monitors and ensures the welfare of pets, agricultural animals, aquatic and wildlife, and the quality of animal-derived foods, the minimum length of chain it prescribes to secure dogs is ignored by many Costa Ricans who improperly chain their dogs to limit their movement by using leads that overly restrict them or that cut into their necks (e.g., wire). Many shelter and rescue workers would rather see dogs roam than be tied up in ways that are potentially cruel. So, for example, the shelter director says, "We tell people not to tie up their dogs. A dog should not be tied up. I don't like dogs tied up. Maybe if it has a cable for roaming ability. But I hate tied up dogs. I don't like it."

Workers also see roaming as intractable because the practice is so deeply anchored in Costa Rican culture and history. They adjust their expectations accordingly because many Costa Ricans look at roaming from the animal's perspective, believing that dogs and cats are very "street smart" and "savvy" and will not get hurt. While people knowingly take a risk when they let their dogs roam, they also think that most are clever enough to avoid danger, as are cats who are thought to be smart enough not to be eaten by snakes, eagles, or other predators.

Sometimes shelter and rescue staff members also take the animal's perspective to adjust their expectations about roaming, aligning themselves closer to how Costa Ricans view street dogs. Costa Ricans and workers alike believe that some dogs do not want to be owned by anybody or at least by one person or family. As one shelter worker said of street dogs, "They always want to roam around and want this life. They're like monkeys. I've seen them in an enclosure—they crawl up and dive over. They want to roam free." One such dog, Macho, was adopted from the shelter but then returned. Macho was adopted out again but came back on his own when roaming. His last owner was Rosie, a woman who apparently gave him everything, yet he again returned to the shelter. Rosie did not understand why Macho did this and was told by the director that Macho was probably a stray who wanted his freedom. He lived out the rest of his life at the shelter but would roam every day. He would return at exactly four o'clock, when the shelter dogs were fed. All the shelter dogs knew and greeted him. At night he slept with a poor Nicaraguan family, only to roam during the day and make routine stops at places like the shelter.

Rather than reducing their expectations for what Costa Ricans will do with their animals, shelter and rescue workers sometimes manipulate their interactions with Costa Ricans to change their behavior. Knowing that many Costa Ricans are unaccustomed to getting or paying for veterinary care, shelter and outreach workers sometimes coax pet owners into being more responsible for their dogs and cats when they are initially reluctant to do so. One way is to tell them they will save money if their animals get sterilized, which they would be reluctant to do otherwise. For example, sometimes Costa Ricans who bring in unsterilized animals for veterinary problems are told they will be charged less for treatments if they let the shelter sterilize their animals. Most of the time the director or other staff members will try to pressure them into it, as happens when a Costa Rican brings in a dog with an inflamed and infected ear but does not want to neuter it. The director will say, "'Well, if you don't neuter it your cost is so much, but if you do neuter it, your cost is so much [less].' So, touch their money and that's the way to get them to do it, although that's more cost for us."

Another way staff members force Costa Ricans' hand is to tell them that their animals might die if they fail to follow advice. For example, an owner brought to the shelter a nine-year-old pregnant dog whose health was so severely compromised she could die giving birth. Former attempts to have the owner agree to sterilization had failed, but this veterinary emergency provided a window of opportunity to shelter workers to save the dog and get it sterilized. When told the dog should be sterilized, the owner said it would be "terrible to have an abortion now" because the dog was pregnant, to which the shelter worker asked, "Do you want her to die? There's a big chance she will die if she has the puppies." The owner then consented to sterilization.

Even without their pets' lives threatened, Costa Ricans may be warned that without sterilization their animals will face expensive veterinary care in the future. For example, some outreach workers tell Costa Ricans who are reluctant to sterilize that without the procedure their dogs are likely to acquire sexually transmitted diseases, including a form of cancer that can kill their animals and entail huge veterinary bills. "That's how I try to rope these people into getting their animals spayed or neutered," said one shelter worker, who modified her comment by adding, "but even then some people don't give a shit and throw the dog out when it's sick and get another one."

The shelter and other groups providing low-cost sterilization also use tragedies as opportunities to motivate people to get their animals spayed or neutered, thinking that Costa Ricans might be more likely to seek veterinary care if the value of receiving services is put in a local cultural context. A case is Hurricane Otto, which struck eastern Costa Rica in 2016. People living in the areas particularly damaged by the hurricane saw animal loss in addition to destruction of property. Relief workers there made sure to point out that had owners sterilized their animals, there would have been fewer on the streets when the hurricane hit. Nor is the need for sterilization the only teaching opportunity created by tragedies like hurricanes. For example, administrators of Otto relief efforts encouraged donors to see that victims of disasters—whether human or animal—needed and deserved help. For the first time in Costa Rican history food donations after a major disaster were greater for dogs and cats than they were for farm animals. This shift, according to shelter workers, was indirect evidence of the growing importance of pets to Costa Ricans relative to animals having only instrumental value.

A different kind of tragedy can also be transformed into a teaching moment to change public awareness about the need for sterilization. Animal advocates take advantage of highly visible and tragic dog attacks in the area to get more Costa Ricans to sterilize their animals. For example, a tied-up, unneutered rottweiler attacked and killed a girl that was getting a chicken. After this untoward event Costa Ricans started calling the shelter to say they did not want their rottweilers anymore. In response, shelter workers would tell callers that it was not the dog's fault because it was tied up on a short chain. "They made a monster of it. You neuter it and you see the craziness goes out." In another case a pit bull went over a fence and killed a man, leading to a rash of pit bull owners calling the shelter wanting to surrender their dogs. "People would say they have a one-year-old pit bull and were afraid of it. We try to convince them to neuter if it's not an old vicious dog that's been chained. Then there's nothing you can do. But if it's a young dog. . . ."

Whether increasing Costa Ricans' motivation to sterilize animals or modifying their own expectations for what Costa Ricans will do, shelter workers are adjusting to the liminality of street animals. On the one hand, they create a working definition of responsibility for pets that reflects local cultural norms and traditions as well as the reality of how Costa Ricans keep their homes and yards. The result is that their expectations become realistic for how Costa Ricans will manage their animals and whether they provide basic veterinary care for them. To be clear, this realism does not mean that shelter and rescue workers abandon their efforts to improve the welfare of dogs and cats; they just let culture weigh in as they calculate the likely benefit or detriment to animals of Costa Ricans' actions toward the dogs and cats in their lives. At the same time, shelter and rescue workers redouble their efforts to get as many animals sterilized as possible by manipulating their interactions with Costa Ricans so they see the advantages of having this surgery done on their dogs and cats.

Our findings serve as a reminder to all animal welfare NGOs, not just in Costa Rica but in any developing or third world country, that diffusing basic veterinary services calls for an awareness of and sensitivity to well-entrenched beliefs and behaviors toward animals that are possessed by those targeted for change. Without a baseline understanding of local cultural practices toward cats and dogs, it is easy for animal advocates to assume that the initial willingness to accept veterinary services will incrementally spread and have a "domino effect" among everyone in the general population, making it, in theory, easier for everyone to be responsible for their animals, if responsibility means getting animals sterilized, along with caring for their basic needs and health problems. If aware of these potential cultural barriers to change, programs can adapt their strategies for delivering veterinary services to reach the most underserved pet owners, or at least accordingly temper their expectations for changing the behavior of these people.

For the diffusion of veterinary services in Costa Rica, this means that animal advocates cannot assume that most people will think of dogs and cats as either unowned strays or pets in the modern Western sense. Indeed, dichotomous thinking that distinguishes stray dogs from those owned is not relevant or useful to many Costa Ricans, as we have seen in this chapter. Even the term "semi-stray," used by some scholars to acknowledge the limits of this dichotomy (e.g., Pręgowski, 2016), does not fully capture the range of social roles that can develop between humans, dogs, and cats in poor urban or rural areas of Costa Rica. In their interactions with Costa Ricans and tourists, they become companions, mascots, vacation pets, neighbors, guards, beggars, and pests.

Depending on the particular roles assumed by street animals, the degree of attachment to and responsibility for them will vary from fondness to indifference and from taking some responsibility for their basic veterinary needs to taking none. Those that stay close to one home but are still allowed limited roaming or that roam particular neighborhoods will likely be fed, played with, named, and perhaps even sheltered. Of course, this care and attention can be inconsistent for some street roles, especially if an animal hangs out during the week at a workplace as a mascot or guard, when workers are gone over the weekend. Others who roam more remotely do not fare this well, as they lose their pet-like behaviors when they temporarily join packs of roaming dogs that are unowned, only to return to their homes or neighborhoods at night. These latter dogs, the beggars and pests, are lucky to find any food as they scavenge and can even be harmed by people.

What distinguishes these roles from each other is not merely the degree of attachment to, interest in, and responsibility for these animals but, at a more abstract level, the degree to which they are dependent on and controlled by individual Costa Ricans and the local culture. They are most dependent when roaming close to home in pet-like relationships and least dependent when roaming far from home in packs of dogs. Given this declining slope of control over animals and their distance from the people and neighborhoods that think of them as theirs, it might be useful to think of the human–street dog or cat relationship in parts of Costa Rica as one of graduated dependence, an idea suggested by Sandoval-Cervantes (2016), who used this concept to describe the shifting views of dogs in Mexico from pets to pests, which we also saw in Costa Rica. At one extreme, dogs seen as pets have most of their agency controlled by humans, while at the other extreme those viewed as pests are more agents themselves.

Supporting the idea of graduated dependence are long-standing, culturally entrenched beliefs about dogs and cats, held even by many Costa Ricans whose animals are regarded and treated much like modern pets. They see these animals as independent creatures capable of fending for themselves, finding their own food and water somehow, somewhere. They also believe that their innate "nature" makes them want to be independent and roam, so curtailing this biological drive is wrong, impossible, and perhaps even cruel. These beliefs deter owners, neighbors, and most others who have contact with street animals from taking much if any responsibility for their daily care, let alone for providing them with basic veterinary services, especially as they move along the slope of graduated dependence toward greater agency.

As El Refugio pursues its goal of sterilizing as many dogs and cats as possible, the shelter bends but does not completely surrender to the cultural norm that some if not most street animals are independent from their owners. Instead, it acknowledges that owners or others concerned about particular animals will take limited or inconsistent responsibility for them in certain respects, while not abandoning its attempt to reduce animal overpopulation and further the welfare of cats and dogs.

Culture obviously presents a barrier to the shelter's mission, but it also becomes a bridge to understanding the realities of pet owners and knowing how best to convince them to act in the interests of animals, at least sometimes. However, the beliefs of Costa Ricans are only part of the shelter's social world that it must understand and work with to diffuse low-cost veterinary care. Other shelters, rescue groups, and sanctuaries that work outside urban, higher income, and more educated pockets of the country will too. As we see in the next chapter, these animal advocates must deal with each other, as well as with private-practice veterinarians, when trying to sterilize, vaccinate, and medically treat dogs and cats in the underserved parts of Costa Rica. Depending on the degree of trust between groups and the extent to which they have similar philosophies of sterilization, relations among advocates can range from collaboration to conflict, helping either to provide animal care and veterinary services or to deter their diffusion.

CHAPTER TWO

Who Speaks for the Underserved?

COOPERATION AND CONFLICT AMONG
WELFARE AND VETERINARY GROUPS

In the big picture, groups seeking to further the welfare of animals share the same general belief or aspiration—they want animals to be given food, water, shelter, and at least basic veterinary care as well as to be safe and comfortable. Yet disputes among animal advocates are common and well known in the U.S. and U.K. humane communities, sometimes occurring within advocacy organizations or between them. These disagreements are hard to understand—especially to those outside the animal welfare movement—because all of these activists and service providers want the best for animals.

In reality, these organizations often must strain to share the same beliefs about defining animal welfare, let alone furthering it, because of intergroup differences. Unequal distribution of resources within this community as well as different beliefs about the ideological or theoretical nature and value of nonhuman animals, the appropriateness of particular veterinary or sheltering practices, and the perceived urgency of intervening to improve animal well-being all contribute to separating more than uniting animal welfare groups and animal activists, at least in the modern Western context (Arluke, 2003; Balcom & Arluke, 2001; Garner, 1998; Greenebaum, 2009; Guenther, 2017; Peterson, 2018; Winograd, 2009).

Individuals and groups wanting to further animal welfare in Costa Rica are no different. They too share the same general hopes for animals, but in practice sometimes have tense and distrustful relationships with each other, as we see in this chapter. Understanding why this tension develops, or not, and how groups like El Refugio respond to doubts about or disagreements with other groups is important because these relationships might impact the extent to which innovations, like the delivery of low-cost veterinary services, will be diffused in developing countries.

As with any innovation, the diffusion of these services takes place within a social and geographical network of actors and organizations that influence the likelihood that new behaviors are adopted (Young, 2006). This system includes many organizations, grassroots groups, and individuals in Costa Rica working to manage or reduce the animal overpopulation problem and provide basic veterinary care to Costa Rican dog and cat owners. So El Refugio, as the only large animal shelter with a veterinary hospital and adoption facilities, exists side by side with other "shelters," humane NGOs, sterilization outreach programs, sanctuaries, rescue groups, fosterers, and small, community-based grassroots efforts to help animals as well as the country's Colegio de Medicos Veterinarios—a professional organization representing private practitioners. El Refugio's ability to sterilize and provide basic veterinary treatments to as many dogs and cats as possible in Costa Rica will be facilitated or hindered by its relationships with these other groups.

This complex and somewhat confusing organizational landscape of animal advocacy groups has changed dramatically over the last three decades. Thirty years ago, only a small handful of organizations existed in Costa Rica to manage the animal overpopulation problem. Since then, the country has experienced rapidly escalating interest in animal protection and welfare, both wild and domestic (Drews, 2001, 2002), expressed by the growth of organizations and small groups dedicated to finding homes for dogs and cats, providing veterinary care for them, and offering low-cost sterilization. If one includes any group, regardless of size and whether it is formally recognized by the Costa Rican government through SENASA (El Servicio Nacional de Salud Animal), then today there are approximately 100, although it is impossible to obtain a precise number since groups frequently emerge and disappear.

For the most part, even if humane organizations do not consider some of these groups to be legitimate, they operate in a complacent atmosphere that allows them to coexist without much if any intergroup tension. This lack of conflict in much of Costa Rica is largely due to the fact that there is very little, if any, territorial overlap in the services they provide, so it is easy to find an impoverished town in need of low-cost or free veterinary services that is not being helped by another group. Although Costa Rica is not a large country, there are many parts that are isolated from other regions where an animal group may be the sole welfare-promoting organization. For example, one such group in northern Costa Rica that provides low-cost veterinary services, performs rescue and rehabilitation, works with a foster care network, and operates a trap-neuter-release program has no local rivals and works cooperatively with the only other animal organization near the three towns it serves. And in less isolated areas like the central valley around San Jose, there is ever-present, if not expanding, demand for sterilization and basic veterinary care.

Although cooperation among groups that sterilize or otherwise deal with unowned animals can still develop when there is territorial overlap, intergroup differences make tension or conflict more likely. In particular, a group's beliefs—as much as or more than its location, size, gender, and even resources—can facilitate intergroup support or create strain. Rescuers, shelter workers, and veterinarians have different perspectives about spaying and neutering as well as animal overpopulation, euthanasia, the well-being of animals, and the responsibility of pet owners toward their charges. Adherents to these perspectives make implicit judgments about what is correct, or not, to do regarding the value and role of sterilization as a tool to manage overpopulation, the duties of owners, and the responsibility of shelters and other advocacy groups for street or unowned animals. They are moralities of sterilization.

Moralities of sterilization can affect how animal advocacy groups and veterinarians view and interact with one another, and ultimately the extent to which basic veterinary services are diffused throughout the country. Depending on the degree to which groups share and act on the same morality, this perspective toward sterilization, animal overpopulation, and empathy for pet owners and animals can either provide the basis either for cooperation or for strain and distrust among them. For a humane organization like El Refugio, pursing its goals of providing low-cost sterilization and encouraging more responsible pet ownership requires it to cope in different ways with these other groups, whether their sterilization moralities are compatible or conflicting.

As we see next, when different advocacy group share the same morality of sterilization, their relationship tends to be complementary and requires few if any adjustments, exchanges, or sacrifices to coexist. Different groups can then assist each other as they jointly pursue the goals of both helping impoverished owners deal with the costs of veterinary care and using sterilization as a tool to reduce overpopulation and animal suffering. For the most part, El Refugio tries to support these complementary approaches, while enabling women to become empowered in the process.

Compatible Moralities

The sterilization morality expressed by El Refugio and other established sterilization programs is shared by many grassroots animal advocates who aid the efforts of larger and more established organizations to sterilize and rehome stray dogs and cats. Known as "independent rescuers," they often have reputations as the "animal lovers" in their villages or towns. They can act alone or in very small groups. In some areas, there can be multiple rescue groups of varying sizes and legal statuses. For example, in San Ramon there is only one legally recognized animal rescue group that sends its mobile unit, in which sterilizations are performed, to 10 different towns in its vicinity and is manned by about 20 to 30 volunteers and a veterinarian, the latter being paid approximately $10 per sterilization performed, but several other unrecognized rescue groups exist in the area.

Support for these rescuers is strongest in areas of the country where there are no shelter facilities. Here, grassroots efforts take up some of the slack left by the absence of conventional shelters because they find homes for stray animals, whether sterilized or not, treat those that are sick or injured, funnel unsterilized animals to outreach sterilization clinics, and supply needed manpower to support the operation of remote outreach sterilization clinics.

Grassroots rescuers often turn to local town governments and larger humane organizations for help because they have few resources to run their operations. Towns can subsidize sterilizations or provide free use of a building for clinics, although a minimum of 10 volunteers is required for a rescue group to be legally recognized as a formal association that can seek public donations. Some rescuers depend on El Refugio and sterilization-only groups because they do not have enough capital, cages, or access to veterinary care to take care of rescued animals. Since El Refugio has more resources and experience than other shelters or sterilization-only groups, it sometimes pitches in and helps them.

Some tension can result when smaller shelters or rescue groups want to give some of their animals to El Refugio because they are unable to care for them or choose not to do so. If El Refugio accepts these animals, most will be difficult to adopt out and many will probably need veterinary care. This forces the shelter to expend additional resources to cover the added personnel, overhead, and animal care costs, leaving it with fewer resources to share with smaller advocacy groups that struggle to stay afloat. The shelter's director and some staff members resent this dependence on them for expensive services that are often unpaid and question why other groups do not try to better their financial situation by hiring a veterinarian who could raise revenue from providing veterinary care. In turn, these resource-lacking grassroots groups fail to understand why El Refugio chooses not to share its resources since it has much more compared to them.

Despite the occasional frustrations and complaints aired on both sides, El Refugio's efforts are more than simple interorganizational charity. Its support of independent rescuers means that the shelter as well as some of the other sterilization-only groups are grassroots support organizations (GSOs). As a GSO, El Refugio helps these struggling groups sterilize dogs and cats at the lowest price and gives them advice about how to increase donations by having a sterilization program. This support can diffuse the idea and practice of sterilization as a method to control animal overpopulation, not as a requirement for accepting the shelter's aid but as a consequence.

The shelter's involvement with rescuers can also empower many of them, especially women, as is often true of NGOs (Martínez, 2008) that deliver services to disadvantaged communities in developing countries (Miraftab, 1997). The vast majority of independent rescuers are women between the ages of 20 and 30. The few men who help these groups are usually husbands of advocates and are thought to be much less involved or committed to helping animals and the sterilization clinics. That independent rescuers are commonly women—indeed, that women are so heavily represented in Costa Rica's animal welfare and advocacy groups—should not surprise us since women heavily outnumber men globally in animal rights and welfare movements (Gaarder, 2011; Jasper & Nelkin, 1991; Kruse, 1999).

Helping women assume roles as animal advocates in grassroots organizations can empower them in Costa Rica because many do not have access to modestly paying jobs, let alone work. Only 56% of Costa Rica's female population is currently engaged in the workforce, although a majority of the population aspires to occupational success. Consequently, some women forfeit their professional ambitions to fulfill domestic responsibilities and refrain from confronting obstacles in the way of occupational success (Osborne, 2013). This stunts their socioeconomic development and constrains them to traditionally prescribed gender roles. Participation in animal advocacy groups, even though they usually are volunteering, may provide them with a sense of purpose and mission as well as leadership roles, absent in their lives.

One important function is for rescue volunteers to help establish and run sterilization outreach clinics. They contact veterinarians at outreach organizations to come to their towns to run clinics; help create awareness in their communities for the need to sterilize animals; provide information to local people about the dates and locations of clinics; administrate clinics, including arranging for appointments, having forms signed, and collecting sterilization fees; buy and serve food for the volunteers and veterinary staff; and set up, shut down, and then clean the facilities. Leftover food is sometimes fed to street animals. For example, one volunteer emptied the remaining food (i.e., rice, chicken, beans) from the lunch served to staff members at an outreach clinic into a single container, the contents of which she then left on the streets for strays to eat.

Some volunteers also gather dogs, and occasionally cats, needing to be sterilized so they can be operated on at the outreach clinics. Some of this effort involves collecting apparently unowned street dogs. Volunteers may keep up to

10 of these dogs at a time in their own homes until the day they are driven to the shelter to be sterilized. They also take animals that neighbors give them into their homes, without any money for the surgery and often with a threat to release them back onto the streets unsterilized or simply to kill them. It is common for volunteers to keep those animals that are not adopted out as their own pets, whether indoors, confined outside by fencing or a chain, or allowed to roam the neighborhood.

At times volunteers helping outreach programs also transport Costa Ricans and their pets to sterilization outreach clinics. Some even arrange and pay for taxis, if available and affordable, to get people and their animals to the clinics. If taxis are not an option, they will pick up and transport animals to the sterilization clinics when residents are unwilling or unable to take responsibility for doing this. In one such case, a San Ramon volunteer working with El Refugio's outreach team retrieved five dogs and cats from two homes and drove them to be sterilized because the pet owners had no cars, could not afford to take taxis, and had no public transportation to the clinic.

If an extra hand is needed, volunteer rescuers might assist the veterinary team during pre- or postop. For example, a volunteer might help the veterinary technician shave and clean a dog's stomach in preparation for sterilization surgery. Other volunteers might pick up from the floor and carry dogs and cats still under postop anesthesia, where the veterinary technician lays them, to a more comfortable and perhaps quieter corner of the room where they are then covered in blankets and occasionally watched.

Outreach programs also depend on volunteers to help with costs, such as relying on their personal knowledge of local residents' ability to afford the $12 sterilization fee, $4 of which the volunteers raise. By living in the community, volunteers know local people who have cats or dogs and can reliably assess whether these owners cannot afford even the modest payment requested by the shelter. This knowledge is helpful, especially when mobile clinics first begin visiting towns, because some local people try to take advantage of the reduced fee and bring animals to the clinic, claiming that they are unowned street animals so they should not be charged anything for the surgery, when in fact they are owned. Volunteers also raise funds by informally asking other residents of the villages for donations or by setting up and collecting money from donation boxes strategically placed in restaurants and popular locations to help pay for the costs of renting spaces to be converted to temporary clinics, hiring veterinarians, and buying supplies and food for workers. A few advocates also donate their own money to help defray the costs of the sterilization outreach programs.

Other community rescuers facilitate a different outreach model. Once a week they gather dogs and cats needing sterilization, whether somewhat stray (these animals hang around outside an individual's home and are fed and given water but are not considered house pets) or owned as a pet by neighbors, and drive them not to a mobile clinic but to El Refugio, at great distance, for spaying or neutering. Pet owners and concerned residents drive or use taxis to drop off their cats and dogs at the rescuer's home, where they are put on a truck to El Refugio for sterilization. While driving to the shelter, the truck and the volunteer will make stops along the way in neighboring towns to pick up a dog or a cat that could not be brought to the rescuer's home. After surgery they are returned to their owners' homes, sometimes as far as a two-hour drive from the shelter.

For example, one community rescuer in the greater Cartago area has been working with outreach sterilization organizations like El Refugio for over 20 years. At one time she allowed her home to be turned into a temporary surgical suite, with sterilization surgery conducted on top of her washing machine. More recently she has furthered El Refugio's sterilization mission by coordinating remote sterilizations and using her home as a drop-off point for animals that will be taken to and fixed at El Refugio. Because she is so well known in the extended community, people usually call her when they have animals to be sterilized; occasionally people from as far away as a two-hour drive have heard about her and bring their animals to be sterilized. On drop-off days a truck from the shelter arrives at her home and picks up approximately 40 animals after each person pays for the sterilization and signs the required paperwork that she administers, along with a general registration sheet to identify animals and owners. Additional street animals she finds and temporarily keeps at her home are also put on the truck for sterilization at the shelter. She then drives back to the shelter with the animals, while making several stops along the 45-minute drive to pick up additional dogs and cats from people who could not get to her home. After animals are sterilized at El Refugio, they are loaded back on the truck and returned to Cartago to reunite the animals with their owners by late afternoon. If she cannot find homes for the sterilized street animals, they are released in the neighborhood.

Nor is her work with animals, like that of other rescuers, limited to sterilization. Occasionally, someone calls regarding a sick or injured animal, perhaps a dog with a broken leg, which she drives to the shelter for veterinary attention and takes monthly payments if the owner cannot afford to pay the entire bill. If it is impossible to get the animal to the shelter for help, she calls the shelter veterinarian for advice and does what she can to alleviate the problem because over the years she has acquired some skills, such as removing stiches or injecting antibiotics, that enable her to function as an unlicensed veterinary nurse when called upon. She also educates owners whose animals are neglected or tied up for most of the day so they can better care for them.

While the relationship between this rescuer and El Refugio is one of long-term trust and respect, that is not always the case with other rescuers or rescue groups. There are a few cases of outreach workers not fully trusting rescuers when the latter appear to behave "fanatically." For example, one such rescuer did not want the shelter to euthanize a dog with distemper and fought with the manager to not euthanize it, even though it was unadoptable, and pressured the shelter to operate on a dog with a serious eye problem that could not be fully corrected, even though the surgery would not increase its already very low chance of being adopted.

There have also been occasional allegations of questionable or unethical business practices by some rescue groups. For example, sometimes new rescue groups will fight over rescuing a dog or cat to get good publicity from a dramatic rescue that might be covered in the newspaper or on TV news. Donations usually follow these media reports because the rescuers ask for money to allegedly cover the cost of veterinary care. While donations might be used to pay for these costs, some critics of these groups claim that the money is often used to cover the personal expenses of those operating the programs. In one such case, after a woman allegedly paid a neighbor to get rid of her dog, he tried to kill it by cutting off its head with a machete, but missed and seriously cut the dog's snout, and the dog ran away. A neighbor found it and called one of the humane organizations for help, but before someone could rescue the injured dog the head of a small rescue group scooped up the dog and took it to a veterinarian. The rescuer ultimately got enormous publicity from this extreme case and asked for donations to cover her expenses.

Less common are charges of questionable practices by more established rescue groups. For example, a dog in an empty lot was found suffering from a bad case of worms and covered with maggots that were eating her alive, leaving euthanasia as the only humane option. A senior staff member from a rescue group was present when this dog was examined by a veterinarian. Allegedly she asked the veterinarian, "Could you keep her alive for a week so we can ask for more money?" The dog died shortly after her request, but the staff member published photographs of the dog to raise money. Neither SENASA nor the Veterinary Colegio currently try to coordinate the activities of rescue groups or monitor the integrity of their actions.

Despite occasional reservations about the enthusiasm or judgment of a few rescuers, El Refugio relies heavily on many of them to help it provide low-cost sterilization in remote or underserved towns. Doing so enables the shelter to further its larger mission of sterilizing as many animals as possible to reduce overpopulation while empowering many women who rescue in the process. Their underlying moralities of sterilization facilitate this exchange. However, as we see next, having similar moralities does not always ensure a trusting relationship between the shelter and the grassroots activists with whom it works and supports.

Circumspect Moralities

Unlike independent rescuers who facilitate the sterilization of animals, other grassroots activists help to deal with the overpopulation problem in a different way. Although moralities of sterilization can be shared with these activists, there can be serious doubts about their professionalism and caretaking abilities. Such doubts are overlooked or lived with by El Refugio and sterilization-only groups in part because there is no regulation or control over the behavior of grassroots activists, but also because larger and more established humane organizations and groups depend on activists who work alone or in very small groups, known as *casa cunas*, to fill in some of the service and care gaps they cannot provide, while the casa cunas in turn depend on established organizations for resource support.

The casa cuna model of homing dogs and cats is loosely based and vaguely similar to the casa cuna approach to helping homeless children. Cuna houses are homes in Latin and Central America for abused children and/or those received by voluntary surrender. They are administered by a municipal government and are licensed as a home institution and adoption agency. These homes are often attached to municipal offices, such as the Department of Community and Social Development. The houses are considered to be temporary shelters for those minors from birth to three years of age who have been mistreated and/or voluntarily surrendered. These temporary homes allow the children to live in a safe environment where they can hopefully receive love, attention, and respect, until they are located in a permanent home.

El Refugio, along with most outreach programs and humane organizations, informally depend on individually run dog or cat casa cunas, akin to what is considered "animal fostering" in the United States, to find homes for as many as possible as well as to sterilize and perhaps vaccinate and treat them for veterinary problems. They generally support the casa cuna approach because there are too many homeless animals and too few shelters to expedite their adoption, so any help is welcomed to increase the number of adoptions and reduce animal overpopulation. The animals, usually only one or a few at a time, are temporarily kept in a person's home—the casa cuna—until someone adopts them, often because there is no shelter in the area to keep them and because they might have veterinary problems that need monitoring. While in these homes the animals are given food, water, shelter, and perhaps veterinary care if necessary until they ideally find more permanent homes. Social media like Facebook as well as word of mouth are used to aid their adoption efforts.

But in the end, most casa cunas need help caring for their charges and finding them homes.

Support from established shelters or sterilization-only organizations, whether ideological or material, is not just because casa cunas are filling a service gap unmet by organizations like El Refugio. Larger and more established sterilization groups are comfortable working with most casa cunas and endorsing their efforts because these groups share a similar morality of sterilization that is enough to bridge whatever doubts they have about the results and behavior of some casa cunas. For example, one casa cuna is run by a young unemployed woman who lives with her son in a small village on the outskirts of San Jose. They see an urgent need to take in and care for street dogs that are very young or injured with the hopes of sterilizing and finding them homes rather than turn their backs on the animals, allow them to potentially suffer, and contribute to the overpopulation problem by breeding. To them, animal care is not a business but a larger commitment not to their own pet keeping but to addressing a wider problem. This view, shared by many other Costa Ricans who have animal casa cunas, is close to how most workers at El Refugio think about animal welfare, animal overpopulation, and sterilization. Although the shelter obviously has to be concerned about staying afloat financially, its program to sterilize animals is not profit making, as it can be for private-practice veterinarians. They are there to provide a voice for the many dogs and cats that would go unnoticed, uncared for, and unhomed.

Despite their similar sterilization moralities, and their mutual dependence, El Refugio and some of the sterilization-only groups do not always agree with the conduct of some casa cunas. Lack of monitoring or regulation by the state or SENASA leads to certain limitations or problems.[1] For one, the casa cuna approach sometimes does not lead to finding homes for animals, or what are called "failed fosters," when animals never leave the casa cuna or are abandoned on the streets. For example, one young woman and her mother served as a casa cuna for a dog brought to the clinic for sterilization. The dog was a neighborhood stray that the woman felt sorry for because it was being aggressively pursued by males and had a litter the prior year. She befriended the dog, gave it some food, and kept it in her backyard until taking it to an outreach sterilization clinic. After its sterilization she would keep the dog in her yard for about a week to make sure its postoperative recovery went well and then try to find a home for it. Although her daughter liked this dog, her mother made it clear that they would not keep it if no adopters were found. The outreach worker confided that she thought it would be very unlikely to find a home for the dog because it was about seven years old and had some medical issues, predicting that the dog would end up back on the streets but at least would be sterilized. It became a failed foster.

Failed fosters are an unfortunate but accepted outcome of this approach, but the humane community has criticized other practices by some casa cunas. Although it is rare, money is sometimes raised for injured animals by casa cuna staff who then allegedly spend it for their personal expenses, a trend that is allegedly increasing. For example, if a dog who has been hit by a car is found by a casa cuna staff member, people running the group might exploit the injury as an opportunity to get public donations, presumably to pay for the animal's veterinary care. Sometimes this money is raised through social media, like Facebook, where a posting might say, "Please help me with money, I'm trying to help this dog that was just hit by a car." The larger outreach organizations and rescue groups are aware that these incidents occur and would prefer they did not but just live with them because they are so rare and difficult to control.

The casa cuna approach can also encourage "unintentional" hoarding and result in unadopted animals ending up at the shelter when the people running the casa cunas cannot find homes for the dogs and when they can no longer afford or manage their care. For example, in one extreme case a woman claiming to run a casa cuna acquired almost 75 dogs without finding homes for any. Over time her husband became impatient with the large number of dogs and threatened to leave. Shortly after his threat, the woman apparently poisoned all the dogs out of desperation, according to a well-placed and knowledgeable respondent close to this case.

Finally, casa cunas can become a problem for outreach groups like El Refugio when they unduly pressure these organizations to provide free food and medications for their animals as well as help them adopt out animals. Facing this pressure, on occasion the shelter, somewhat reluctantly, provides food or medication to casa cunas, while other animal groups more regularly help them to feed their charges. In addition, El Refugio helps local casa cunas find homes for their dogs online, but it is difficult for the shelter to take animals that casa cunas cannot adopt out because it is filled to capacity most of the time and because caring for the animals would further tax the shelter's already lean budget.

These issues with some casa cunas lead El Refugio and other more established advocacy groups to have a somewhat uneasy—if not distrusting—relationship with them and to fall short of officially endorsing the casa cuna model, despite their similar sterilization moralities. They still work with and rely on them to help care for and rehabilitate street animals to facilitate their adoption but cannot assume that all casa cunas will home most animals temporarily taken in and behave ethically or professionally with their charges. The result is a somewhat leery intergroup dependence where, despite their doubts, established sterilization organizations provide some support to these grassroots efforts to care for and find homes for unowned animals because they themselves cannot do this everywhere, while casa cunas need resources from more robust humane groups to carry out their mission. In the end, El Refugio's relationship with them is guarded and practical yet works well enough most of the time, with most casa cunas to be worth supporting.

Although uneasy at times, intergroup relationships among groups with compatible or even circumspect moralities of sterilization are, for the most part, unproblematic—they coexist with little friction and can work together to support each other's aims. However, coexisting with some organizations that deal with street or owned animals can become problematic for El Refugio and sterilization-only groups. Distrust rather than dependence prevails when sterilization moralities compete or clash.

Competitive Moralities

Despite the generally complacent and dependent informal network that can develop between El Refugio and grassroots advocates who, for the most part, share similar sterilization moralities, the shelter and sterilization-only groups can sometimes feel as though they operate in a competitive environment rife with tensions that can damage the reputations of individuals or particular groups. The major source of this intergroup tension is economic competition for veterinary clients. How this competition manifests itself and plays out can hinder El Refugio's ability as well as that of some sterilization-only groups to provide free or low-cost basic veterinary care to Costa Rica's underserved pet owners.

Most economic competition is between organizations providing sterilization and private-practice veterinarians who are represented by the Veterinary Colegio. At the core of this tension are different moralities of sterilization. The Veterinary Colegio exhibits a different ethic of responsibility regarding the delivery of low and no-cost animal services than does El Refugio. When it comes to providing interventions like sterilization at below-market rates to disadvantaged pet owners, the Colegio and many if its members see the issue as one of professional rights and fairness to them. Sterilization is viewed narrowly as a service provided to specific owners rather than approaching it more broadly, as does El Refugio and grassroots groups who conceive of the practice as not just a device to control overpopulation but an expression of empathy for owners and communities overrun with the burdens of too many animals as well as a way to empower Costa Ricans by giving them new control over their environment.

Since the Colegio views its members as potentially in competition with low-cost spay/neuter groups for clients, it seeks to protect private-practice veterinarians through regulations it creates and imposes on groups like El Refugio. The Colegio requires outreach programs to apply to it for "permits" to conduct low-cost sterilization "campaigns" and to provide it with the names of the veterinarians who participate. Although it does not have the authority to forbid outreach clinics, the Colegio can issue a "directive" indicating its disapproval of a campaign. In practice, almost all campaigns are approved, but at least one outreach group believes that the Colegio declined its campaign proposals because the group offered public support for a new animal cruelty law that threatened the practice of some of the Colegio's veterinarians who work with bulls and farm animals. This outreach group is also the focus of the Colegio's wrath because it has given free veterinary consultations at "animal fairs," including deworming, advice on proper feeding, and prescriptions. Allegedly, the Colegio's protest has been strong enough for the group to limit what it does at some animal fairs to sterilization surgery.

The greatest conflict with the Colegio stems from members who are in private practice and feel threatened by the work of low- or no-cost veterinary clinics in the greater San Jose region. These threatened veterinarians have gone so far as to create a Facebook page, "Veterinarians for Veterinarians," to protest perceived encroachment on their practices by outreach clinics because they feel that low-cost spaying and neutering is a form of unfair and illegal competition, which they claim undercuts their businesses by taking clients away from them. To support their allegation of unfair practice, Colegio veterinarians usually cite different versions of the same type of anecdote, featuring a well-off woman driving a black Mercedes who takes her dog to the clinic for low-cost sterilization to avoid paying a higher fee elsewhere, which suggests that outreach programs are taking away clients who could afford private-practice veterinarians.

In their defense, outreach workers point out that the vast majority of Costa Ricans using low-cost clinics can hardly afford the heavily discounted clinic price, let alone the much higher fee charged by private-practice veterinarians. The rare person who could afford to use one of these veterinarians to sterilize his or her animal will not go there, for whatever reason, having the surgery performed only if a cheaper option (10,000–11,000 versus 30,000–35,000 colones) exists. If outreach workers challenge these wealthier pet owners or refuse them this low-cost option, they would not get their animals sterilized at a higher price, and sterilizing as many animals as possible is the shelter's priority and an essential piece of its sterilization morality. Rather than being threatened by low-cost spaying and neutering, then, members of the Veterinary Colegio should be comfortable with if not supportive of this practice because they are not losing clients, according to outreach workers.[2]

Many Veterinary Colegio members do not accept this defense and pressure veterinarians to quit working at sterilization clinics. Outreach programs closer to San Jose are frequently visited by Colegio veterinarians who "harass" and "intimidate" clinic veterinarians as they stand next to them to observe surgeries, question their procedures or techniques, or tell them that what they are doing is an ethics violation because it is a "disloyal practice" that might result in their licenses being revoked. Allegedly, one clinic veterinarian was told, "It's because of you that our profession is on the ground. You're prostituting yourself."

The Veterinary Colegio has also threatened veterinarians sterilizing animals for low-cost spay/neuter groups with professional censure to prevent their future practice, although there is no evidence that the Colegio has pursued such action, let alone stopped a veterinarian from providing low-cost sterilization. However, one American veterinarian who migrated to Nosara obtained a Costa Rican licensure through the Colegio, but sensed some degree of suspicion about his interest in practicing there. After he brought in several veterinarians from around the globe to help with an animal welfare campaign in Nosara, the Colegio bureaucratically blocked his request to use them, hoping to make things difficult enough to force him to abandon his plan. When he went forward with the plan and veterinarians arrived and started working, the Colegio put him through a disciplinary process because it felt his campaign created unfair competition for local veterinarians in private practice; he found this scrutiny "a bit humiliating." As with other conflicts with the Colegio, the reality was that the veterinarians in Nosara were not offering their low-cost services to people who could afford or seek the services of private-practice veterinarians if they were close enough to reach.

Occasionally, the Colegio finds out about and is displeased with veterinary interventions or prescriptions given at clinics that go beyond sterilization and puts pressure on the outreach programs to prevent or obstruct the operation of their clinics. But such intimidation has not stopped the larger, more established outreach programs from having clinics. "The Colegio is our biggest enemy," claims the director of one of these outreach organizations, because its veterinary hospital was seen as taking away private-practice clients. Despite pressure from the Colegio, this group's efforts to provide low-cost services are undeterred. However, the Colegio has stopped the operation of some smaller and newer outreach groups. In one instance, it disapproved of a building being used as a clinic because it was allegedly too small and filed a complaint, which made the clinic veterinarian so uncomfortable he refused to work if the clinic stayed in that location.

Some outreach programs, such as El Refugio's, have learned to avoid the Colegio's monitoring by focusing their efforts on shantytowns or remote locations that are underserved by private-practice veterinarians, far from San Jose where the majority of private-practice veterinarians work. These towns do not have a small animal veterinarian to do sterilization surgeries, and many residents cannot afford the higher cost of having this surgery done by a veterinarian in another town, if they are able and willing to travel that distance.

Other low-cost programs, such as the one in Puntarenas, try to ease the concern of private-practice veterinarians by assuring them that while they are being cut out of the sterilization profit, animals sterilized at the clinic will generate new revenue for them after the fact by creating demand for other services, an argument similar to the one posed by El Refugio. As one outreach worker said to a private-practice veterinarian, "Now that their animal is sterilized, they'll be coming to you for shots, they'll be coming to you when it's sick, they'll be buying your food." Also, this outreach program buys its veterinary supplies from local private-practice veterinarians to show its intent to cooperate with them, provides rather than reduces revenue, and smooths their relationship overall.

To deter the success and inroads made by low-cost veterinary outreach programs, some of the Colegio's veterinarians capitalize on very rare instances when the former programs sterilize an animal and serious complications or mortality results. For example, if an owner's dog becomes infected after surgery, she may take the animal to a regular veterinarian who already "hates" outreach clinics. When the veterinarian examines the animal, he blames the outreach clinic for having poor veterinary technique and then charges a substantial fee for his work to repair the alleged mistakes. These owners, in turn, might then go online and post criticisms of the outreach program for providing substandard veterinary care, citing the words of their veterinarians as proof that sterilization clinics practice unsound medicine. They might paraphrase the veterinarian's words, saying, "Everything was bad. I can't believe I had to open the dog again. I had to do this and that." So outraged, they may also post online that it cost them 100,000 colones or more for this veterinary care, suggesting this huge expense was due to inept veterinary practice at the outreach clinic.

Negative online reviews can damage the reputation of outreach programs, especially if the postings focus on deaths of animals after sterilization, even though such untoward events are very rare. In one alleged case, improper staffing at an upstart sterilization-only group had veterinary students performing sterilization surgeries and allegedly had very high mortality rates, ranging from 80 to 100 percent, compared to about one or two deaths per 2,500 surgeries a year for one of Costa Rica's more established sterilization-only outreach organizations. The latter is a very low mortality rate considering that thousands of these surgeries are performed each year and the few animals that die were likely seriously compromised by prior illness or were not given proper care by their owners postoperatively. Yet affected and upset owners will, out of anger and misinformation, post highly critical comments on Facebook and other online sites, making incorrect and inflammatory comments such as "Don't go to the clinics, they kill animals" or "They use bad materials or expired drugs."

Friction over veterinary clients is not limited to El Refugio's relationships with private-practice veterinarians. Some of this economic competition is between groups offering low-cost spay/neuter clinics, especially when an interloper creates territorial conflict in certain parts of the country. An upstart outreach program might set up its operation close to an established sterilization program to draw clients by undercutting prices. For example, one long-standing sterilization-only outreach group faces competitive challenges from a newer and smaller upstart low-cost sterilization group seeking to encroach on the former's territory and success. It does this by having its clinics nearby and on the same day as the established clinic, while charging about 1,000 colones less, a difference of about $2, or the equivalent of about one to two hours of wages.

While there is no indication yet that the presence of upstart clinics has reduced the number of people seeking to sterilize their animals at established outreach programs, there is another worry. Some of the latter are less concerned about the potential loss of clients than they are with the potential for new outreach groups to have a higher morbidity and mortality rate because they are less experienced and may hire less competent veterinary staff, in turn hurting the reputation of all sterilization outreach clinics in the community, including those run by El Refugio.

Other conflict happens when a small number of people informally set up a spay/neuter program, sometimes even in a garage. They may use veterinary students who are unsupervised by trained professionals, such as the group Vida, not ask for proper permits from the local authorities, or not have a protocol as do the established outreach programs.[3] The latter often have a set of requirements for hiring veterinary doctors and assistants, so that only certain people can work at these clinics. And, of course, many sterilization-only groups and El Refugio believe that their own moralities of sterilization are different from those held by interloper or novice groups who are usually seen as selling spay/neuter surgery primarily or only to make a profit rather than offering the service, first and foremost, to reduce overpopulation and help disadvantaged Costa Ricans and their animals.

Whenever economic competition occurs among these groups, in the big picture it is not just a dispute over the control of veterinary patients. This competition is about El Refugio, sterilization-only groups, and the Veterinary Colegio jockeying for authority and influence in the dog and cat domain about

how best to manage the overpopulation problem and provide low-cost veterinary services to the poorest of Costa Ricans and the neediest of animals.
In other words, it is a frame dispute (Goffman, 1974) where groups differently
interpret an event, activity, or technology (Benford, 1993)—in this case sterilization and other basic veterinary services—according to their own organizational realities and mental models (Snow et al., 1986). What results is a
competition over whose morality of sterilization is best when it comes to the
need for this surgery to control overpopulation, the right of Costa Ricans to
access it, and the qualifications of advocates to provide it to street animals
and the pets of the poor.

While this dispute is mainly driven by economic competition and the drive
for professional power, as we see next, there are other serious disputes over
sterilization moralities. These, too, prevent intergroup beliefs from being
shared about animal welfare and fuel more distrust than trust among these
groups, but their nature is different. In these instances, there are clashes of
sterilization moralities over the propriety of sterilizing animals, the surrendering of unwanted animals, and the keeping of those sheltered.

Clashing Moralities

Although economic competition for the control of veterinary patients is a major source of intergroup tension, disagreement can also occur over the appropriateness of certain practices to manage the animal overpopulation problem.
Some advocacy groups have a view of animal rights and suffering that puts
them at odds with the sterilization moralities of groups like El Refugio. These
clashes are not technical disputes over whether certain approaches work or
not or the degree to which they are effective for certain populations. They are
moral disagreements over how best to manage overpopulation and unwanted
animals.

Sterilization moralities occasionally clash over the use of euthanasia as a
technique to manage overpopulation. This tension occurs between groups
morally opposed to euthanasia as a technique to control overpopulation and
El Refugio because of the latter's ill-deserved reputation as a kill shelter, which
follows it and taints its relationships with animal groups that do not shelter
or euthanize animals. This reputation originated over 25 years ago before the
HSUS stepped in to help the current shelter director change the shelter's prior
approach and operation, whose image of "killing everything" caused many
people in the community to avoid going there. Nevertheless, the reputation
lingers. For example, one of the established sterilization-only groups prefers
the casa cuna approach to dealing with animal overpopulation rather than El
Refugio's because it still suspects that the shelter sometimes euthanizes other-

wise healthy animals, despite the shelter's claim that it now performs euthanasia only to relieve suffering. Some of the large rescue facilities also share this
suspicion about El Refugio's alleged use of euthanasia and do not endorse or
use this method themselves. In the end, even if euthanasia is rarely used to kill
unadoptable animals or those that linger too long in the shelter, the idea of euthanasia is a symbolic lightening rod that can separate animal groups from
each other in Costa Rica as elsewhere (Arluke, 2003).

More commonly, sterilization moralities clash over the surrendering process. Groups providing low-cost sterilization and basic veterinary care often
do not operate shelters because they are so expensive to maintain, but also
because these groups are opposed to the shelter's policy of allowing Costa Ricans to surrender their animals. They claim that Costa Ricans who do not feel
much if any responsibility for their dogs or cats can "donate" them to the shelter because it allows this "dumping" and the shelter is then forced to become
the responsible party for these animals, albeit an organization rather than an
individual. The argument is that the shelter, as an institutional enabler, by taking in unwanted animals, removes whatever guilt surrenderers might have re-
linquishing their pets,[4] making the process of giving up animals too easy emotionally and perpetuating the larger overpopulation problem. Critics of the
shelter also feel that if animals are sterilized they are better off on the streets
than caged in shelters; such "urban fauna" are thought to keep pests such as
insects, mice, and pigeons at bay and create balance in the urban ecosystem.

Defending itself, the shelter points out that in Costa Rica there are few options for people to surrender animals to legitimate shelters. For people who
want to get rid of dogs or cats, if they do not take them to El Refugio, they often turn to groups mislabeled as shelters that are at best large sanctuaries and
at worst hoarders, or they abandon the animals on the street. This situation
creates significant demand on the shelter to accept unwanted animals. Indeed, approximately 90% of the calls taken by shelter workers are from people
who no longer want their pets or have found animals on the street and are trying to "dump" them at the shelter without paying anything for taking the animals, despite the subsequent cost to feed, care, and house them. As the shelter manager explained, "They think they're a good person, so they won't throw
it onto the street. They want us to take their responsibility. If we took the dog
from them, they'll just get another dog because they don't want the dog they
have now."

El Refugio tries to shift responsibility for these surrendered animals back to
the Costa Ricans who want to "abandon" them. Responsibility for unwanted
animals is put back on these owners by trying to convince them to find homes
for the animals, which is easier if their dogs are sterilized. A typical scenario
would be a Costa Rican who calls the shelter saying they would like to drop off

a nine-month-old pit bull because it allegedly had gotten too big and the family is afraid of it. In response, the shelter will then tell the owner that no one wants to adopt an unneutered adult dog and that it is their responsibility to find the dog a home, but that if they agree to neuter the animal and take responsibility for its adoption by keeping the dog, the shelter will then help the person find it a home by listing the dog on its Facebook page, which has about 80,000 followers. If this is successful, the Costa Rican, not the shelter, places the animal.

Otherwise, to discourage this practice and shift responsibility back to people wanting to surrender dogs or cats, El Refugio will not accept animals unless the surrenderers pay a fee of approximately $50. During sterilization outreach, the shelter's veterinarians also refuse to accept such drop-offs. For example, at one outreach location two women walked over to the shelter's truck and spoke with the veterinarian sitting inside. They said they had a cat to give to the shelter but were told there was a fee to take their cat back to the shelter. The woman was irate and said that was "robbery." In cases like this, if people cannot find an adopter and El Refugio will not take the animal, it may be drowned if it is a kitten or puppy or simply abandoned, much to the chagrin of the shelter's staff. Despite El Refugio's efforts to shift responsibility for pets back to their owners, the perception lingers among some animal advocacy groups that it still makes it too easy to surrender animals, while the shelter feels it alone must accept the burden of providing a legitimate option for owners to surrender their pets.

Clashes of sterilization moralities can also stem from different notions of what an animal shelter should be and how animals are accepted into a facility and subsequently treated. Groups like El Refugio position themselves as more mainstream or legitimate shelters by questioning the practices of other groups that allegedly mask themselves as legitimate animal shelters, sanctuaries, or rescue groups. Unlike more mainstream humane organizations, these marginal groups refuse to sterilize or euthanize their animals, accept all dogs or cats being dropped off whether they are owned or stray, adopt out few if any animals, do not have veterinary support on site, and do not have cages for their animals.

To some degree, these tensions stem from the ambiguous and casual use of terms like "shelter" (i.e., *refugio*) to describe a variety of animal groups that have very different philosophies of animal care and adoption, services, and missions. For example, as the term is commonly used in Costa Rica, shelters are places that keep animals so they can in theory be adopted. When generally defined this way, dozens of organizations can be labeled as shelters, with only a few being roughly comparable to what in the United States would be regarded as shelters. Indeed, as of 2014 SENASA had certified only 13 shelters as legitimate veterinary operations, making the vast majority of groups calling themselves shelters to be "off the books" (TCRN, 2014). Using a narrower definition of shelter, more consistent with use in the United States, the only shelter in Costa Rica is El Refugio, in San Rafael.

Unfortunately, many marginal or unofficial groups that label themselves as shelters and aspire to this status quickly run into problems as the number of animals in their charge grows precipitously. For example, in its early stages, one group called itself a shelter and went from 40 to 200 animals within two years of its origin as adoptions paled by comparison to the number of abandoned litters deposited on its doorstep each day. Neighbors complained about the nuisance of roaming dogs and noise, but the small organization lacked the funds to put up fences to contain the animals. By 2000, the group had shuttered its shelter and decided to focus entirely on preventive strategies, then calling itself an adoption center that did not take animals, and finally closing the adoption center and selling the property six years later with 17 dogs remaining.

Indeed, a few of the mainstream animal care and welfare groups suspect that some of these marginal organizations hoard and neglect animals in their charge, an accusation vigorously denied by the latter. Although there has not been an official investigation of these practices, informal reports occasionally leak out from visitors, some of whom are veterinarians or veterinary students, who describe a large number of animals often in poor health with little or no chance of adoption. These reports also allege that some of these marginal groups restrict access to their facilities to only a few hours a week, do not permit visitors to observe animal care practices, and do not share detailed admission and adoption records, all of which, if true, raise suspicions.

Even if these reports are unfounded, marginal humane organizations can create problems for more mainstream animal groups. For one, when marginal organizations adopt out a dog, it is likely to be returned to a legitimate shelter rather than to be permanently kept by an adopter because the adoption process is so casual and the dog can have behavior or medical problems unbeknown to the adopters. When this happens, the capacity of the shelter receiving the animal is strained and a potentially unadoptable animal that might have to be euthanized is left there. And if the animal has to be euthanized, it gives ammunition to the shelter's critics who accuse it of excessively and unnecessarily killing animals.

For another, when marginal rescue groups or "no-kill shelters" can no longer care for or adopt out some of their charges, they sometimes try to pass these animals on to more mainstream humane organizations to care and find homes for. However, some of the latter are sterilization-only organizations that do not have the facilities to house the animals until adopted or to be kept permanently if unadopted. Expressing her reservations about dealing with some rescue groups, the director of one sterilization-only organization lamented, "They [rescuers] say if you're working on prevention you should be taking in animals—but we're not a shelter. They think we should take in every box of abandoned kittens or puppies someone drops off, and if we don't they don't feel they should help us."

Mainstream humane organizations have few options for dealing with this intergroup tension, so the clash of sterilization moralities festers and occasionally surfaces. If nothing else, they can avoid having contact with certain rescue or other groups who are thought to be doing a disservice to their charges. For example, one mainstream organization refuses to take any animals from marginal groups, while maintaining its focus on sterilization until there are fewer and fewer abandonments. And to avoid continued pressure to take rescued animals, this organization tries to keep as much distance as possible from this type of rescuer by not accepting their offers to volunteer to help with things like putting up signs to publicize forthcoming sterilization clinics.[5]

Apart from such avoidance, it is challenging if not impossible for organizations like El Refugio to curtail the operation of marginal groups, whether that would be to shut down questioned facilities or monitor them more closely to improve their animal welfare, because of the connections among them. Some so-called shelters or sanctuaries work in concert, so any kind of meaningful regulation of questionable practices would entail simultaneously monitoring and controlling a number of groups. For example, a common allegation is that some interconnected marginal groups are institutional hoarders with substandard animal care, but investigating this charge and potentially correcting this practice, should it exist, become all the more challenging when there are multiple groups or organizations who communicate with and support each other's efforts.

In one such case, a facility with approximately 400 animals that rarely get adopted has ties with another organization, often referred to as a "no-kill shelter" or even "paradise" for dogs (e.g., Billock, 2018) that has over a 1,000 strays. The former allegedly "taught" the latter how to acquire animals, run a large facility, and represent itself to the public as a legitimate organization. These two facilities also have informal ties with independent rescuers and casa cunas; when the latter become overwhelmed with dogs they give them to the former, which exacerbates any tendency to hoard animals. In one such case, a woman who operated a casa cuna eventually acquired over 50 dogs and had to pawn many of her valuable possessions to continue keeping these animals as well as work full-time every day to manage them. She finally became depressed when she realized it was too much for her to care for these dogs, so she got in touch with one of the above organizations, which agreed to take all her animals.

If any organization were to monitor these groups for possible hoarding and take corrective action, it would be SENASA, the governmental organization, but it has investigated and seized animals only in small hoarding cases. While SENASA is aware of potential cases of institutional hoarding, some of the suspected facilities are impervious to official investigation and potential closure because the public is convinced they are doing good work. Indeed, one such facility has garnered favorable international attention, making it a popular tourist destination. Serious investigation of these cases appears beyond SENASA's current abilities and agenda.

In the end, mainstream humane organizations leave these groups alone, neither formally investigating or informally pressuring them to change their animal care practices. Clashes of sterilization moralities dissolve into suspicions about animals being mistreated or even allegations of incompetence causing animals to suffer. Charges of needlessly euthanizing animals and making it too easy for owners to give away their pets are hurled at El Refugio, while it questions whether some advocates fail to medically care for their charges. They cannot arrive at some shared meaning for how unwanted or unowned animals should be managed.

El Refugio is not the only advocacy group that wants to improve the welfare of dogs and cats as well as reduce animal overpopulation. It pursues these goals as part of a humane network of animal advocates in Costa Rica whose relationships with one another can be loose and informal, supportive and helpful, or suspicious and tense. El Refugio's ability to reach as many animals as possible, and ultimately change the behavior of Costa Ricans, is both supported and curtailed by these other network actors, whether that makes the shelter depend on the help of grassroots animal advocates or restrict what it does due to economic and ideological disputes with veterinarians, sterilization outreach groups, and rescue facilities.

When tense, intergroup relations are more than internecine squabbles over limited resources or domain control. Objecting to how other groups care for animals and approach the overpopulation problem is significant, even if organizations are powerless to do much more than withdraw their moral or fiscal support, because these disagreements—especially when the underlying sterilization moralities are different—reflect an attempt by some animal advocacy groups—each with very different expertise, resources, facilities, membership, and beliefs—to become the voice for unwanted or street dogs and, to a lesser degree, street cats. Rather than sharing their beliefs about promoting animal welfare, they strain to coexist. Indeed, when sterilization moralities clash, they present an opportunity to extol a group's beliefs, instead of trying to craft some common ground with other groups—not just about how over-population should be addressed, but about how dogs and cats should be regarded and treated.

At one level, these beliefs are about whether advocates or veterinary personnel should have and act on sympathy for the plight of street animals and for the pets of people in or near poverty. The sterilization moralities of many rescuers and shelters come close to the ethic of care developed by Gilligan (1982) and elaborated by Donovan (2007), who argue that sympathy, compassion, caring, and politics should be the grounds for how humans treat animals. Groups professing this morality, such as El Refugio, take a wider view of the larger problem they are trying to combat and have more empathy for impoverished Costa Ricans, their needs, and their pets than do groups like the Veterinary Colegio. The latter are more concerned about who profits from spaying and neutering rather than who might suffer less from its application.

At another level, these beliefs are about who should be responsible for these animals and what that responsibility should entail. Some sterilization moralities share a similar sentiment with Hens's (2009) argument that humans should have the same ethical responsibility to provide for the physical and mental well-being of their pet dogs as they would for a child or other family member. Consequently, advocates like El Refugio raise questions about the quality of animal care provided by some rescue facilities or casa cunas, suggesting they may be irresponsible caretakers of their charges. When the latter's sterilization moralities insist that the shelter makes it easy for owners to be irresponsible, it counters with a more realistic view of pet ownership while pushing back on owners to be more responsible for their pets. In the end, these disagreements are a moral as well as a practical struggle over what our human relationships should be with these animals.

Reducing intergroup tensions produced by divergent if not conflicting beliefs would be desirable. Under certain circumstances, instead of multiple and dissonant voices, friction between organizations can be the space in which groups are transformed into more than the sum of their parts by acknowledging what connects them and how they can reinforce each other's efforts (Dobbie & Richards-Schuster, 2008). Taking this step is essential in Costa Rica because no one organization has the capacity to provide low-cost veterinary services to all or even most of the country's underserved pet owners, control if not reduce animal overpopulation, and raise the general standard of animal health and welfare. Perhaps, over time, jockeying for the best approach to overpopulation will clarify the current entangled and uneasy relationships that make up the country's loose network of advocacy and veterinary organizations.

However, in the short run this is unlikely. Much of the humane and veterinary network in Costa Rica is too fragmented, resource dependent, competitive, and varied in their sterilization moralities to establish commonalities and unity. Network disputes overwhelm the ability or interest of any one or more organizations to try to construct common ground and bring groups together across their differences. Moreover, even when these participants coexist with little or no friction, it stems more from their dependency, territorial separation, and lack of regulation than from trust. Instead, the network is shot through with doubts about other participants' competence to care for animals, their fairness, honesty, and willingness not to harm other groups in the network, and their ability to commit effort and resources necessary to complete their humane goals, even when they have similar sterilization moralities. Given these suspicions, the extent to which an organization, like El Refugio, can cooperate with others to achieve its main goals—sterilizing, homing, and providing veterinary care to as many of Costa Rica's dogs and cats as possible—will be less than it could be, as others have observed when studying networks lacking trust among their participants (Newell & Swan, 2000).

Despite the incoherence of and tensions in this network, El Refugio and a few sterilization-only groups continue to offer low-cost spaying/neutering in underserved communities. Providing this basic veterinary service, as we see next, does more than medically intervene to control animal overpopulation. It culturally intervenes to change how Costa Ricans think about and behave with dogs and cats.

CHAPTER THREE

Sterilization as an Agent of Social Change

CHANGING HOW COMMUNITIES THINK ABOUT PETS

Improving animal welfare is a long-standing concern for activists who want to encourage the adoption of new humane behaviors by pet owners, those who work with animals, and the public at large (Grandin, 2015; Whay & Main, 2010). The adoption of a new humane behavior, as is true of any behavioral innovation, is a multistage process that is thought to begin with an individual's awareness of a new behavior and end with the decision to implement and continue it (Dearing, 2009). Attempts to intervene in this process have focused on identifying barriers to changing behavior and how to overcome them, such as providing information about the new behavior as well as motivation and empowerment to undertake it (Whay, 2007).

However, narrowly focusing on the end stage of adopting one particular humane behavior may underestimate the impact of interventions on the targeted population because doing so ignores the nature of norms and situational learning. When adopters are at the stage of trying on a new behavior for the first time, they may also be made aware of a host of other related behavioral expectations or norms. That this exposure should occur is unsurprising because a single behavior is often part of a cluster of similar actions that may be introduced simultaneously by groups trying to further the adoption of humane behavior. They may intentionally plant a number of new ideas about how targeted individuals should think, feel, or act (Greenhalgh et al., 2004) by piggybacking the introduction of these norms on the adoption of a primary behavioral outcome. Reinforcing this deliberate norm seeding is an unintentional process: those adopting the new behavior may observe peers enacting other behaviors that may inspire them to behave similarly or at least plant that possibility in their minds.

Such norm seeding, whether intentional or not, can potentially change behavior because it allows for informal learning (Eraut, 2004) among those exposed to new ways of thinking and acting. Unlike formal learning that is structured and based in institutions, informal learning can grow out of everyday encounters as people use or work in a given situation (Marsick & Watkins, 2001) and can learn from others (Eraut, 2004). In that context, experiences occur that might influence how people interpret the situation, their choices, and the subsequent actions they take. As people make sense of this situation, insights are prompted and they may question old assumptions and customary ways of behaving.

This questioning begins with some sort of trigger that tells people they are unsatisfied with or at least question how they formerly behaved. The learning trigger at outreach clinics is to get Costa Ricans to surgically spay or neuter animals. This is the implementation stage for many who attend the clinics because they are trying on this behavior for the first time and most do not regard and treat their cats and dogs in modern Western ways. For outreach workers, then, getting these Costa Ricans to bring animals to their clinics provides an opportunity to change their behavior, and subsequently their thinking, toward animals.

That outreach clinics use sterilization as a behavioral hook to plant animal-related norms among Costa Ricans runs counter to popular and some academic thinking about the relationship between attitudes and behavior. Although it is often assumed that beliefs determine behavior, the link between attitudes and behavior is bidirectional (Fazio, 1986), so the reverse influence can occur as well and might be true among Costa Ricans using outreach services. That is, getting Costa Ricans to go to sterilization clinics exposes them to outreach workers who, in their interactions with Costa Ricans, get them to behave in novel ways that might change how they regard animals. Indeed, in addition to their contacts with outreach workers, Costa Ricans also interact with others bringing animals to one location where they register, pay, and wait for the surgery to be completed. They see friends and neighbors also behaving in a new way, and just being in their presence can also support these new steps and perhaps contribute to changing practices toward animals.

Outreach workers believe these interactions with Costa Ricans can change their behavior toward dogs and cats. Although it is indirect, some evidence suggests this norm seeding may have contributed to Costa Ricans becoming more responsible for their animals' welfare and more modern in how they interact with and view dogs and cats on or near their property. Changes in pet owner behavior in the eight years between 2003 and 2011 indicated by surveys

(WSPA, 2012) and by the growth in the membership of the Veterinary Colegio are large, given the relatively short time involved (societal behavioral changes usually take decades to shift by 10 points or more). The changes are all in the direction of increasing control of and care for household dogs and indicate that it is possible to evolve from a culture of street dogs to a culture of "controlled" pets relatively quickly. These changes (accompanied by increases in the rate of ownership of both pet dogs and cats) occurred in the United States in the 25 years (1950–1975) following World War II.

If this cultural shift is real, getting Costa Ricans to sterilize their animals might have some part to play in making this change. But until more is known about what outreach workers exactly do to accomplish this sought-after goal, we can only speculate that norm seeding at sterilization clinics is linked to subsequent changes in Costa Rican behavior toward animals. Indeed, we know little about the norm-diffusing roles of NGOs in general and those who work for them (Greenhill, 2012), let alone what outreach workers at sterilization clinics do to diffuse pet-keeping norms.

We found that outreach work in Costa Rica is as much or more about social interaction and change as it is about technically delivering a surgical procedure. Interaction with Costa Ricans at these clinics is an opportunity for outreach workers and volunteers to change Costa Ricans' thinking about sterilizing dogs and cats specifically as well as how they regard them more generally. As we see next, the process of seeding new norms starts from the moment a community is chosen to have an outreach sterilization clinic.

Expecting Sterilization

There usually is little awareness of or demand for sterilization surgery among residents of Costa Rica's remote and underserved towns and villages before outreach teams set up their first clinics. Most view animal overpopulation, and the frequent litters and roaming behaviors that entails, as normal and natural, albeit a nuisance. However, the goal of these teams is not merely to provide this surgery but to make the idea of sterilization something that targeted communities expect and view as normal.

Getting Costa Ricans to think of sterilization as a normal and expected veterinary intervention starts when outreach groups first identify and contact poor communities that have an apparent animal overpopulation problem and no access to veterinary care. At this early stage of delivering this service, outreach workers cannot assume there will be a demand for it or a suitable location for a clinic that can be set up to provide surgery. They must improvise to create this demand, find a spot in town to conduct their clinics, and convert this space into a temporary surgical suite and recovery area.

At this stage, outreach workers' efforts are a form of bricolage because they are creating something out of nothing by improvising what is available (Lévi-Strauss, 1967). This process can refer to making do with found materials to create something new, as car mechanics do when they cannot get needed parts but fashion their repairs using whatever can be found (Harper, 1987), or it can describe improvising ideas, as entrepreneurial organizations do when they use preexisting symbols to forge new identities for themselves (Perkmann & Spicer, 2014). Outreach workers trying to provide sterilization in temporary clinics also engage in bricolage because they too improvise both tangible materials and intangible ideas, but in their case it is to create demand for a service—in this case sterilization—and a location and facility where sterilization can be performed.

The first step is to get villages and towns to take some responsibility for the need to have sterilization clinics and therefore for the larger problem of dog and cat overpopulation. With this goal in mind, outreach programs prefer that someone from the town reaches out to them and requests a visit, but this does not always happen. When not contacted by officials to intervene, workers or volunteers will knock on doors to find local leaders who can help them gain access to the community if outreach groups suspect or see significant dog and cat problems because of poverty. In particular, they visit the *pulperias*, or the little shops that are omnipresent in poor communities, where store owners and regular customers know everyone and everything about the town's population. As one outreach worker says, "You ask who is the man in charge of the community rooms or building where they do weddings, birthdays meetings, classes. Now we have the first name. We ask where he lives. We go there, knock on his door. 'Are you in charge?' 'Yes.' We would like to come and spay/neuter dogs and cats but we need a room to do this.'"

Outreach groups hope that local leaders in targeted towns will take responsibility for the need to have sterilization clinics by donating public space for workers to use when providing this community service. Most obliged when outreach programs began years ago; in many cases, local leaders or public officials supported the idea of controlling animal overpopulation and reducing the number of animals on the streets. However, in recent years, more have been trying to charge fees for the use of public spaces because they think these programs make a lot of money from the clinics, although they do not factor in the costs for veterinarians, travel, equipment, and supplies. Given this trend, some outreach directors make a point of identifying "animal-friendly" officials in local towns that see the need for these clinics, accept responsibility for dealing with animal overpopulation, and therefore will not charge for the use of public spaces. Other outreach groups simply pay towns for their use of local facilities, often the rough equivalent of eight surgeries.

Once a location is picked and payment, if required, is agreed upon, out-reach programs set a date for their first sterilization clinic in that town. Be-cause there are no preexisting veterinary or medical facilities to serve as tem-porary clinics, outreach workers improvise surgical suites, recovery rooms, and waiting areas in whatever public space they can find, no matter how un-accommodating, small, cluttered, dirty, or hot they may be. They also need to find and get the cooperation of any local people—usually from nearby animal rescue groups—who can help outreach workers set up, operate, and otherwise make the outreach clinics as effective as possible, given the circumstances.

Outreach workers compare creating and running these sterilization clin-ics to what the military faces in wartime combat zones. As in combat, a few described occasional dangers they encountered when visiting certain villages and towns to set up clinics. Local gangs in very poor shantytowns have al-legedly burglarized or assaulted outreach workers to steal valued items. In one case, a town in Cartago where low-cost sterilization is urgently needed also has a dangerous reputation as a hot spot for drug deals and high rates of crim-inal behavior. During one visit to this town, men with machetes assaulted out-reach workers to steal Christmas toys and cookies they were bringing for local children. Equally rare, but perhaps even more dangerous, is economic ten-sion created between outreach groups and dogfighting gangs in certain very poor towns. Local gangs breed pit bulls and think their businesses are threat-ened by spay/neuter campaigns because if people start taking care of their an-imals and are more responsible for them, there will be fewer bait dogs on the streets. One outreach program director cannot go into certain areas where gang members have threatened to kill him.

And as in a warzone, outreach workers have to deal with a lack of on-site surgical and recovery facilities. Volunteers and veterinary staff, like those in mobile military hospitals, adapt whatever space and conditions are available; just a few years ago, some of these outreach workers created surgical suites in horse stables. More recently, they set up and performed their surgery in a pet store having a second floor with two rooms—one for surgery and one for re-covery; in another they used a multipurpose municipal building that had a large lobby, and in yet another they used a small office, after removing its fur-niture, for both surgery and recovery.

In the buildings they use, outreach workers repurpose found space or rooms for pet owners to register and wait as well as for animals to have sur-gery and recover. For example, in one remote town, a storage closet and a kitchen were transformed into a surgical suite that included two operating ta-bles and space on the floor for pre- and postoperative patients, while a front porch became a waiting and registration room. Larger spaces without walls can present a challenge to partition into different outreach needs. One outreach sterilization group uses a corner of a public parking garage for its clinic when visiting a town near San Jose. The registration area, the recovery room, and the surgical area are sealed off from each other with blue and red tarpon, flanked by anxious owners waiting for their dogs and cats to come out of anesthesia so they can go home.

It is worth improvising temporary surgical facilities only if local residents are aware of low-cost spay/neuter programs and want to use them. People living in these towns are alerted in various ways. Organizations providing this veterinary service will periodically revisit the same location from one to four times a year, depending on local interest and demand. Over time, these visits become a recurring part of the town's culture, so many local residents know about and expect this service. For example, one sterilization-only group's outreach clinic periodically revisits the same sites, in addition to having a campaign set up two weeks in advance to ensure the target communities know about the impending clinic. These campaigns communicate information about the clinics through social media posts, flyers, and handouts listing the dates, location, and cost ($20) of the sterilization.

Some outreach groups also have volunteers who live in the targeted towns go door-to-door with this information trying, with various degrees of success, to convince people to fix their unsterilized animals. While these encounters relay information and provide reassurance, they do not always succeed in getting Costa Ricans to sterilize their animals, in part because it can be difficult for volunteers to develop instant rapport and not come off like "some stranger walking up to your door and saying, 'hey, we see you're not taking care of your animals.'"

Outreach workers and volunteers have to do more than establish rapport; they have to overcome a common fear among Costa Ricans that spaying or neutering animals is dangerous surgery, a lingering concern from the past when most Costa Ricans were afraid that surgery or anesthesia would kill animals. Despite advances in technique, equipment, and anesthesia that make sterilization routine and safe, most Costa Ricans are still somewhat apprehensive about having it done for the first time. For those who have never had an animal operated on or taken one to a veterinarian, going to the sterilization clinic can be anxiety provoking. These people often appear nervous during the two to three hours they are at the clinic, especially when they give their animals to veterinary assistants for preoperative care and when they see their dogs or cats postoperatively recover on the floor of the improvised clinic. Increasingly Costa

Ricans appear to have become more receptive to sterilization as they see their animals recover from surgery. Overtime, they bring other dogs and cats to future clinics and tell neighbors who are reticent to do so that the surgery is safe.

However, outreach workers must also deal with Costa Ricans' fear that sterilization surgery will adversely change their animals' behavior. A few worry about how sterilization might impact their cats' behavior, fearing that the surgery might reduce the animals' predatory instinct toward mice and snakes. Far more commonly male Costa Ricans worry about surgery's impact on their male dogs' behavior. This gendered fear is somewhat different in other developing countries. For example, male Bahamians are likely to project human traits onto dogs and appear more reluctant than women to neuter them, especially when they are kept for long-term breeding (Fielding et al., 2002). For male Costa Ricans, the fear is not about breeding but about changing the behavior of dogs that serve as guards or as aggressive status symbols rather than being just companions. Male Costa Ricans fear the operation will reduce the animals' aggressiveness, thereby lessening their ability to protect property or make the owner look tough or threatening. Some male Costa Ricans who are closely bonded with their dogs also see the surgery itself as an assault on their machismo. Paraphrasing one Costa Rican who expressed discomfort with castration, neutering would somehow taint his own identity by making both him and his dog lesser men.

Outreach workers use several tactics to change the attitudes of these men, although this gendered fear has started to lessen in recent years. To reduce this discomfort with or fear of sterilization surgery, workers can be humorous, although it is not always effective. For example, one worker jokes with male Costa Ricans by saying, "It's either you or him." Also, male Costa Rican staff members might approach and talk with men about the surgery when they are reluctant to have it done, hoping words from another man will reassure them that sterilization will not change their dogs' personality or nature, but that does not always work, and some men still refuse to sterilize their male guard or status dogs.

By contrast, more women are willing to sterilize their animals, including male dogs, although some who are married decline because the dogs are their husbands' animals, and without their permission, these wives will not neuter them. However, outreach workers co-conspire in keeping a secret with other wives who ignore their husbands' wishes and bring their male dogs for sterilization when they are at work and cannot find out about the surgery. Wives resort to this secret surgery because they see the dogs return home bruised from battles over female dogs and realize that if neutered these dogs would probably not roam in search of females, thereby avoiding scuffles over females in heat. In addition, they are tired of having to take care of litters and do "not want the trouble of eight more puppies," as one woman exclaimed. In these cases, outreach workers understand the domestic dilemma faced by these women and perform the surgery. Supporting these efforts to overcome domestic obstacles to sterilization, wives take solace when hearing from outreach volunteers that sterilized male dogs will not behave very differently if at all after surgery, so husbands will not discover what happened. Making them even more confident, many wives also think husbands will never notice if their dogs' behavior changes after surgery because they rarely if ever interact or spend time with them, given that they are not kept for companionship.

Efforts by outreach workers and volunteers to support women's backdoor approach to sterilization, along with their attempts to provide information, reassurance, and humor for men, can help to normalize sterilization in communities that have no prior experience with veterinary care or surgery. In these rural and coastal villages that are periodically revisited by outreach teams, pockets of cultural acceptance of sterilization and perhaps an openness to considering other kinds of veterinary care are created. Here, clinics become part of the local community culture, such that people living in or near targeted towns expect to bring animals for sterilization without needing persuasion because they now are more likely to understand its purpose and to not be fearful of the surgery.

However, such normalization falls short of outreach programs' goal of wanting to also change Costa Ricans' larger perspective toward sterilization so they understand how it can benefit the community and not just individuals. The reality is almost all Costa Ricans have decided to sterilize animals for "personal reasons." For example, some bring dogs and cats that hang around their homes or neighborhoods but are not regarded as pets even in a loose sense because they see litters being born, kittens and puppies dying, and street animals in poor health or being abused. They say they do not want to see more litters because it is unpleasant to see them suffer and deal with such unpleasantries, so they round up as many as they can catch and carry for sterilization at the clinic, where it is less expensive than with a regular veterinarian, if there even is one nearby.[1] Although the programs hope to see a shift from Costa Ricans having purely personal motivations for sterilizing their animals to appreciating why the wider community benefits from this surgery, it is still not the main reason most get animals sterilized at the clinics. Nevertheless, even though Costa Ricans' wider perspective remains unchanged, normalization of sterilization has changed their behavior as they increasingly accept the presence of outreach clinics and the need for this surgery.

Feeling Responsible for Animals

Outreach workers also try to increase owners' commitment to caring for the animals they bring for sterilization. The most obvious way to instill some sense of responsibility for their pets' welfare is getting Costa Ricans to bring animals to be sterilized at the clinics, since most have never sought veterinary care. Just bringing animals for surgery can enhance their perceived worth—and desire to be responsible for them—because Costa Ricans making this effort have invested hard-earned money and time (close to half a day) to improve animal welfare, in addition to reducing the nuisance of unwanted breeding and litters. As one outreach worker observed, "The act of bringing an animal changes their perception of it, maybe seeing it more as a pet, and makes them feel more responsible for it and want to take care of it more."

Another way to make Costa Ricans feel responsible for their animals is to have them sign some form of documentation relative to their animal's care that is as important symbolically as it might be practically. Even creating a small behavior, such as signing a consent form or a postoperative care sheet, can trigger feelings of responsibility for their animal's care or reinforce that sentiment if it already exists. As one outreach group worker said, "We make them fill out a shitload of paper" to instill a sense of "investment" in the animal, so they will not "kick it out" on the street if the animal gets sick or injured or if they simply lose interest in it. Some organizations, such as El Refugio, have people sign a release and consent form, while others operating outreach spay/neuter clinics have people sign a two-page information sheet before their animals are taken home. The sheet has information about postoperative care, such as stopping animals from licking their stiches.

Outreach workers also try to heighten owners' perception of their animals' worth—and responsibility for them—by asking people to pay something for the surgery, whether the animals are owned by one person or family, a neighborhood pet, or a true stray. Spending money can be symbolically important for what it stands for, telling the spender that whatever they are paying money for has value, by definition. In turn, if owners think their animals are worth something, they will want to care and be responsible for them, especially since in poorer villages and towns there are many people who spend nothing on dogs or cats. The $20 for the operation represents a large sum relative to what most people in shantytowns earn; apart from buying dog food, if purchased at all, probably no other money is spent on pets.

Outreach programs and their staff members believe that it is crucial for people who cannot afford the $20 sterilization fee to pay at least something to create a sense of investment in animals and to heighten their perceived value.[2] Although some people refuse to spend any money for sterilization and threaten to release the animal back on the streets if sterilization is not provided for free, most pay something. If people allegedly cannot pay the full amount, they are asked to pay what they can, which can be as low as $2. Since staff members live in the community with many of the people who avail themselves of these services but cannot pay the full amount, they know whether individuals are sincere and trust that the full amount cannot be paid. In cases where people claim they are unable to pay anything, some sterilization programs ask them to symbolically pay by doing some service to help the clinic, such as cleaning the clinical facility or picking up people who cannot afford to take a taxi to the clinic to have their animals sterilized. Outreach programs let slide the few people who can afford to pay for regular veterinary services but who choose to save money and bring their animals to the clinic because workers fear these people might not otherwise get their animals sterilized.

Finally, recovery from surgery can itself encourage responsibility for animals going forward. After seeing their animals bounce back from surgery, Costa Ricans often claim that they will at least consider seeking veterinary care, if affordable, should injury or illness befall their animals, although realistically most cannot afford it and many do not live near a veterinarian. Instead, after their visits some Costa Ricans call outreach workers if they have problems with their animals or revisit the mobile clinic with their sick or injured pet, which they would not have thought to do before because their awareness has changed—they now know there are knowledgeable and skilled people who might help their dogs and cats. For example, one Costa Rican in a poor town on the outskirts of San Jose visited the clinic months earlier to sterilize her dog, only to have the animal, which was allowed to roam during the day, get hit by a car, breaking its rear leg. She could not afford to take it to a private veterinarian but did not want to abandon or kill it, which is what she said would have happened before she first met the outreach team. Although she hoped the team could fix the injury, they lacked the proper equipment and time to mend the leg and instead gave her some money to take the dog to a private-practice veterinarian who sometimes worked with them and reduced his charge for poor pet owners.

These efforts by outreach teams have both practical and symbolic consequences. Controlling dog and cat overpopulation obviously requires the help of Costa Ricans who bring in animals needing spay/neuter surgery, and outreach clinics need paperwork for record keeping as well as money to defray their costs. But getting Costa Ricans to go through the effort of bringing their animals to the clinic, making them fill out forms when sterilizing animals, having them pay something for the surgery, and helping them feel relief that surgery goes well are also acts that can convey symbolic meaning and seed pet-keeping norms among Costa Ricans sterilizing animals. In these cases, workers are manipulating their interactions with Costa Ricans so they will perceive greater value in and responsibility for their animals as well as a need to provide veterinary care in the future, if possible.

Becoming Closer to Animals

Many poor Costa Ricans who sterilize animals are unaccustomed to caring for or nurturing cats or dogs, although they are at least trying to be responsible by seeking veterinary services. Nevertheless, they tend to be emotionally distant from their animals, which are primarily kept for instrumental rather than affective reasons. This customary view of dogs and cats, commonly found in many rural villages and the poorest urban areas, results in animals not having their movement restricted so they are free to roam the streets, not being pet, played with, or shown affection, not being fed and watered regularly if at all, not being treated for injuries or diseases, and not being walked on leashes.

Outreach workers are keenly aware that many people coming to the clinics do not have close or caring relationships with animals in their charge and believe they can spot Costa Ricans who are not used to relating to dogs or cats as pets by the way they stand with their animals. While waiting to register them for sterilization, owners' uncertain and detached body language with their dogs makes them appear uninterested in them. They are not a sociological "with" (Sanders, 1999) in that the animal is separate from rather than an extension of the owner's identity (Belk, 1996) or a unit in their mind when entering public places. Because these people do not think of themselves as being a twosome with their animals, their behavior together will reflect what outreach workers see: the absence of a shared relationship or meaningful connection.

However, as they wait at the clinics to register animals and pay for sterilization, Costa Ricans watch others interact with their own animals and sometimes witness entirely new ways of being with or treating dogs and cats. Once home with their animals they may repeat or imitate some of what has been seen, as reported by a few Costa Ricans who were interviewed during the weeks following the clinic. That their observational learning might have such an impact is supported by research on socialization, which finds that people are more likely to copy or imitate behavior that appears to lead to positive consequences (Simons et al., 1998), and some of these new ways of interacting with pets appeared to have such a result.

Control of animals using leashes is a case in point. Local people in destitute shantytowns often bring dogs and cats "that have adopted them," a phrase used by locals that suggests limited responsibility for animals because the individuals did not intend to have an animal or seek to create such a relationship. Because these areas are rural, animals are rarely kept from roaming and leash use is uncommon, although is starting to appear in these areas. So when rural Costa Ricans bring their animals to the outreach clinic, they are often unleashed and carried by owners who try to prevent them from running away during their hour-long wait for surgery. Dogs are more likely leashed when clinics are held in dense, urban neighborhoods, but many leashes are improvised from available materials and not used at other times.

Costa Ricans also see new ways of interacting with and caring for dogs and cats at the clinic that have apparent positive consequences. Those who do not interact with their dogs and cats as modern pets watch other Costa Ricans or expats handling their animals in close and affectionate ways, such as touching, holding, grooming, or talking to their pets. They might see people hugging them, speaking to them in baby talk, or perhaps touching noses with them before undergoing surgery. Importantly, observing attempts to reassure animals that appeared to be anxious from the loud noise and novel environment of the clinic had a similar impact and lesson as did observing people who controlled their pets with leashes—they both seemed to produce positive results. Seeing people in the clinic gently stroking and talking to stressed animals seemed to result in animals becoming more relaxed as owners gave them this special attention—or at least that is what the observing Costa Ricans believed.

More deliberate education takes place by outreach workers who try to instill responsibility and closer interactions with cats and dogs by making practical suggestions that ostensibly make it easier for them to bring their animals to the clinic. If followed, these suggestions might make Costa Ricans feel closer to their pets or deepen existing bonds. For example, because people in targeted communities are often poor and do not consider animals they bring to the clinic as theirs, they often do not own expensive carriers. Outreach workers tell them to bring smaller animals in pillow cases rather than simply carrying them because this teaches the importance of restraining or controlling animals when in public for safety and to prevent their escape. But this is more than a practical suggestion since these people are then forced to pick up and carry animals they may never have touched previously and perhaps clutch their animals in an unfamiliar, nurturing way. Outreach workers believe this opens the door to closer contact with their dogs at home in the future. Of course this strategy does not always work; some bring animals stuffed into pillow cases as though they are carrying sacks of trash to the local dump.

Outreach workers also model caretaking behaviors for Costa Ricans to potentially copy when they get home with their pets, fostering not just caretaking but closer interaction with animals. Much of this modeling happens when animals are postoperatively coming out of anesthesia in the recovery area, a time when workers usher Costa Ricans into this area just to let them observe their animals as they wake up because their whining or apparent distress, such as shivering, stirs compassion in some owners who, perhaps for the first time, feel sorry for their pets. The modeling occurs when workers deliberately demonstrate various caretaking practices, such as how to clip a dog's nails, as well as how to massage the animal to help it wake up faster from anesthesia. Seeing workers or volunteers caring for pets and making sure they are alive and healthy shifts how many Costa Ricans regard their own animals, at least during and shortly after the clinic visit. As one outreach veterinarian said, "We're petting them, trimming their nails, cleaning their ears. They're standing around watching this. They see us do all of this for their pet and I see them change. I see their faces soften." Costa Ricans exhibited this change in less ambiguous ways than having their faces "soften." For example, many come to the clinics roughly dragging their animals with makeshift leashes or carrying them over their shoulders in laundry bags, having never carried their pets in a nurturing way or touched them affectionately, but end up leaving the clinics holding them like newborns.

Sometimes clinic staff and volunteers intentionally model affection for pets as an informal way to teach Costa Ricans new ways to interact with and be closer to their dogs or cats. For example, one outreach worker says that she escorts children to their animals when they are recovering from anesthesia and still asleep to show them how to pet dogs or cats, with the worker first petting the animal, then guiding the children's hands so they touch it the same way. At other times the modeling is unintentional but also demonstrates that stroking, petting, grooming, talking to, and otherwise comforting and closely interacting with animals is enjoyable for pets and owners alike. This was the case for one outreach worker who said she frequently "kisses" dogs in the clinic, sometimes knowing that Costa Ricans are watching this interaction, while at other times more spontaneously kissing them as Costa Ricans watched.[3]

And finally, sometimes situations emerge at sterilization clinics that can become opportunities for Costa Ricans to try on new pet-related behaviors that bring them physically and perhaps emotionally closer to their animals, if only briefly. Such a forced situation happens when pets are coming out of anesthesia and must be carried to the car or all the way home by people who were very reluctant to touch their dogs or cats. "At first, they're like 'Oh, I don't want to touch him,'" said one rescue worker, but most people quickly embrace this new behavior, especially after they are told that the animals are clean and free of fleas. Workers also tell these Costa Ricans to carefully monitor their animals' recovery for a few days after surgery, thereby forcing them to pay extra attention and perhaps feel closer to their animals.

A common thread runs through all of these teaching opportunities, whether unwitting observations made by people coming to the clinics or intentional coaching of them by outreach workers. More than merely modeling some valuable practical behaviors with pets, such as how to use a leash or cut a pet's nails, the various teaching moments, when viewed as a package, can potentially chip away at long-standing cultural attitudes toward animals. Sentiment and behavior toward dogs and cats are being nudged in the direction of modern Western human-pet relationships by encouraging people to care for and be emotionally close to animals.

Seeing Animals as Patients

Some outreach sterilization programs announce in the weeks leading up to clinics that minor veterinary treatments in addition to fixing animals will be provided. Offering these extra services draws many additional Costa Ricans. For example, one sterilization-only group periodically offers deworming and a basic veterinary examination for free at some of its outreach clinics—a point of contention with some regular veterinarians in private practice who see these free services as unfair competition and an infringement on their professional territory. When this sterilization-only group did not offer these services at one clinic, only 40 people came with dogs and cats for sterilization, compared to 250 to 300 at another one of their clinics that did offer deworming and other veterinary services. Offering these extra services for free draws Costa Ricans from distant towns who hear about clinics outside their communities through Facebook announcements that note the date and location of forthcoming appearances by outreach teams. Despite the distance and concomitant expense, going to the free clinic is far less expensive than visiting a local veterinarian in private practice to get the same basic treatments.

Some veterinary problems also get treated when veterinarians take care of unsolicited problems they spot that owners are unaware of or insensitive to. Veterinarians conduct an initial examination of animals brought to the clinic to ensure they are healthy enough for surgery. During this examination, veterinarians occasionally find medical problems that prevent safe surgery. When this happens, they are usually careful to not violate their understanding with the Veterinary Colegio to only make recommendations and not treat an animal beyond sterilizing it. However, in the course of preparing an animal for surgery or during the procedure, the clinic veterinarian might find a medical problem and tell the owner what the problem is and how it might be addressed, suggest that the owner take the animal to a veterinarian for further care, or actually do the procedure while under anesthesia, despite warnings from the Veterinary Colegio to do otherwise in these situations.

Other Costa Ricans come to sterilization clinics soliciting veterinary help for their injured or sick animals, hoping the pets will get treated because they have no other options for veterinary care. Private-practice veterinarians are too far away and most Costa Ricans in poor towns do not have access to transportation or the money to afford treatment even if they could get there. So they come to outreach clinics with animals having medical problems running from tick disease to injuries from crocodile attacks to severe anemia, knowing that these problems are unrelated to sterilization surgery but thinking, sometimes with desperation, that the staff will make an exception or look down on them with pity and at least offer advice on how to manage the problem.

In these cases of owner-solicited help, the veterinarian, at his or her discretion, can decide to medically intervene if it is a relatively minor issue by giving owners free medication or writing them a prescription. Sometimes staff members do this without the owner's solicitation. For example, at one clinic a veterinarian clipped the long toenails of an aggressive dog while the animal was under anesthesia since the owner could not easily do that as well as treat it for mange and heartworm; the owner was not charged for this service, nor was the local advocate group or cooperating shelter expected to pay an extra fee to this veterinarian.

With most urgent veterinary problems, outreach sterilization clinics can do little to immediately intervene medically but might try to help animals get treatment elsewhere. Whether or not veterinarians were worried about the Colegio punishing them for overstepping its regulations, very serious veterinary problems were untreated because the clinics lacked needed equipment to intervene, such as x-ray machines to diagnose broken legs. Occasionally, some clinics offered help by paying for taxis to take sick or injured animals to private-practice veterinarians or by paying for the treatments themselves. For example, at one clinic in a poor town bordering San Jose, a woman brought in a dog not to be sterilized but hoping to have veterinarians fix its broken leg. She claimed to not own the injured dog but to have found it roaming the streets with its leg injury. However, the staff did not believe her and instead assumed she was attempting to shirk financial responsibility for its care by claiming it was not hers. Despite their doubts, the clinic veterinarian examined the dog and injected it with analgesic for pain reduction, but that was all he could do because the clinic had neither x-ray equipment nor permission from the Colegio to mend the broken leg. The outreach staff strongly encouraged her to immediately take the dog to a nearby veterinarian they contacted for an appointment that day and who was reassured that the outreach organization would pay the $175 bill if the woman could not. At first the woman seemed unable or unwilling to pay the taxi fare needed to get to this veterinarian, but she ultimately did and the dog was seen and cared for that day. The outreach group subsequently had to seek sponsors and donations to cover this bill.

In rare instances the outreach veterinarian will, at no cost to the owner (and at no extra pay), medically or surgically intervene if an animal presents with a life-threatening problem. As with minor veterinary problems, intervening with more serious medical issues presents an opportunity to both help animals and change people. The team's efforts not only can be life-saving but also can encourage Costa Ricans' sense of responsibility for dogs and cats by getting them to bring very sick or seriously injured animals to veterinarians, while underscoring the importance of doing this in the future should animals need urgent veterinary attention.

For example, in one case someone brought to the sterilization clinic a dog that was "clearly not well," according to the veterinarian on duty, because it had a mammary tumor that, without surgical intervention, would kill it. The veterinarian felt that "ethically" he had to perform this surgery, even though his intervention would violate the Veterinary Colegio's rules. However, he did not fear sanctioning by the Colegio because the only people observing his surgery were the other veterinarian and the dog owner who would not report his off-the-record surgery to the association. Days after the clinic, this dog owner emailed photographs of the recovering dog to the operating veterinarian to show that the dog was fine. These actions suggest that both the medical and interactional interventions succeeded because the dog was doing well and its owner took responsibility to follow-up on its progress.

In short, treating or helping Costa Ricans manage veterinary problems presents an opportunity to outreach programs. Rather than turning away Costa Ricans who bring animals for issues other than sterilization or ignoring veterinary problems that are discovered, treating or even just evaluating medical issues acknowledges that pet owners are doing the right thing by seeking veterinary care in these circumstances and encourages them to seek it in the future should animals become sick or injured. So by helping people who bring sick or injured pets to sterilization clinics, outreach workers not only can help the animals but also can potentially instill, reinforce, or enhance Costa Ricans' sense of responsibility for their dogs or cats.

Yet helping animals that need veterinary care can also present challenges to outreach clinics. For one, outreach staff members worry that doing so might embolden Costa Ricans to bring sick or injured animals to their clinics for care, quickly overwhelming their limited resources. Also, by raising Costa Ricans' expectations for receiving veterinary care, outreach clinics risk disappointing and frustrating pet owners in the future who want such care for their animals only to be turned down by clinic veterinarians and not have the means to afford private-practice veterinarians.

For another, treating medical problems other than the most basic might result in reprisals from the Veterinary Colegio. While a few outreach veterinarians with bolder styles of intervention do not worry about reprisals from the Colegio and sometimes treat gray-area medical problems, especially if they have medical and surgical resources in their clinic to help these animals, most are more circumspect. The latter fear overstepping the Veterinary Colegio's restrictions on what they can do and often curtail what they think might be best to do medically for animals in need. The result is that the decision to treat animals for problems other than sterilization—and the ability to seed pet-keeping norms—is decided on a case-by-case basis by individual veterinarians, each of whom has a different tolerance for challenging or complying with the Colegio's limited view of what they can perform during outreach.

––––––––––

Despite their primary focus on sterilizing animals at remote clinics, outreach workers can affect people as well. Veterinarians, veterinary assistants, rescue workers, and volunteers can change how local people think about using veterinary care as well as what they feel for their dogs and cats. Doing so is neither outreach workers' primary mission nor something they always do with intention, but that does not lessen the significance of what transpires—local culture is being nudged to alter long-standing customs for interacting with and being responsible for dogs and cats.

Indeed, the influence of outreach workers as norm seeders should not be underestimated, along with volunteers and some local pet owners who serve as role models. Their efforts are sustained as they return to the same village or town to sterilize more animals, their interactions are powerful as they meet and get to know pet owners face-to-face, and their goal is formidable—to change behavior, at minimum getting Costa Ricans to sterilize animals—but in general suggesting new ways for Costa Ricans to think about and behave with dogs and cats. In addition, larger cultural changes bolster these efforts to seed norms, as happens with the diffusion of innovations elsewhere (e.g., Fujii, 2004). Factors such as increasing tourism, greater access to the internet, and rising socioeconomic status in Costa Rica have likely accelerated the diffusion of pet-keeping norms, including willingness to sterilize animals.

Getting Costa Ricans to change their perspective toward sterilization in particular and toward pet keeping in general is not as simple as just offering low-cost spaying and neutering to underserved communities. Like norm diffusion elsewhere, this process generally progresses from coercion or persua-

sion to learning and emulation (Gilardi, 2012). This change in perspective involves a complicated, multistep process of improvising demand for surgery
and facilities to conduct sterilization, routinizing local expectations for this
procedure, increasing Costa Ricans' investment in and commitment to their
animals, changing how they interact with them, and treating some veterinary
issues beside sterilization. In other words, if these norms are diffused, the hesitancy of those coming to the clinics for the first time gives way to openness
toward the pet care perspective of outreach workers and animal advocates if
not conversion to new behaviors.

Such perspective change can have far-reaching social and cultural implications. Individuals who adopt these new behaviors can change, but so can their
local cultures. As people adopt new behaviors, what they and many of their
peers come to see as expected, normal, and part of everyday life also changes
as networks of people try on a new way to think and act. In this regard, sterilization clinics have the potential to impact not merely the behavior of individual Costa Ricans but the social world they inhabit, which includes dogs and
cats. This social spillover from one Costa Rican to the next can occur as converted pet owners establish their innovative behavior as a local norm by re-
cruiting converts nearby, thereby expanding the network of sterilization users
as a whole, as happens with diffusion in other international settings (Kincaid,
2004).

This process of norm seeding has the potential to do more than increase
sterilization rates and exert greater control over dogs and cats. It can change
how Costa Ricans view these animals—their nature, desirability, and social
worth, just as animals are framed and then reframed in other social contexts.
For example, residents in some American urban locations have become more
willing to view certain animals as neighborhood cohabitants rather than as
unwelcome pests (Rupprecht, 2017), while people in China are increasingly
viewing dogs and cats as pets rather than as meat (Doi & Pettier, 2018). Although these examples illustrate how animals can be reframed in cities or societies, framing animals can also be an interactional resource to communicate thoughts and feelings to other people (e.g., Tannen, 2004), as happens
when outreach workers try to shift Costa Ricans' view of dogs and cats.

Indeed, understanding this potential shift in Costa Ricans' definition of
dogs and cats is at the heart of the efforts of sterilization outreach teams as
well as many animal advocates in Costa Rica, who want to change how everyday people regard and treat dogs and cats. Encouragement of and support for
Costa Ricans to sterilize animals can start to chip away at long-standing conceptions of the meaning and significance of dogs and cats that have traditionally created distance between humans and animals, particularly in Costa Ri-

ca's poorest areas. When Costa Ricans commit to sterilize their animals and interact with staff members and neighbors at outreach clinics they are given an alternate perception of dogs and cats, or at least one that questions how they have viewed them in the past. No longer unwanted and "dirty" nuisances or objects that serve only instrumental purposes, such as guarding homes or killing mice, they become something akin to modern pets.

Typical neighborhood served by El Refugio's sterilization outreach team, Cartago, Costa Rica.

Dog considers public garage to be his home, Los Guidos, Costa Rica.

Dog returning to same family every day for occasional water or occasional scraps but is not regarded as their pet, nor are they viewed as its owners.

Cat "adopts" guard at hotel entrance and becomes a mascot during the day, Puntarenas, Costa Rica.

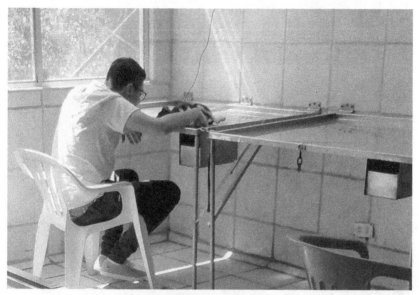

Owner grieving over dying pet at El Refugio's veterinary hospital.

Dropping off dogs and cats (often brought in cloth bags) at pickup location to be driven two hours to El Refugio for sterilization and then returned later the same day.

Numbering of dog and owner to indicate their turn in the day's 230 surgeries performed by a sterilization outreach team, Ipis, Costa Rica.

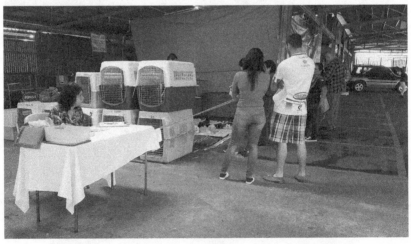

Registration, waiting, recovery, and operating rooms set up for the day in a parking garage by sterilization outreach team, Cartago, Costa Rica.

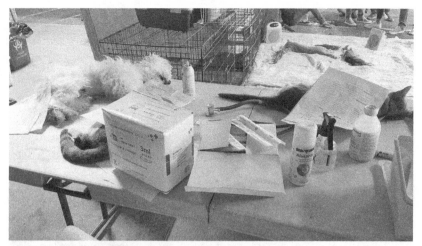

Postop recovery table, sterilization outreach team, Heredia, Costa Rica.

Operating room repurposed by sterilization outreach team on second floor of farm feed store, San Ramon, Costa Rica.

West Charlotte neighborhood near the Humane Society of Charlotte; downtown Charlotte in the distance.

Dog chained in West Charlotte backyard, a common sight.

Dogs more often leashed in West Charlotte than in most Costa Rican villages and poor urban areas.

Volunteers building a backyard fence for West Charlotte dog owner.

Owners waiting in line for the Humane Society of Charlotte's Food Bank, held twice a month if supplies are available.

Owner with pets waiting to be examined, microchipped, and vaccinated at the Humane Society of Charlotte's Wellness Clinic.

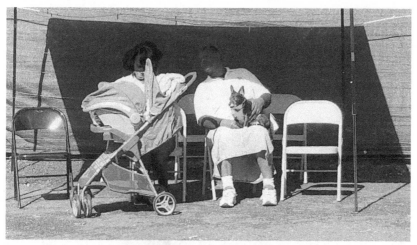

Spay/Neuter Clinic at the Humane Society of Charlotte with outdoor waiting area.

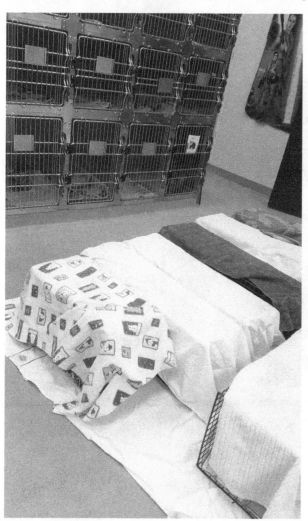

Preop room for community cats (feral or neighborhood) before sterilization at the Humane Society of Charlotte.

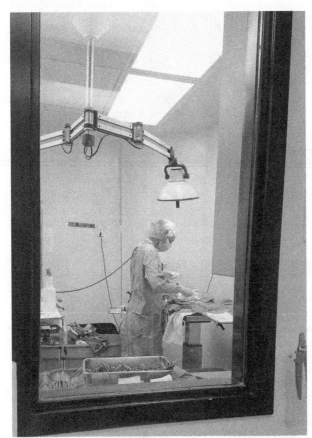

Operating room,
Humane Society
of Charlotte.

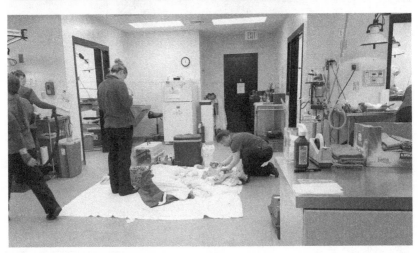

Postop, Humane Society of Charlotte.

West Charlotte, North Carolina

CHAPTER FOUR

Underdogs and Their People

LIVING WITH PETS IN
RACIALLY CONCENTRATED POVERTY

We saw how culture can impact human-street animal relationships in traditional parts of Costa Rica. Long-held beliefs and customs about the nature of
animals and the extent of human involvement with or commitment to them
shape Costa Ricans' willingness to care for and control dogs and cats. This
cultural take on human-animal relationships means that humane advocates
wanting to control overpopulation and provide low-cost veterinary care do
not have a tabula rasa to work with. On the contrary, perspectives conflict as
to whether street dogs are viewed as problems and, if they are, what kind of
problems they cause and their severity. The result is that both Costa Ricans
and animal advocates adjust their expectations and behavior regarding animal care.

However, cultural norms and beliefs are not the only constraints on how
people think and act. The structural features of society, like race, gender, and
social class, can intersect to oppress and exploit people. With this intersection, the oppression of people becomes the oppression of animals (Gaard,
2011), as feminist scholars in particular have pointed out. Gender, as one of
these structural features, has been shown to influence human-animal relationships because of the connection between the oppression of women and
animals (Deckha, 2012). Other feminist scholars have gone further to point out
not only the joint oppression of women and animals but also the simultane-
ous domination of people of color, the poor, and animals (Warren, 2000).

Does this intersectionality affect the way pet owners in predominately
black, low-income communities interact with their animals and, if so, how?

Some suggest that the plight of being poor and black, especially when combined with the cultural norms of disadvantaged communities, could prevent people from being attached to pets. Attachment is weakened, it is thought, because the disorder of life in or near poverty and the added pressure of trying to survive in such a world leave pet owners little time or opportunity to become emotionally invested in the lives of their animals. The image that follows from this line of thinking is a poor inner-city neighborhood having many large barking dogs chained in driveways to stand watch while scores of semi- or un-owned crying cats decimate and dirty the few existing green spaces.

Some people also think that pet owners in America's disadvantaged neighborhoods are more "irresponsible" than those in more advantaged communities. Rather than considering their inability to provide a certain level of veterinary care, this line of thinking assumes that poor pet owners are unwilling to live up to middle- or upper-class standards of ownership. That they are pictured as faulty or deficient owners who do not care enough about their pets to provide them with basic veterinary care likely stems from cultural stereotypes of poverty. People continue to blame poverty on the poor (Adeola, 2005; Greenbaum, 2015) because they see them as lazy, dependent, helpless, or not valuing work (Burton, 1992; Lewis, 1966). If the poor cannot be responsible for their children, for example, why would they be any more responsible for the welfare of their pets?

Rather than blaming pet owners in or near poverty for their presumed detachment from and irresponsibility for their pets, we wanted to allow for a different possibility to emerge from the data, if these assumptions were untrue. So we listened to how these people regarded and interacted with their pets, how they experienced the problems of everyday life and what impact this had on their pets, how they bonded with their animals and demonstrated this connection, and how they cared for their pets' welfare, given all the difficulties faced by both people and animals in this community. In other words, we asked how subculture, race, and social class affect the lives of pets and owners and the kinds of relationships they form, how they affect the need of animals for the shelter's low- or no-cost services, and how they affect owners' ability to use these services.

Expressing and Regulating Bonds

Attachments to pets in West Charlotte can be as profound and lasting as among pet-owning residents in any neighborhood, but the conditions fanning or restraining attachment are somewhat unique to this community. Low-income pet owners or those living in poverty have fewer resources to express or act on their attachment. Disposable income for this population is very limited and needs to be stretched to take care of basic everyday needs such as food, utilities, medical, care, and home maintenance. Under these demanding conditions, West Charlotte pet owners try their best with what they have access to, even if it is less than ideal. For example, one pet owner grieved over her recently deceased 14-year-old cat but never had a photograph taken of "Chloe." So she scoured magazines to find a likeness of her cat and found one that she framed and hung in her living room.

With fewer resources, some residents who are strongly attached to pets claim to make personal sacrifices in their own lifestyles and welfare for the animals' sake, just as they routinely do for other family members when they are in need.[1] One pet owner allegedly spent his entire social security check for a sick dog's veterinary bill, making him forgo what little entertainment he had and miss credit card payments despite incurring penalties. To be clear, these sacrifices are sometimes inseparable from the ways pet owners managed scarce resources in general. For example, a few cut back on their use of utilities to save money not only to care for their pets but also to pay for other things they and family members needed. To wit, one pet owner claimed she did not pay her electric bill for over a month and lost power to have enough money so she could buy food for her children as well as take her dog to a veterinarian so it could be treated for worms and mange.

Often these sacrifices involved not purchasing food for themselves or family members to find extra money to pay for pet food. One cat owner started getting food for herself at a food pantry so the money she normally spent for her own food could be spent on pet food, which she otherwise could not afford. Another owner of two pit bulls claimed that when she could not afford pet food, she fed table food to her dogs, although she knew that doing this was not as healthy for the animals as giving them pet food. Feeding her pets table food also meant she ate less herself. This was also true for another person who could not afford pet food, so he fed a week's supply of hot dogs, which he normally would have eaten, to his Chihuahua.

Of course, a few pet owners say in jest they would "go without eating" or "not feed my kids" in order to feed their pets. But even in these cases pet owners are likely to make concessions in their lives to feed animals, putting their pets' needs before their own, as also observed among homeless veterans (Fink, 2015) and users of a pet food bank (Rauktis et al., 2017). The latter found that about three-fourths of clients who did not have pet food shared human food with their pets, a practice we commonly observed among West Charlotte pet owners. So in these cases they may have eaten less as opposed to not eating at all, but that constitutes a sacrifice.

However, there are times when pet owners cannot make certain sacrifices for their animals because doing so would be too catastrophic for them. For example, some pet owners who had children were reticent to sacrifice their diet or the home's heating because the state's Department of Social Services would "have a field day for not taking care of my kids." Other pet owners could not take their pets to the veterinarian for examinations or treatments because they were worried about being fired if they took time off from work to do this; missing even a day of work could be economically devastating.

Pet owners in West Charlotte cope with more than a routine lack of resources that makes it difficult to care for pets. They also frequently endure trauma and changes in their everyday lives that are seen as normal but from a middle- and upper-income perspective would be seen as unstable, unpredictable, chaotic, fragile, disorderly, and perhaps dangerous (Maholmes & King, 2012). Doing something like opening the door of a heated oven in the winter to warm a house is not unusual or strange, nor is not hanging pictures on walls because they expect to be evicted again. It is also normal for them to face job insecurity, bouts of unemployment, a hand-to-mouth existence, multiple transitions in family structure, financial struggles on a fixed income, loss of electrical power and heating because they cannot pay for them, sickness, injuries, or disabilities where they cannot obtain medical care, and neighborhood or domestic violence. Of course these problems can occur to anyone regardless of their social class, but they happen more often in lower classes, and those stricken are less able to deal with and overcome these problems.

As Gans (2014) observed, little is known about how people living in poverty develop solutions, if any, to deal with regularly occurring and cumulative crises. When disorder and uncertainty are normal and day-to-day existence is a constant struggle, these conditions can fan particularly strong attachments to pets as they take on a special role. For the most part, the chaotic and disorderly nature of West Charlotte life does not prevent bonds from forming with pets, and perhaps exaggerates their importance if they are latched onto as small beacons of stability. Low-income pet owners may rely on their pets as anchors to get through the disorder and challenges of everyday life because pets represent the only stability and predictability in their lives, just as pets provide stability for military families undergoing frequent transfers (Anderson, 2016; Cain, 1985) or play a positive and protective role for stressed pet owners in the aftermath of disasters (Tanaka et al., 2019). Even simple routines required by pets, such as feeding, can be counted on to provide some degree of structure in lives that are otherwise in disarray.

This anchoring role may make the depth and importance of owners' bonds with pets stronger than human-pet bonds in families that have less trauma and more ability to manage it. Many West Charlotte pet owners appeared to develop deep and even profound bonds with their animals because they were older blacks in or near poverty who relied on their pets to get through the many difficult challenges they faced every day. One such person was John. John thought God sent him Sparkles because the cat made it easier for him to cope with his hard life, but after many years of close companionship the cat ran away and was lost. Now that Sparkles was gone, John had no idea how he could go on. After some time he got a new cat that resembled Sparkles, with whom he formed an equally intense bond and dependency. Even if it is argued that the strength of the bond is the same regardless of the owner's social class and race, the social conditions facilitating and maintaining the bond can still be quite different. At least to some extent adversity can create or facilitate bonding with pets.

Especially close ties may be fostered when owners identify with the plight of their pets as both owner and pet endure significant, although not necessarily identical, misfortune. Indirect support for such underdog bonding comes from studies reporting intimacy among breast cancer patients (Lugton, 1997), concern for animal well-being by people who themselves have been treated unequally or have experienced economic hardship, such as women, younger people, and blacks (Kendall et al., 2006), bonding between homeless pet owners and their animals (Gillespie & Lawson, 2017), and identification with abused animals by at-risk children (Arluke, 2010). For example, one owner and her mixed-breed dog Chubby both lived precarious lives and were hanging on to their relationship and home, even though time was running out for both of them. She found the dog when she moved into her current home; one of the tenants owned Chubby but cared little for it and frequently hit him with a stick when it was tied up outside all the time. When the tenant moved away, she convinced him to leave the dog with her. She rapidly formed a bond with Chubby and wanted to give it the best possible care and home, given the dog's traumatic history—making sure it had a stable home inside, was well fed, was given lots of affection, and certainly was never physically harmed. Simultaneously, her own health and home were severely threatened as she faced a life-threatening illness and eviction. Suddenly both she and Chubby faced an uncertain future—nowhere to live and perhaps death. In her own case, the cancer gave her little time, and if Chubby had been surrendered to animal control, he would likely have been euthanized.

Close ties with pets can distract West Charlotte owners from the unique kinds of distress and disorder they face, as the bond survives despite, or even because of, these difficulties. For one, unemployment is a common stressor in this community, and having a pet can sometimes mitigate this stress, as suggested by studies of coping by other unemployed groups (Ribton-Turner & De Bruin, 2006). This was the case for one resident who was a bus driver with one child. After getting hurt he was laid off and faced a series of problems, such as being unable to heat his house with the electric kitchen oven in the winter because his electricity was cut off. He continued to encounter additional problems that created high stress, but the two of them always had their dog. Hanging out at home with the pet was apparently a source of joy in an unideal and difficult situation, enabling their attention to be distracted, even if briefly, from the significant problems surrounding them by doing things like putting outfits on the dog.

For another, pet bonds appear to lessen the impact of isolation and health problems common in communities of color that are predominately poor (Kawachi & Berkman, 2003), just as they do in the general population (Krause-Parello, 2012). One such pet owner bonded very tightly with her dog because she had no meaningful human social contacts other than with shelter workers, in part due to her poverty that left her unemployed for years without the daily contact of coworkers and a modest income, while being estranged from her daughter and nephew. As the outreach worker on the case commented, "Everything was unpleasant and bad in her life," topped off with worsening personal medical problems that were difficult to face and afford. When her dog developed severe mange and other veterinary problems, she cared so much for it that she got a second mortgage on her house just to pay the veterinarian rather than euthanize it, in part for the dog's sake but also because she clung even tighter to the dog as her own life seemed more precarious and challenging to live. "All of her joy in life was wrapped up in this animal" and seemed to grow stronger, observed the shelter worker, as this pet owner seemed to battle harder to keep the dog and herself alive with virtually no social support system and almost no money.

While attachment to pets survived and even flourished in West Charlotte, often because of the difficulties faced by their owners, other aspects of this subculture of poverty and race suppressed, but did not eliminate, these bonds. One suppressor of bonds occurred when a pet had an instrumental function, as also observed among pet owners in middle-class communities had guard dogs (Shore et al., 2006). People sometimes seemed less attached to larger dogs, such as shepherds, akitas, and pit bulls, that were kept outside as guards—chained or kept behind a fence all the time in the driveway or backyard where they were rarely interacted with or treated as pets. And people were less attached to cats when they were kept outside to deter or kill rats and snakes on the owners' properties. One consequence of this instrumental behavior is that it reinforced the idea that animals "naturally" wanted to be outside and were "happier" there, a widely held belief in West Charlotte.

However, people often appeared to be at least somewhat attached to their pets even when instrumentally valued, bonding with and appreciating them for companionship while simultaneously valuing them for their ability to protect property and provide a general sense of security. For example, one pet owner was very attached to her two pit bulls, who were acquired to be companions. Yet pit bulls could simultaneously serve as guard dogs in this community. So in this case the owner was grateful that they served as sentries in her backyard to protect her old iron porch furniture that she feared would be stolen and sold as scrap. Even smaller dogs could serve as both companions and guards because they were often kept inside as alarm dogs more than guards—their barking would alert the owner's outdoor dog of a threat. Chihuahuas, in particular, were popular choices to serve as alarm dogs because they barked loudly at the slightest possibility of an intruder. One West Charlotte resident compared owning a Chihuahua in his neighborhood to wealthier people owning a German shepherd. "The same way in rich neighborhoods, you're going to have a German shepherd that's been trained in all these fancy places. You cross into his territory, you're going to get bitten. It's the same thing with a Chihuahua. But the cost of a trained shepherd is out of the price range of a poverty-stricken neighborhood. A Chihuahua is a lot more common and cheaper." In the end, the instrumental value of pets in West Charlotte can hinder but not necessarily prevent attachment to them.

Bonding can also be hindered by subcultural norms that create multiple caretakers for animals in disadvantaged communities. Compared to middle- and upper-class pet owners, West Charlotte's residents are more likely to befriend stray or feral animals of unknown origin by occasionally feeding them or briefly letting them into their homes to the point where they start to regard the animals as more pet than stray, although their bonds with these animals tend not be as intense or as long-lasting as those with more permanent and clearly owned pets. Some of these "strays" are owned by neighbors who let them roam the neighborhood and "adopt" multiple homeowners for additional food and attention, going into and staying for hours in various homes, with or without the temporary owner knowing the animal's source. For example, if you go into Don's house, at any one time he has about 10 cats as well as two or three dogs, but not all are his pets. He encourages neighbors to bring their dogs when they visit his home, and when they do, the dogs tend to stay for about three days. A neighbor's dog, Chocolate, was a frequent visitor who stayed for days. Although Don even buys food for Chocolate and other neighborhood pets that visit, he does not regard them as his pets. This type of neighborhood sharing of pets allows for a community of ties to local animals, as well as with their owners, where bonds are less intense with animals but more common than if owners sequester their pets.

Allowing pets to roam neighborhoods is another subcultural norm that hinders bonding by making pets less dependent on families and less present with them. Dogs are less likely than cats to be allowed to roam, but it does sometimes happen in West Charlotte. Owners believe dogs "need" to be free and will come back. In one case the owner felt his dog "needs to sow his seed." But some do not return; they get hit by cars or buses, shot by police officers if seen as aggressive and dangerous, or picked up by animal control. If animal control officers seize these roaming dogs and take them to their facility for assessment and holding, most West Charlotte owners cannot afford the fee to recover them, so there is some chance they will be euthanized, especially if they are larger, are older, or have behavior problems. More commonly, pet cats are commonly allowed to roam in West Charlotte. Most owners permit them to roam because they believe cats want to be outdoors and feel they should not be stopped. But because these owners do not understand the full risk of doing this, they minimize its danger. For example, while they know their cats can get fleas, everything has fleas in most West Charlotte neighborhoods, and residents think that fleas cause only itching (as opposed to getting diseases from fleas, such as tape worms, which most residents think pets get from eating table food). In the end, their autonomous behavior on the streets makes roaming cats less of a "family member" than are dogs in terms of how much they are included in family rituals and routines.

Subcultural norms can suppress attachment in yet another, more protective way for some West Charlotte pet owners. They may stop themselves from becoming very attached to their pets to prevent or minimize future emotional distress. Restraining attachment to prevent possible sadness often happened when West Charlotte pet owners adopted a puppy or had a litter, yet were unsure that the puppy or litter would make it into adulthood. For example, one resident's dog had a litter of puppies, but two of them developed parvo, as did prior puppies in her care. While she asked the shelter to treat the parvo, "Let's do what we can to save them," she was not distraught by their potentially fatal condition because she was resigned to the idea they might not live like other dogs before.

Such subcultural norms, then, work in two converse ways to influence the nature and extent of pet attachment in West Charlotte. On the one hand, these norms sometimes constrain emotional investment in pets. People routinely expect trouble and trauma in their lives and brace themselves for pain by sometimes taking a step back from deeper bonds with animals that they know would come back to hurt them were they to allow these bonds to deepen. People are also accustomed to thinking about most, but not all, pets as somewhat autonomous creatures that are distant from them because they can fend for themselves outside with the help of neighbors who also sometimes feed them and given their natural abilities to hunt or forage in the wild. But on the other hand, subcultural norms can encourage stronger emotional investment in pets in ways that protect the welfare of these animals. Most owners expect to make sacrifices for their animals, as they forgo and do without in the rest of their lives for the welfare of family members and themselves. Cutting back on food, entertainment, clothing, or utilities is an expected coping device that enables pet owners to express their affection for and attachment to their charges by taking care of them as well as possible, given challenging circumstances.

Mirroring Misfortune

Bonds between West Charlotte residents and their pets exist despite—and to some extent because of—the chaos, stress, and hardship of everyday life that people face in this community. Pets who live in this community are not immune from these pressures and problems. Their lives will mirror those of their owners, as intersecting structural factors, such as race and class, can oppress both humans and animals. Pets in this community are likely to experience misfortunes similar to the people around them, as they are cotravelers with their owners in a life where both are prone to the vagaries of everyday life, injury, disease, disability, accidents, violence, and early death, with limited or no access to adequate health care. The result is that West Charlotte's pets have relatively shorter life spans compared to those kept in middle- and higher-income households.

While most owners in West Charlotte want to be responsible for their pets, the stressors of living in a disadvantaged community make it difficult for them to do so, as misfortune falls on them and their pets. For example, it is normal that "shit happens" in the everyday work and personal lives of West Charlotte pet owners. These unexpected problems are difficult to manage because the affected individual does not have the disposable income to deal with sudden complications (e.g., to pay for a taxi to transport children) or a network of friends and neighbors to pitch in and help spontaneously. Nor are they likely to have salaried jobs with paid time off or time accrued that would give them some flexibility to deal with personal matters. Since they have fewer resources, a small issue can become an unmanageable problem, a situation not faced by most middle- and upper-income pet owners who have the financial and social resources to rely on for help when emergencies or unexpected everyday stressors arise.

These unpredictable and difficult-to-manage events can complicate the care of human dependents as well as pets by creating barriers to using health, social, and veterinary services. The result is that West Charlotte pets as well as children receive a lower standard of care compared to pets and children living in more prosperous communities. Having such a lower standard of care means that the former's pets are less likely to get veterinary attention when sick or hurt or preventive care to stave off illness, such as heartworm medication that can prevent early death. West Charlotte pet owners would like to provide this level of care, but their lives make it difficult to do so.

When West Charlotte pet owners face capricious and often uncompromising misfortune, something as "simple" as taking a pet to get vaccinated at the shelter can be challenging or impossible. One resident had two dogs scheduled for surgery but called the shelter the night before to say her boss said she had to come in to work the next day, and there was no one else to take her dog to the shelter. Or because they have to make an extra trip to pick up a child at school, they find that they do not have enough gas to get to the shelter and cannot borrow a few dollars from a neighbor to pay for extra fuel. The likelihood of "shit happening" is even greater among West Charlotte's elderly pet owners who have diseases or disabilities with unpredictable symptoms from day to day that can prevent or complicate the use of the shelter's services. For example, if an elderly pet owner on dialysis goes for a treatment, she might not be able to take her dog or cat to the shelter the next day if, unexpectedly, she feels sick afterward. Lacking a safety net, she has no one to fall back on to take her pet to the shelter.

Problems in the lives of West Charlotte pet owners can also make it difficult if not impossible for them to keep animals. Pets are commonly abandoned, given temporarily or permanently to another family or person, or surrendered to the shelter or animal control. Going to jail ("he went away for a while"), being evicted, having to care for a sick out-of-town relative, being deported, moving away, or changing jobs or work schedules that keep owners away from home are some reasons for this displacement. This pet turnover means that West Charlotte pet owners will own more pets over the same period of time than will higher income pet owners because each time a West Charlotte resident's pet dies or is abandoned, given away, or stolen, it will likely be replaced with another pet when opportunities present themselves, unless the original animal is reclaimed from whomever is holding it.

In the end, the misfortunes facing West Charlotte's owners and their pets can make having them seem like a transitory and short-lived experience rather than a stable and enduring one spanning many years. In one typical household, pets seemed to stay alive for just a few years, to be replaced with another until that pet died or disappeared too at an early age. As this pet owner said of her family, "We always have a few dogs, when one is gone, we get another one," suggesting that she did not expect the family's dogs to lead long lives, instead appearing and disappearing routinely from her home. However, the unpredictability and lack of control over everyday problems that make pet ownership so tenuous is merely one source of misfortune for West Charlotte's pets.

Pets in West Charlotte are also likely to experience misfortune because of the community's subcultural pet-keeping norms. Many pets there are likely to be sicker, even from birth, than their counterparts in middle- and upper-income communities. Having more health problems stems from many factors but starts with the pathway to acquiring pets in West Charlotte, which is different from that in higher income communities, where aspiring pet owners are far more likely to acquire their animals from pet stores, professional breeders, and animal shelters that usually screen new pets for disease and ensure that they have been or will be properly vaccinated and sterilized. But only 2% of the pet owners who live in the shelter's West Charlotte zip codes of interest acquired pets from the shelter, and 6% did so from legitimate breeders.

West Charlotte residents are aware they can adopt pets fairly easily and inexpensively from the local shelter, but they do not because many are convinced their adoption requests will be rejected. They think the shelter will perceive them as inadequate pet owners because, for example, many do not have full-time jobs and fenced-in yards, instead chaining their dogs outside, sometimes without a doghouse, a practice that is relatively common in low-income communities. For example, in an economically comparable community on the Texas border, about 62% of households chain their dogs outside (Poss & Bader, 2007). They may also be intimidated by the shelter's adoption contract, which makes it sound like the shelter can take a pet away from a family after it has been adopted if some fault has been found in its animal care, even though the contract has no legal standing that would support such an action by the shelter.

Instead of obtaining pets from the shelter, professional breeders, or pet stores, the pathway to pet ownership in West Charlotte tends to be opportunistic, random, and local, which increases the likelihood that the new pet might be in ill health, need vaccinations, and be unsterilized. Because they often get their pets from backyard or onetime breeders, West Charlotte residents are more likely than middle-income pet adopters to get dogs that need veterinary attention. Although some backyard breeders may try to get their litter vaccinated and/or treated for worms at the shelter before selling them, this is not standard practice. Because of this, West Charlotte adopters can acquire vulnerable and sick puppies or kittens in need of veterinary services and treatments rather than starting their pet ownership with animals that are already disease free as well as sterilized and vaccinated or soon scheduled for these procedures.

The impulsiveness of the adoption decision can create misfortune for pets because it is more likely they will be given away or abandoned rather than kept. West Charlotte residents often get animals from neighbors, friends, or family members who no longer want them or need someone to take care of their pets temporarily, inherit dogs or cats after relatives die, or take them in off the streets. Acquiring pets this way means that some people will not have carefully thought through this decision and do not fully understand the responsibilities of owning a pet. For example, children will hear about a litter of a friend's or fellow student's dog and bring a puppy home without consulting their parents, only to return the dog a week or two later because "it was too much work" or because the parent made them return it. One puppy was returned to the original owner twice because its adoption was so casual. Another resident was not looking to adopt a dog but took it in to help a coworker who discovered two days after getting it that her apartment banned pets, so as a favor to his friend he took the dog. However, he was undecided about keeping it because of unruly behavior and considered finding the dog another home or releasing it on the streets.

The practice of leaving many pets outside in disadvantaged communities can also cause them misfortune. Compared to middle- and higher-income pet owners who are more likely to confine their pets, West Charlotte pet owners tend to keep most cats and large dogs outside all the time. Leaving pets outside makes sense and seems reasonable, from the perspective of most residents in West Charlotte. While there is an increased risk of pets getting hit by cars or attacked by strangers or animals or acquiring some disease, West Charlotte residents too face a precarious reality every time they venture out into their community where they too can be injured or killed. So the risk of pets dying or being injured outside is not a paramount concern to these owners because it is a routine risk they and their family members also face. In addition, deciding to keep pets outside the home reflects the limited resources that low-income pet owners have. For one, they cannot afford to pay for training their animals. Because there is no accessibility in the community to free or even discounted dog training, it is understandable that owners get frustrated when they find that, when kept inside, their new dogs start chewing up furniture, rugs, fixtures, doors, or walls, especially if they have to pay their landlords to fix the damage. When this happens, keeping dogs outside seems like the only rational solution. Since fencing money is rarely available, the only option is to tie the dog to a tether or chain, so it cannot run away. For another, many residents there cannot afford air conditioning in the summer, so being outside can be cooler for pets. And winter months tend to be temperate, so animals can usually handle the cold.

Keeping pets outside the home, whether behind a fence, tied or chained to a stake, or freely roaming the neighborhood, means these animals are at increased risk of disease, injury, or escape. They can be infested by fleas and ticks, hit by cars, and attacked or eaten by other animals. For example, a West Charlotte owner of several cats, over the course of a few months, had one killed by a neighborhood dog, a second went missing and never returned, and a third was run over by a car. Outdoor dogs can also escape even if they are chained or behind fences. If they escape, they then encounter the same problems faced by street dogs. Even inside dogs can escape and get outside for brief periods. For example, one pet owner claimed that she kept her dog inside at all times, but when asked to describe her everyday life, she confessed that often when cooking Latin dishes, she needed to open the kitchen door because of the heat and odors, at which time the family dog ran out.

Even if chained or behind a fence, dogs can be harmed. High rates of violent crime are common in disadvantaged neighborhoods like West Charlotte (Krivo & Peterson, 1996), where gun violence and domestic abuse can affect both pet owners and their animals' welfare. In some cases pets are given away or even euthanized when their owner is shot and killed. After a mother's son was shot and killed, she "had to put down" her son's pit bull because it was so aggressive, although when alive her son could manage the dog's aggression. Dogs also get passed on to new owners after their owners' tragic deaths; one man "inherited" his teenage niece's dog after she was shot and killed. Pets can also be direct victims of gun or other violence, such as physical abuse or poisoning. They may be fired upon by juveniles looking for moving targets or simply because they hate dogs or cats, or by adults "tired" of hearing the barking of their neighbor's dog. One West Charlotte resident did not let her pet dog run free in her fenced-in yard because she was afraid it might be shot or stoned by the armed juveniles who lived nearby. And an eight-year-old West Charlotte girl saw her family dog gunned down in front of her for no apparent reason.[2]

Outdoor dogs can also be stolen by strangers, ex-boyfriends, spouses, and dog fighters, although the latter claim is probably exaggerated. The belief that pets are stolen for dogfighting bait persists in this community, despite the lack of evidence to support it. Owners do not know what bodily evidence is truly a sign of a dog having been used as bait; there are other possible explanations beside dogfighting for the physical changes seen by owners on their pets. To wit, one pet owner was sure that her dog had been used as bait because it had marks on its head, face, and legs, but shelter workers who inspected the dog thought it lacked the kind of scrapes and wounds typical of bait dogs. While residents do not question the veracity of this assumption, some shelter staff members do, claiming that media hype about dogfighting in low-income neighborhoods—some fed by animal welfare groups themselves—exaggerates its presence and the escapades of dogfighters. They also point to the disappearance of dogfighting indicators, such as the decreasing presence of shredded tires in backyards, as evidence for its decline in West Charlotte, although the increasing stigmatization and criminalization of dogfighting may have pushed it underground.[3]

Nevertheless, local dogfighting is used by West Charlotte residents as a default category to explain why dogs go missing or are inexplicably bitten or injured because it is assumed they were stolen to be used as bait for training dogs to fight. This was the case with one person whose dog was snatched from her yard by several young men and put in their car, never to be seen again. Other pet owners are convinced that their dogs were used as dogfighting bait because of scars and cuts of unknown origin. For example, one resident had a young pit bull acquired from a friend who denied knowing anything about the dog's history. However, the dog's appearance suggested to its owner that it had been used for fighting because it had bite marks, deep scratches, a shredded ear, and a burn mark consistent with dog branding.

And if West Charlotte's pets are not stolen, lost, or killed, they are more likely to suffer at the ends of their lives compared to pets in middle- and upper-class communities. Many disadvantaged owners do not know that euthanasia is an option to spare their animals from suffering, so they are often allowed to die a slow death from natural causes, however long that takes. And it is unlikely West Charlotte owners, even if aware of euthanasia, could or would want to pay for this service, just as palliative and end-of-life care are underutilized in the African American community at large (Crawley et al., 2000). Instead of taking their pets to be euthanized by a veterinarian, some of these owners think that when a dog or cat is old and sick one should drop it off at animal control, which outsiders criticize as "dumping," but for pet owners in poverty doing this is an act of compassion.[4]

The inability to get such palliative help for pets, as well as preventive or interventive veterinary care, parallels the lack of child and adult health care in disadvantaged communities like West Charlotte (Yerby, 1966). These parallels remind us that the welfare of pets can be directly linked to that of their owners (Doane & Sarenbo, 2019), such that the race and class of owners intersect species. Pets are underdogs living in an underclass culture where opportunities to flourish, be safe, and be healthy will be as limited or precarious as those of their owners. The misfortunes they face are a product of their owners' hardships and way of life.

Mirroring Barriers to Care

Problems shared by owner and pet alike can create barriers to seeking affordable care, best illustrated by looking at the plight of transportation for residents in West Charlotte. Transportation problems can become a major obstacle for West Charlotte residents, as low-income or poverty-level pet owners, who want to be responsible and take their animals to the shelter for veterinary care and pet food. In this part of town there are few if any private-practice veterinarians, veterinary clinics, veterinary hospitals, or pet stores (e.g., Petco) selling nutritious food. Indeed, for some Pets for Life programs, there may be no private-practice veterinarians in the targeted neighborhoods.[5] Although the shelter is in West Charlotte, getting there can be difficult for many pet owners who want to take advantage of its free or discounted services, such as its Food Bank and its Wellness and Spay/Neuter Clinics. This is also true in other cities having similar programs, such as Milwaukee, where the shelter is about three miles from the targeted neighborhoods, but "we might as well be a world away for some people," commented a shelter worker there.

Not every West Charlotte pet owner has access to a car or even a license to drive one. About half of the adult men between 18 and 35 years of age in targeted Pets for Life neighborhoods in Milwaukee are, or were, incarcerated and can no longer obtain a driver's license because of their prison record. Even if residents have a car and a license to drive it, the car may be undependable or used by someone else in the house to get to work. And even if they have a car that can be used to get to the shelter, paying for gas becomes an added expense to use discounted veterinary services if pet owners have a long drive to the shelter—a major barrier for pet owners in rural Montana who want to use Pets for Life services in that state because many live so far from the nearest shelter.

Some West Charlotte pet owners have cars but will not use them to take their pets to the shelter because they are unaccustomed to doing so. Compounding this custom, many owners are very proud of their cars and see a lot of value in them, spending time and money to keep them in good working order and clean, in contrast to their homes and property, which are not always kept as well.[6] As one shelter worker said, "Their cars often look immaculate, but their houses are a wreck." To be clear, neglect of homes and yards, in contrast to cars, is not always the pet owner's fault; in many cases they rent a run-down apartment or house and the landlord does not maintain it, so the only well-kept possession they own and are responsible for is their vehicle. Since their cars have symbolic value to them, these pet owners will keep animals out of their cars because they might be dirty or might damage them. However, valuing cars to this extent means that getting pets to the shelter for free or low-cost services becomes a problem for these owners.

If pet owners do not have access to cars, they can ask a neighbor, relative, or friend to drive them and their animals to the shelter, but these arrangements are not always possible to make or keep. For example, one pet owner was taking her animal for a veterinary appointment she "desperately" wanted. It was an important appointment that could improve the dog's health and she was "thrilled" to have access, with the help of subsidies paid by the shelter to cover most of the visit's cost. But despite her efforts, the appointment was missed because no one could be found to drive them to the veterinarian's office. And when these alternative arrangements are available, they may not be free; neighbors who offer to drive pet owners to the shelter, or let pet owners borrow their car, will likely charge the latter around $10, allegedly to cover the cost of gas or more. Unfortunately, that $10 could also go toward paying for some pet food, for example.

In theory, taking public transportation should be an option to get animals to the local shelter, but only designated service animals under a certain weight are permitted on buses. Even if the animal is small and caged, some bus drivers, unfamiliar with this exception, will prevent the pet owner from getting on. And using a taxi or Uber is not an option because of the expense and animals are sometimes prohibited in these cars. Walking to the shelter with one's pet is also not feasible for most pet owners because they live far from the West Charlotte shelter, they have to bring animals (except for the Food Bank), and they can be elderly and/or disabled. Nevertheless, some will walk. To get his pet examined and treated for mange, one man walked over a mile each way with his dog on a huge and heavy chain because he did not own a leash, but it was a hot summer day and his dog became overheated from the walk. At some Pets for Life shelters around the country, walking with pets to obtain free or low-cost services is dangerous because owners cannot walk safely and dogs will get stressed from the noise and traffic. For example, to walk to the Charleston Pets for Life program, people and their pets have to use a narrow sidewalk that runs next to an eight-lane highway where the traffic rushing by scares most pets.

Related to transportation problems, the timing of free or low-cost services can become an access barrier, given that some pet owners work full-time and/or are responsible for children and/or elders. Getting one's pet to the shelter has to be squeezed into very busy days, where, for example, single-parent pet owners have to drive and pick up their children at school, go back and forth to work themselves, oversee very young children or elders at home, run essential errands, and manage unexpected problems that can appear from day to day, while fighting traffic on heavily congested roads. One resident, who brought his dog for vaccinations because it was less expensive than going to a regular veterinarian, said that he took a "long lunch hour," even though driving to the shelter, waiting for his appointment, and driving back to work would take almost two hours and infringed on his time on the job. A woman with two dogs, also updating her dogs' vaccinations, ended up using about half of her only day off from work to go to the shelter. Those residents with children, relatives, or elders who cannot be left home unattended often bring them all to the shelter with their pets. With the Food Bank, some residents do not go because it is "too much hassle to come on the first or third Saturday" and they desperately need that day to run errands and do things they cannot do during the week.

Barriers like inconvenient timing, lack of transportation, and others commonly exist for pet owners and animals alike in West Charlotte. Despite such barriers to accessing affordable care, many owners do not disregard their pets' welfare. They try to behave responsibly according to the customs, limits, and guidelines of their subculture. However, these indigenous ways of coping result in responsibility being expressed differently than in mainstream society for similar problems.

Coping Indigenously

Pets and their owners jointly face certain misfortunes that can make it difficult for people to keep and be responsible for their animals. But part of living in West Charlotte's subculture means that residents often have improvised unique ways of coping with these problems. Such natural or embedded ways of dealing with misfortune were readily apparent when housing issues made it difficult for people to keep their pets. When this happened, people often found ways to manage so they could maintain responsibility for their animals and not abandon them on the streets or turn them into animal control where they would likely be euthanized.

A major source of pet misfortune stems from the fact that many West Charlotte pet owners rent an apartment or house or stay in a "pet-friendly" hotel, where they are vulnerable to landlords who can impose regulations that restrict the number, weight (e.g., no dogs over 50 pounds, no cats over 10 pounds), and/or kinds of pets permitted, if permitted at all.[7] They also can charge an upfront pet deposit (about $300 to $450) or monthly fee ($30) to pay for the privilege of having a pet on the premises. Hotel and apartment managers justify the fees on the grounds that they must pay extra for insurance that covers animals or certain breeds as well as to pay for any property damage caused by animals.[8]

Some of these restrictions occur in government-subsidized Section 8 housing in West Charlotte operated by a private landlord who at any point can decide to no longer rent the property as a Section 8 home and make their own rules about whether pets can be kept, what size, or how many.[9] There is also government housing that has no private control, where people can have pets but must pay $500, half of which the shelter or animal control can pay, and they cannot have pets over 20 pounds. In the worst-case scenario, actions by landlords, whether in privately controlled housing or not, can lead to pets being frequently relocated, given away, surrendered to the shelter or animal control, abandoned, lost, or euthanized.

A few pet-friendly or indifferent landlords choose not to enforce these regulations. For example, in one apartment complex that officially prohibits pets, the manager likes pets and allows tenants to have as many as they want of any kind, as long as they have been spay/neutered and have up-to-date vaccinations. Despite the manager's relaxed stance toward the building's pet restriction policy and apparent fondness of animals, she did not always act in the best interests of her tenants' animals or their owners. In one case, a resident put her dog outside on a chain during the day. While doing so did not violate any code, a neighbor who lived two doors away felt that this chained dog was being neglected and reported it several times to animal control. Rather than telling the neighbor to stop filing complaints when there was no code violation, the manager told the pet owner to get rid of her dog to end the dispute.

However, most landlords and hotel managers enforce the regulations and may use them as a tool to exclude tenants they think will be problems. Some informally exclude certain people by imposing extra costs on prospective renters who own certain breeds, especially pit bulls or pit mixes, and less so rottweilers and boxers. By charging high fees to limit stigmatized breeds or ban them outright, landlords think they are filtering out "certain types of people" seen as "riff raff." Another way that property managers can use pet regulations to keep out certain types of renters who they think will be undesirable tenants is to ban dogs over 20 pounds or those deemed large and dangerous. Or landlords and managers can selectively enforce pet regulations on a case-by-case basis as they size up potential renters. If a property bans all pets, landlords can choose to ignore these regulations for smaller pets while imposing them for larger, more threatening dogs and/or owners seen as undesirable, hoping, for example, to kick out renters who own pit bulls. That happened to one West Charlotte mastiff owner who had his dog for nine years but surrendered it to animal control because his landlord forbade him to keep it. The owner lived in several different apartments over those nine years, but moved into his current apartment a few months earlier. Expecting trouble with his current landlord over the dog, he kept the mastiff at his grandmother's home until she died, forcing him to keep the dog in this apartment until the landlord noticed it. He waited until the last day before being evicted so he could be with his dog until the end. When he surrendered it to animal control he broke down and cried, knowing he would not see the dog again and that it would likely be euthanized. He left animal control not knowing that in a few days a rescue group rehomed his dog.

Tenants unable to pay a pet fee can sometimes get help from the shelter, animal control, or other groups like the American Pit Bull Foundation (APBF). Unfortunately, tenants usually do not know they can get this financial help until they are surrendering their pets to the shelter or animal control. For example, one resident had a shih tzu in public housing and could not afford this fee but was unaware of the shelter's possible support, so she felt she had to relinquish her dog to the shelter or be evicted. When she came to the shelter to surrender her dog, she was told that the shelter would pay half the pet fee so she could keep the dog, enabling this dog and owner to stay together. Sometimes landlords are paid off more informally. If tenants live in homes or apartments not run by large property management groups but where landlords prohibit dogs, the APBF might offer to pay a pet fee to get around the outright ban. Some of these landlords accept the offer and agree to allow dogs on their properties because they assumed that paying this fee would be beyond the tenants' means.

However, the shelter or other organizations cannot always prevent the surrendering of pets, even if they can help pay pet fees, because some renters are unable to pay their rent and subsequently face eviction. In one case, a woman dying of cancer lived alone with her mixed-breed dog Chunky in Section 8 housing. Diane first met Chunky when she moved into the home. He was owned by the elderly tenant who was fond of Chunky, although a roommate mistreated the dog by often hitting it with a stick. Having always been a dog owner, she gravitated to Chunky and took him in as her pet when the two tenants left. She viewed Chunky differently than did the prior tenants, who kept the dog chained outside and did not provide him with veterinary care. Although the elderly tenant would sometimes pet Chunky or cut his hair, the roommate either ignored or harmed the dog. Instead, Diane kept Chunky inside, set up a large dog bed in her living room, bought many dog toys, took many pictures of Chunky, improved his diet, and enlisted the help of the shelter in getting Chunky the necessary vaccinations and treatments. As attachment deepened to Chunky, Diane's own life became more challenging because her sick mother needed care and financial support, and she continued to undergo her own cancer treatment, making it difficult for her to pay the monthly rent. Because she does not want to relinquish Chunky to the shelter, she is now searching for a pet-friendly hotel as an option if she is evicted from her current housing. However, paying for such a hotel could be costlier than her current rent, so she would be forced to give up Chunky to the shelter, which would reject the relinquishment because he is somewhat aggressive around humans, leaving Diane no choice but to relinquish the dog to animal control where it would be euthanized as unadoptable.

In cases where pets are banned, some owners may try to move out of their rental properties in search of other places to stay where they can keep their pets. When doing so is impossible, the consequences can be tragic for the animals. For example, in one case, a woman with 14 cats lived in Section 8 housing, where the landlord suddenly dropped Section 8 coverage and decided to ban pets. Although she gave one cat to a friend who had recently lost hers, she did not want to give away the others, so she tried to temporarily move in with her cats at a friend's house, which was also government-subsidized housing. But this failed because government regulations prohibited guests from staying for more than a few days. Without a place to stay with the cats, she was forced to surrender them to animal control, where all were euthanized. Several years later, she still cries when recounting this loss.

A more common strategy is for pet owners to have neighbors, friends, or family members temporarily keep their pets, without getting any money in return, until owners reclaim them after ideally finding a better housing arrangement where they can keep pets. Although friends or family members are just fostering or helping them, some of these temporary pet keepers accommodate difficult animals that are unpleasant to interact with because they are aggressive or very shy, or because they require special maintenance or patience, as with one dog that liked to chew on furniture and otherwise destroy property. In the latter case, the fosterer decided to use a crate indoors to restrain the destructive dog, which she gave to the dog's original owner, who in turn also started using the crate to minimize damage and make her pet relationship more amicable.

While substitute owners often take on quite a bit of responsibility to manage their temporary animal guests, they will not assume ownership over them, akin to a foster home without a right to keep a pet. All parties informally understand that the temporary keeper does not own the pet, even if it lives there for weeks, months, or perhaps years and is only occasionally visited by its true owner. Important decisions about the animal's welfare are left to the original owner. Thus, temporary keepers will usually refuse to take their fostered pets to the shelter for basic services because they do not own them. For example, if shelter workers suggest that the guest pets be sterilized, the substitute owners will refuse because they are only temporarily keeping the pet and do not feel they have the authority or right to make this decision. In one such case, a West Charlotte resident cared for five kittens—one of which belonged to her evicted cousin but was staying with her until the cousin could find a permanent home. When the outreach worker asked her about fixing all five kittens, she declined to have her cousin's kitten fixed because she wanted her to make the decision. In rare cases where the temporary keeper does sterilize a fostered animal, the owner is unlikely to reclaim it because they do not like their autonomy over their animal being taken away. At the same time, it is also understood that if the person does not reclaim the pet it is theirs, although it is unclear how long the temporary keeper has to wait before this can happen.

The crisis of finding a temporary pet home can happen when property managers change and new landlords decide to enforce pet regulations entirely or selectively, suddenly challenging pet ownership rules, whether formal or informal, that may have existed for months or years in the same building. This happened to Tex, a huge dog that had the face of a pit bull but probably was not one. Tex's owner was a 70-year-old man who had a month-to-month lease for years in an apartment that officially prohibited dogs, but his prior landlord ignored this regulation. He contacted an APBF outreach worker and told her that he now had a new landlord who told him he could not keep Tex. The outreach worker was convinced that the landlord did not want pit bulls and their owners in his building, so she came up with a few strategies to try to keep Tex in his owner's home. Because the owner was a war veteran, the outreach worker offered to certify Tex as an emotional support dog and use that status to override the exclusion in the lease, but given that the lease was month to month, the landlord could evict him for any reason and he would have no recourse. The outreach worker also called the landlord and offered to pay a fee so Tex could remain with his owner, but the landlord would not return these calls. Tex's owner was forced to give him away to a friend living in the same zip code whom he met playing chess at a local community center. He also gave his friend contact information so he could reach the outreach worker on Tex's case, who was soon called to help the dog get needed vaccinations and transportation to the shelter, since his temporary keeper also did not own a car. Tex's original owner takes a bus every few weeks to go to the new owner's home, something he probably would not do if Tex were living with him, yet doing so brings him in contact with his chess friend as well.

These arrangements to manage dog evictions last only as long as the substitute owner stays in his or her home. When Jerry moved into public housing, rules required him to give up his dog Nevada that he had before moving in, when he was homeless. The two had been through a lot when they lived on the street and forged a tight bond because of their joint experience, so rather than give up Nevada entirely he asked a friend in a nearby neighborhood to keep and feed the dog for him. He would bike over about once a week to clean up after Nevada, chained up in his friend's backyard, and maybe feed him. His friend regarded Nevada not as his pet but still as Jerry's pet. After the substitute owner got evicted from his house because of gentrification, Jerry was forced to find yet another home to keep his dog. But this time the person lived too far away for Jerry to visit by biking there, so he had to take a bus to see Nevada, and because of the distance he could go only once a month. Although

Jerry's friend had his dog all the time except for one afternoon a month when Jerry visited, it was understood that if he could find a place that would allow Nevada, he could have it back—it was still his pet. At the same time, Nevada's temporary keeper loved him and would keep him as her pet if Jerry's interest in the dog waned.

Tenants have other options when they live in rental properties that no longer permit their dogs—they can try to move elsewhere, give up their dogs to the shelter or animal control, or simply abandon them. For example, one West Charlotte pet owner was told that she had to give up her dog because she had a pit bull—one of the breeds excluded by her new landlord. Rather than give up her dog, she decided to move somewhere else with it. She found a pet-friendly hotel but could not afford the hotel's pet fee, and even if she could have paid the fee, the hotel would not permit pit bulls. So she stayed in this hotel but snuck her dog out of the hotel and into her car to drive him around since she was not working. Unable to continue this stealth operation for very long, she moved in with her mother, who insisted that the dog be kept outside. Unhappy with this situation, the owner decided she would have to surrender her dog, but before she could take it to the shelter, it went missing and she never saw it again.

Some pet owners develop strategies to circumvent these regulations. These owners defy the restrictions by keeping their animals "under the radar," a practice that is obviously easier to do with cats. A case in point—one resident named her cat Secret because she kept it hidden from her landlord. When apartment buildings ban pit bulls, owners get creative and call them "terrier mixes." Other pet owners who live in rental properties that do not allow pets work around this restriction by keeping pets outside, at least when landlords visit. For example, one owner had cats that were outdoors much of the time, so he could tell his landlord that they were not inside the house or even that they were not his. Yet he allowed them to come into his home some days, knowing that the landlord visited only once a month to collect the rent. And yet other pet owners who rent apartments or homes having pet restrictions accept that landlords will not maintain their properties (e.g., fixing leaks, plumbing problems, etc.) in exchange for not bothering them if pets are kept inside. But in the end tenants are at the mercy of their landlords when it comes to pet ownership.[10]

Finding affordable housing is itself a difficult task for many residents in disadvantaged communities (Freeman, 2002), let alone also finding housing that permits pets of any breed or size. Despite the barriers that prevent West Charlotte pet owners from keeping their animals with them, they cope by developing different strategies that conceal their pet ownership from landlords or, if that fails, lean on their informal network of friends and family to keep pets for them temporarily until new housing is found that accepts animals. All these efforts reflect pet owners' strong attachment to and responsibility for their pets, while providing a reminder of how powerless they are to control their environment and, subsequently, to prevent misfortune to animals if they must be given up and possibly euthanized.

Despite the vagaries and hardships of everyday life in or near poverty that both animals and people jointly endure in West Charlotte, many pet owners in this predominately black, low-income community appear to be very attached to their charges. Although low-income pet owners or those living in poverty have fewer resources to outwardly express their attachment by, for example, buying toys for pets, this attachment can entail substantial empathy and be as emotionally profound, if not more so, than it is among pet-owning residents in any socioeconomic neighborhood. Indeed, research on working-class people shows they score higher on measures of empathy and are more likely to help other people in distress (Manstead, 2018) than are people of higher classes. Based on what we saw in West Charlotte, this finding may very well be generalizable to human-pet relationships in underserved communities.

However, the conditions fanning attachment are somewhat unique in poverty-level communities. Attachment to pets in West Charlotte appeared to be fueled by adversity because pets were fellow travelers who helped their owners endure everyday difficulties and in so doing fostered strong identification with animals. While certain features of West Charlotte's subculture fanned pet attachment, other features suppressed but did not extinguish it because culture can help people express their identity and emotions while simultaneously regulating them (Holodynski & Friedlmeier, 2006). That culture can both encourage and discourage certain emotions can lead to ambivalence (Weigert, 1991), which could be seen when the attachment of West Charlotte pet owners became guarded or reserved because of their animals' location outside, their instrumental role, or their possible loss or early death.

Even when they were just ambivalently attached, West Charlotte pet owners still tried to be responsible for their welfare. That they tried to be responsible runs contrary to research and popular thinking that suggest low-income or poverty-level pet owners are more "irresponsible" than those in more advantaged communities who make a lifelong commitment to their animals and routinely use veterinary services for prevention, disease, and injury.

Although West Charlotte's pet owners do not demonstrate responsibility for their animals in the same ways as do more advantaged pet owners, they do go to great lengths to be responsible for them. As we saw, these pet owners made every effort to keep their animals rather than abandon or surrender them when circumstances became dire. Most did not want to surrender their pets to the shelter or animal control when property managers forced them to leave or give up their pets. Instead, they struggled to find ways to keep them in their homes or, when that failed, give them to friends or family for temporary keeping while continuing to visit and care for the pets as much as circumstances permitted. Responsibility also means getting pet food and veterinary care for pets. Here, too, West Charlotte pet owners often faced significant barriers, commonly with transportation to either the shelter or a veterinarian's office, which they tried to overcome so pets could be fed and cared for.

This means that responsible ownership is not an either-or proposition in West Charlotte. It is something that is sought after and achieved to the extent that is possible, given constraints imposed by structural oppression, subcultural norms, and the reality of living in or near poverty, whether for humans or animals. The resulting burdens and unpredictability of everyday life in West Charlotte made it difficult for some people to take advantage of free or low-cost pet care because taking care of their animals may be a lower priority than feeding children, heating the home, and being at work 100 hours a week at minimum wage or less. In other words, owners there wanted to provide their pets with food, shelter, and water, give them veterinary care, and keep rather than relinquish them, but had fewer resources and faced more barriers to do so, while subscribing to a subcultural definition of responsibility that differs from the mainstream understanding of this term.

Patently, pet keeping in racially concentrated poverty or low-income neighborhoods will affect whether, how quickly, and how much veterinary care is provided to these animals as well as how their owners regard and interact with them in general. However, some West Charlotte pet owners did not use free or low-cost veterinary services for other reasons that had to do with their perceptions of these services. As we see next, even when there were no financial or logistical barriers to taking pets to the shelter for these services, some owners in West Charlotte still hesitated to take advantage of them.

CHAPTER FIVE

The "Costs" of Care

NONFINANCIAL BARRIERS TO USING
FREE OR LOW-COST VETERINARY SERVICES

Organizations do not always understand social problems the same way as those they serve. When there is such a disparity, the institution's version of what is wrong and the solutions it proposes can be at odds with the lived experiences of those people in the community who must deal with the issue. According to Irvine (2003), how shelters "think" about unwanted animals—in particular those that owners surrender to shelters—is a case in point because the shelter's understanding of this problem does not always match the way clients interpret it. For example, while the shelter she studied reduced to a single reason why pet owners relinquished their animals, this was only a partial picture of the decision process they actually went through before giving up their pets, a finding also reported in other studies (DiGiacomo et al., 1998).

Because the shelter and pet owners have different perspectives about the same problem, confusion or even tense interactions can result between the organization and its clients. The shelter sees pet owners as "bad" because they relinquish pets that they might have kept at home had they taken advantage of programs to manage behavior problems that lead some pet owners to not do the right thing and take steps to try to keep their pets at home. The shelter does not hear the full story from pet owners; if they did, they might be able to intervene to keep pets at home rather than risk being euthanized. Because of this disparity, there is a failure to solve the problem.

As we see in this chapter, there is also a disparity in thinking between shelters and clients when it comes to providing basic veterinary care to pets in disadvantaged communities. The shelter and other humane organizations providing low- or no-cost services to very low-income pet owners frame the problem as one of access and availability, much like the problems of cost and transportation that prevent minority group members from seeking timely and adequate medical care for themselves or their children (Ahmed et al., 2001; Flores et al., 1998). So programs like Pets for Life focus on removing or reducing these seemingly self-evident and easily targeted barriers with structural interventions, if there are funds and personnel to support these efforts.

For example, the most obvious barrier is the cost to owners of getting pets sterilized, vaccinated, examined, and treated for basic ailments (e.g., fleas and ticks, heartworm) as well as fed nutritious pet food. As noted earlier, to do this the shelter heavily discounts the costs of these services or provides them for free through its Pets for Life program. While Pets for Life clients do not pay anything, other low-income pet owners receiving services are asked to pay a small amount, which most do, and those who cannot usually get the services for free. The shelter believes that if pet owners are asked to pay something they will be more likely to use discounted services than if offered the same services for free because by paying even a modest fee the pet owner perceives the service as more valuable.

Even if veterinary services are heavily discounted or free, pet owners must still get to the shelter, and this can be a logistical problem for some, as we saw in chapter 4. When the shelter has sufficient funding and volunteer support, it provides free transportation for almost two-thirds of the animals needing to be sterilized.[1] In addition, the shelter provides transportation for a small number of pet owners who cannot easily get to its Wellness Clinic (discounted microchipping, vaccinations, and basic tests and treatments) and will in a few cases provide taxi money for clients to take their sick pets to private-practice veterinarians, when funding is available.

Focusing on access problems such as cost or transportation by animal advocates and policy makers from outside the community assumes that if these tangible barriers did not stop pet owners in or near poverty, they would provide for their animals' welfare and get their pets fixed, vaccinated, examined, treated for basic problems, and properly fed. In other words, if given the opportunity pet owners will behave rationally by making decisions to maximize their good, or those of family members, including their pets. But it is apparent that not all West Charlotte pet owners behave rationally when the shelter removes access problems to these services by heavily discounting or making services free and by providing transportation to its clinic.

When shelters lower or eliminate financial or logistical barriers to using free or low-cost veterinary care, not all eligible pet owners are quick to take advantage. After West Charlotte owners discover these services, most ultimately use many of them, although often after hesitating to do so or, in some

cases, not using them at all. For example, when offered discounted sterilization, about 25% of the pet owners have already sterilized their animals, 15%
are "low-lying fruit" eager to have the procedure done, but 60% are reluctant
to sterilize their pets, taking weeks or months before they fix their animals, if
they do so at all. Indeed, about 20% of the time they never use any free or low-
cost services including but not limited to sterilization because these pet owners think differently about the services than do the shelter, policy makers who
create such programs, and organizations that fund them.[2]

While financial and logistical barriers influence whether pet owners use
the shelter's free and discounted services, they face other barriers that stem
from living in the West Charlotte community that are different from the shelter's primary focus on cost and transportation. Pet owners evaluate these services much like low-income people who hesitate or fail to seek medical care
for themselves or family members because of barriers stemming from culture,
race, social class, gender (Friedman, 1994), emotions, beliefs (Rosenstock,
1974), and personal circumstances (Verbrugge, 1985). These historical, cultural,
social, and individual barriers are below the surface and more difficult for the
shelter to address, so it concentrates on tangible problems that are on the surface and can be addressed by structural interventions that help many, but not
all, pet owners get basic veterinary care.

Given these invisible barriers, it would be wrong to think that West Charlotte pet owners are behaving irrationally when they do not use free or low-
cost services for their animals. A more complicated picture is needed that sees
their behavior as realistic rather than irrational when they balk at the shelter's offer to help their pets, just as people in general interpret the meaning of
any behavioral innovation and subsequently decide whether or not to adopt
it (Greenhalgh et al., 2004). As we see in this chapter, pet owners interpret the
meaning and value of veterinary services in light of their everyday priorities,
prior experiences with the shelter (and, more generally, white institutions),
knowledge of veterinary health and disease, views of the nature and role of animals, and contacts with friends and family. Because these barriers make pet
owners in disadvantaged communities think differently than the shelter about
using its services, it may be unrealistic to expect them all to have their animals
examined, given basic treatments, vaccinated, or sterilized, even if cost and
transportation were no issue.

Lost Income

Since promoting the sterilization of as many pets as possible drives the shelter's outreach program, it requires people to have their pets fixed in order to
receive certain free services. For example, when it comes to using the shelter's

Food Bank, pet owners, after their first few visits, must show proof that their pets have been sterilized to continue getting free pet food. Most pet owners comply, but some balk at this requirement because they do not want to sterilize their pets. Indeed, in some cases this can be of such concern that pet owners refuse other free services beside pet food that require this surgery. This is particularly evident at the North Charleston Pets for Life program, which operates differently from the one in Charlotte because it offers pet owners only a package of services along with sterilization. But those who reject the package, despite it being free, do so because they do not want to sterilize their animals—a feeling that is strong enough to make them forgo many free services.

The decision by West Charlotte pet owners to breed animals is a major reason why some owners refuse to sterilize their animals, although these "backyard breeders" (Strand, 1993) avoid this surgery for different reasons. Only some refuse to sterilize their animals because they are primarily motivated by profit to breed either pedigree dogs or those regarded as guard dogs (e.g., Fielding, 2010). Not including pet owners who accidentally breed their animals and probably account for most litters, we found four types of breeders in West Charlotte whose breeding varied in terms of its rationale, self-identification, scope, and community visibility, but which in all cases made sterilization unlikely.

Dogfighters who breed dogs are not interested in sterilizing their puppies. To do so would mean lost income from the few local residents who might buy their puppies and perhaps attend their dogfights or buy drugs from them. Dogfighter breeders are also uninterested in sterilizing their animals because they can use some of the litter mates as bait to train fighting dogs, if they do not sell them as puppies. And even if they were interested in sterilizing their dogs, most would still decline to use the shelter's free or discounted surgery, as well as other basic services, because they want to avoid contact with the shelter to protect their identities, given the illegality of dogfighting and any other criminal activities associated with fighting, such as illicit drug sales. In the end, breeding by dogfighters is more of a side note to their activities and is only a small part of their illegal income, unlike other breeders in West Charlotte.

Status breeders, on the other hand, make much of their income from breeding, so sterilizing dogs can be financially threatening. Unlike dogfighter breeders, they are more open about their activity and tend to be locally well known because what they do is not criminal and the more visible they are, the more dogs they can sell. Breeding status dogs can be especially profitable if they have papers alleging that their puppies are purebred and thus in demand in that community (e.g., pit bulls or boxer mixes). For example, a pit bull puppy (litters can average as many as 10 puppies) at six weeks old sells for about $200 to $250, Carolina blue pits for about $400 to $500, and German shepherds for

about $700 to $800. Often as part of the sale, these puppies are already vaccinated because breeders have taken their litters to the shelter for discounted
care. Although the shelter opposes breeding and may know that the pet owner
is a breeder, these puppies are still vaccinated because it has seen too many
dogs die from preventable diseases, such as parvo. Knowing that these breeders will not sterilize their own dogs, the shelter encourages them to at least fix
the puppies they sell to eliminate or reduce their competition, thinking that
this approach will appeal to breeders and result in more dogs being sterilized
in the community. This approach sometimes works. Knowing this, the shelter at least tries to get them to sterilize dogs that have been overbred—a practice that helps to generate a stable income for breeders. Although a few agree
to sterilizing overbred dogs, they usually do this only if dogs have been bred so
many times their litters' health declines. More commonly, if they do not want
to continue breeding a dog, they give it away or trade a male to other local
breeders to avoid the problem of interbreeding their males and females.

Lost income from sterilizing dogs is partly due to the wealth status that
certain dogs confer on their owners in the black community as a form of conspicuous consumption, just as do automobiles, clothing, or jewelry in the
community at large (Charles et al., 2009). However, not all dogs will signal this.
If someone owns a dog without papers—a pit bull mix that was found on the
street or a dog designated as a pit bull that was adopted from the shelter—
it just signals that the owner has a pet that he or she loves. Indeed, one shelter worker acknowledged that their pit bulls do not confer any status on West
Charlotte adopters.

Pit bulls and certain other breeds can serve as visible or portable goods of
black conspicuous consumption if owners "have papers" for them that appear
to certify their pedigree. Getting papers that purportedly verify "purebred" is
important because owning such an animal has some cachet among residents,
just as it does elsewhere (Plemons, 2010). As one shelter worker noted, "That's
how you can tell if somebody has a status symbol, they start talking about
having papers on their dogs." Buying a purebred pit bull with papers signals
to neighbors that the owner has enough money to buy one of these dogs because the cost—$800 to $1,200—is out of reach to most West Charlotte residents, but it is something that people can save up for and is attainable. Having the purebred says, "Hey look, I could afford this." As one West Charlotte pet
owner said, "If you own a certain kinda pit in a crappy neighborhood it's like
you own a $300 pair of Jordans. It's basically like saying you have money." Be-
cause these dogs are pets with added value and are kept outside, some owners
put padlocks on their collars to prevent them from being stolen.[3]

Papers can signal that owners have more than having money. They can also
tell neighbors that the owner is someone who—because the dog allegedly has

papers—can potentially produce income through the animal in an environment where there is relatively stable demand for these dogs. Thus, in West Charlotte the income-generating potential of pit bulls signals a type of neighborhood entrepreneurship that is locally respected and not necessarily because they are a source of fighting dogs, unlike the practice elsewhere of acquiring pit bulls to breed and sell for fighting (Harding, 2013). And finally, a different kind of signaling also occurs with papers. Having papers signals that the owners will not use some or all of the shelter's services because they do not want to sterilize their dogs and, in part, because they often assume that the shelter objects to the ownership and breeding of purebreds.

West Charlotte residents cannot get breed certification from the American Kennel Club because it refuses to certify pit bulls as purebred dogs. Instead, pet owners go to a North Carolina organization that issues papers testifying to this status, or papers are issued by small hobbyist clubs that list these dogs not as American pit bulls but rather as razorbacks or gators, which are breeds within the breed. Even without these papers, some West Charlotte residents claim purebred status when backyard breeders sell them puppies they simply say are purebred, leaving buyers to trust their own visual inspection of the mother and its litter to decide whether the dogs appear to be sufficiently purebred to satisfy their desire to own and perhaps breed them for profit.

Another kind of breeder—the breadwinner breeder—also faces lost income from sterilization. They are pet owners in West Charlotte who have typically spent money for their dogs' veterinary care but believe the pets are responsible for recovering some or all of this expense, along with any other costs of owning them, so the family can stay afloat financially. These pets are expected to provide supplemental household income because they are regarded as contributing family members rather than breeding machines per se. In other words, for these owners, the motto "everybody's got to earn their keep" applies to pets as well as humans. Having this attitude toward pets means that they are viewed, to some degree, like human members of the household, each of whom is relied upon to make some economic contribution to sustaining the household.

Although their dogs are being bred to generate family income, breadwinner breeders commonly express some attachment to these animals and litters, even though the puppies will be sold and likely never seen again. One breadwinner breeder referred to a litter of puppies as her "babies." Unfortunately, animal control took two of her "babies" after a white neighbor claimed she was breeding dangerous dogs—a claim questioned by shelter workers familiar with this breeder and her dogs. A successful challenge of this allegation by social workers enabled them to retrieve the two dogs and return them to the breeder who was overjoyed to get them back, saying that it was her "Christmas present" to have them home again. Despite their alleged attachment to them, some of these economically motivated breeders also trade their dogs with other local breeders in order to have future litters that are different. A shelter worker described one of these traders who nevertheless appeared to be attached to his dogs: "Like this guy, he breeds. He'll have a female at his house who just had a litter with his male dog. So, he'll trade her with somebody else to get another female. He loves his dogs. He really cares for them, but he needs another female to get a litter that's different." In the end, the need to generate income trumps whatever bond these breeders have with their charges.

Finally, casual or ambivalent breeders also delay sterilizing pets, but less so because of lost income. Although they may charge a modest fee for puppies, these owners do not see themselves as breeders and do not have litters to make money. In these cases, if breeding signals anything in this community, it might be a willingness to share a somewhat scarce resource at a very low price, if any. When the breeding household is a single parent, the decision to breed is usually made by the adult, although there can be a teenage son present who sees the dog as his and decides to breed the animal, despite the parent's reluctance. With couples, the decision is sometimes jointly arrived at, although usually one person has stronger views than the other. Whoever makes this decision, contrary to the stereotype of people casually breeding animals without much forethought, deciding to breed is usually not determined quickly or easily. After some indecision and discussion about having a litter of puppies or kittens, these owners often decide to breed their pets only once because they understand the potential difficulty of finding homes for the entire litter and the veterinary problems and costs they might face, but for various reasons feel compelled to breed a single time. For example, some of these onetime breeders have a vague overriding sense that it would somehow be wrong or unfair to the pet to not breed it. Others decline to sterilize because they respect the individual animal and "love the breed," so they want to create more of them. A shelter worker spoke of this type of breeder, saying, "They don't want to take the opportunity away from their animals. Especially with pit bulls, they love the breed so much. They see something in their animal they want to pass down and want other people to be able to experience it." Similarly, other casual breeders love the unique mix or appearance of their pet— usually a small or toy breed dog—and want to breed it so they can hopefully have another one that looks just like it, although they do not understand how unlikely it would be to achieve this outcome. And yet other casual breeders do so because there are children in the family who want puppies and the parents want their children to see the whole process of birth and life, although they never add death to this list, which shelter workers and animal advocates are always quick to inject.

Despite not sterilizing their own animals, some breeders in disadvantaged neighborhoods support the idea that other pet owners should sterilize their animals. They exceptionalize their own resistance, while seeing the value of controlling the pet population in general. For example, one backyard dog breeder in St. Louis was uninterested in sterilizing any of his puppies but supported what the shelter was trying to do in the community. Because he was a longtime resident and knew many local pet owners, he would often refer them to the shelter to sterilize their pets. In fact, on occasion he would personally vouch for sterilization by joining the shelter's outreach workers and going door-to-door with them as they introduced the shelter's services to new potential clients. Nevertheless, he continued to breed dogs because their sale was his principal income. Lost income, though, was not the only reason why pet owners hesitated to sterilize their animals at the shelter or get other basic veterinary care there.

Negative Judgments

Some West Charlotte pet owners delay or even refuse to use the shelter's free or low-cost services because they feel shelter workers view them as irresponsible or neglectful owners, despite efforts by the shelter in recent years to not convey this image. Indeed, the mere suggestion to sterilize an animal is to some West Charlotte residents a commentary on how the shelter thinks they are irresponsible owners who would not take proper care of their pets' litters.

The perception that low-income pet owners are not responsible enough for their animals has hovered for years over many shelters and the communities they serve in America, including but certainly not limited to the one in West Charlotte. This perception has largely stemmed from how they have handled pet adoption. For example, a study of pet owners in Monroe County, Indiana (Blouin, 2008, 2017), found that some working-class participants had unpleasant adoption experiences at their local animal shelter. One woman complained that the shelter was too picky about whom it allowed to adopt, thinking it should be happy that someone wanted to home an animal. She also did not like the shelter's scrutiny, especially its questions about how she planned to feed, house, and care for the pet. Nor did she like the shelter's house visits to ensure potential adopters had an acceptable yard or fence.

West Charlotte's pet owners have similar feelings because of the shelter's former adoption policy, which expected potential adopters to conform to the shelter's ideal of responsible ownership. For twenty years, this policy alienated the pet-keeping community in West Charlotte with its long application for adoption that required potential adopters to have, among other things, fenced-in yards and to make a certain amount of money in order to adopt.

This policy was off-putting and unrealistic to many pet owners in West Charlotte, making them feel like they fell short of the shelter's definition of acceptable standards of pet care, so residents put up their guard. As one shelter worker reflected on this former policy, "We told this whole group you're never going to be responsible pet owners, so they disengaged from us." This disengagement continues today in the West Charlotte community, even though the shelter has changed its former policy and attitude toward local residents so they would be more comfortable adopting its animals.

Even without this judgmental legacy, pet owners still expect to be uncomfortable if they take one of their animals to the shelter for veterinary care. Some fear that because of the staff's experience, reputation, and credentials as "animal lovers," they will be criticized for not taking better care of their pets. This fear has some basis in reality; shelter volunteers and workers can sometimes hold and espouse middle-class norms of pet-keeping in which companion animals are routinely sterilized, fed nutritious often expensive pet food, given routine veterinary checkups, treatments, and expensive surgeries, fawned over and groomed, sent to obedience classes, provided with home visits or sitters when owners are away, buried in pet graveyards or cremated, and otherwise included and integrated into family life such as being allowed in all rooms of their owners' homes and sleeping on their owners' beds (Guenther, 2017).

Because of this bias, new employees and some volunteers might not fully understand or empathize with the perspective of pet owners living in or near poverty and rush to judge the latter's behavior from their middle-class pet-owning perspective. For example, at the St. Louis Pets for Life program, a man came with his "really thin" akita to one of the shelter's outreach events at a local park where it offered free vaccinations. Two novice outreach workers assumed he might have been neglecting his dog and not feeding it. Once they talked with him, they learned that he was feeding the dog "like crazy" but it kept getting thinner because it was diabetic.

More experienced staff members correct new workers if they criticize pet owners and do not consider their perspective. One incident involved a pet owner who allegedly "abandoned" his dog at the shelter's entrance and drove off, figuring that the shelter would not accept his older sick dog because of its limited admission policy. An irate new employee saw this and chased the man as he drove away, copying his license plate number to report him for abandonment, a violation of the state's animal cruelty law, carrying a $1,000 fine. A more experienced staff member told him that the pet owner would not be charged for abandonment and was probably scared to come inside the shelter, thinking that someone would accuse him of being a neglectful owner. But in his mind he probably thought it was better to leave the dog at the shelter than abandon it on the streets or kill it himself.

Fanning pet owners' discomfort is the often crowded and close public space where they gather at the shelter as well as the animal control department. For example, when visiting the latter facility, lack of privacy in the lobby means that people do not always reveal all the details about their pet's history or how they were cared for to the intake staff because other pet owners and some volunteers present might negatively judge them. Such judgments do happen, although infrequently, and adversely affect what pet owners say, much to the chagrin of senior staff members. The following egregious example happened one day in the department's lobby. A Hispanic family came in with three dogs, obviously underweight. They said they could not afford feeding them and realized they should have fed them more. The director of animal control knew that they had come for help and offered it to them, but the entire time the staff was trying to help these pet owners, customers and volunteers from rescue groups took cell phone photographs of them and posted them on social media, with captions conveying the message, "Look at these emaciated dogs that these crappy owners just dropped off." The owners quickly became very uncomfortable, stopped speaking to the staff, and wanted people to leave them alone. The director said, "They were belittled and bullied. I think they started getting scared.... 'Oh, all these people are judging us, what's animal control going to do?' We're still a division of the Mecklenburg police department. 'PD' is on everything here so people automatically assume we're police officers, but we're not. They're just our employers." So the director moved them into a side office, checked the dogs in to place them, and let the owners go.

Because some pet owners anticipate being uncomfortable at the shelter, they might delay bringing their animals for veterinary care even when they are suffering. For example, one woman came to the Wellness Clinic to get vaccinations for a "feral" cat that she routinely fed and viewed as her pet since it regularly appeared at her back door. She hoped that the veterinarian giving the vaccinations would address her cat's apparent ear and skin problem—it had had bloody ears and large patches of missing fur in that area of its head for the past several weeks. She worried that either the veterinary staff or the shelter workers at the registration desk would criticize her for not having brought the suffering cat to the clinic sooner for veterinary attention. The cat's examination revealed that it had a very bad case of ear mites, so the shelter veterinarian told its owner to take the cat to a private-practice veterinarian for treatment since the shelter was not authorized to do this. Whether the cat owner did so is unknown, but she was relieved that no one criticized her for taking weeks to have someone evaluate her pet's problem.

To avoid potential criticism, a few people conceal their identities or lie so they can use the shelter's services and minimize whatever discomfort they might have felt had they been honest with shelter workers or volunteers. For example, West Charlotte residents who fight dogs or have been otherwise cruel to them allegedly often hide from the staff when visiting the shelter. Known or suspected dog fighters who come for services such as discounted vaccinations will stay in their parked cars not far from the shelter while their children take the dogs to the Wellness Clinic sign-in table and stay with the animals as they are being cared for by the staff. Or some owners may lie to shelter workers to avoid discomfort and trouble. This happens with some dog breeders who bring animals for vaccinations and basic treatments but do not admit that they bred them, even though there are obvious signs of breeding like bringing in six puppies that "were just found" for vaccinations.

In some cases pet owners get caught when lying, although this often reveals an owner who is only trying to do the best for his or her animal, given limited resources, little social support, and difficult-to-manage everyday problems. Take the case of a Charleston resident who brought a dog to the shelter he claimed was "stray" and was in very poor health, suffering from untreated chronic and severe mange. But when the staff scanned the dog, its microchip revealed that this resident was the dog's owner, having adopted the dog from the shelter six years prior. When confronted with this information, the resident admitted that he adopted the dog but said that the dog allegedly ran away shortly after being adopted but then reappeared recently. When further questioned by the staff, he admitted that it was his dog and claimed that he had taken it to a veterinarian but did not have enough money to pay for continued visits, so the mange got worse. He heard from a friend that if he came to the shelter and said it was a stray there would not be any questions.

Indeed, while this owner anticipated being criticized for his negligence, from his perspective he was trying his best, just like many of the pet owners we studied. In many cases, what others could interpret as irresponsible behavior was actually an attempt by pet owners to be as responsible as they could be, given their situation. In this sense, pet owners in or near poverty are no different from others who own pets but have the resources and support to provide them with veterinary care. Their motivations are the same, but their situations differ.

Shame

People can feel ashamed or stigmatized when they perform certain group behaviors that others devalue (Link & Phelan, 2001; Major & O'Brien, 2005). To lessen this discomfort and not feel disgraced or rejected, those socially stigmatized often use various behavioral coping devices to protect them (Miller & Kaiser, 2001). Pet owners can also feel stigmatized when they internalize or buy into the negative judgments of others and feel embarrassed or ashamed

when using the shelter's services. And they too, like others who are stigmatized, often cope with these uncomfortable feelings by avoiding or distancing
themselves from others at the shelter.

Historically, at the West Charlotte shelter and others around the country,
the stigma of using the available services stemmed from employees or volunteers who made pet owners feel ashamed because they did so, much the
same way that the attitudes or behaviors of some health care providers can
deter low-income patients from seeking medical help (Kinsler et al., 2007).[4]
While it rarely if ever occurs today, in the past some pet owners felt they were
criticized for using free or discounted veterinary services. They could be of-
fended and unlikely to return after overhearing judgmental comments such
as "Why do you have a dog if you can't afford it?" Because the shelter's culture
has changed in recent years, staff members are more culturally sensitive to
and supportive of pet owners' situation (see chapter 5), so such comments are
rare and are sanctioned when observed.

Now when pet owners feel ashamed, it is rarely due to what shelter staff
or volunteers say or how they act. Rather, it is more a product of pet owners' self-criticism or guilt over accepting free services that they would like to
pay for but cannot. Such service-related shame is not unique to low-income
pet owners; it has also been found to prevent welfare recipients from receiving services because of their loss of self-respect (Kissane, 2003). For some pet
owners, using free services is to admit to being unable to manage a responsibility they have taken on. However, this does not mean that all of the shelter's
services cause pet owners to feel equally ashamed when using them. In general, services that require a modest fee challenge owners' pride less than free
services; the latter can be difficult for some pet owners to accept.

This service-related shame manifests itself in different ways. Some pet
owners who are employed, even at very low-paying jobs, feel that they should
not use the shelter's free services because they have some income, so they take
their pets to relatively expensive private-practice veterinarians. For example,
one pet owner was offered the entire package of free services but declined
them all, and the shelter did not hear from this person for several months. She
got back in touch with the shelter at a later date and said she had been taking
her dog to a private-practice veterinarian but got laid off and now finds caring
for the dog to be a financial burden and needs help from the shelter. Shelter
workers assumed that her sense of pride (i.e., feeling that she could take care
of her own pet without having to rely on the shelter) prevented her from using free services when she worked, even though pet owners do not have to be
unemployed to receive these services. Others who are employed at low-paying
jobs feel they should spend more for veterinary products sold at the shelter
than cheaper versions also sold there. In one such case, a low-income pet

owner who worked would buy at full retail price various pet products sold in the shelter's store, while she could have obtained all of them for free through the Pets for Life program. She reached out for help only after her hours at work were severely reduced and her insurance premiums suddenly increased. And some pet owners feel compelled to spend more money than they have to show not only that they have some income but also that they care a lot for their pet's welfare. This was the case with a few West Charlotte pet owners whose sick pets were seen by the shelter's veterinarian but who accepted an expensive array of diagnostic tests that they could not pay for but did so because they wanted to look like they cared about their pets and had the money to do that.

Asking for free veterinary services can be a public admission that the pet owners are experiencing hard financial times—they might be unemployed or might have a sudden expense they cannot handle. But these excuses for needing help can also be a way for pet owners to cope with the shame of accepting free or low-cost services. That is, by offering various reasons that are socially acceptable for why they need free services, pet owners are providing legitimate and often temporary reasons for needing them. In other words, they are not freeloaders.

Take the shelter's Food Bank as an example. The shelter operates it because pet food is often a significant expense for West Charlotte residents,[5] especially if they have several animals and are trying to buy a better grade of food not typically sold in nearby stores. As of 2016, to help with this expense the shelter opened its Food Bank twice monthly, dispensing about 53,000 pounds of free wet and dry food to supplement pet and feral cat feeding but not to provide all their food. The amount of distributed food varied depending on donations (e.g., local corporations periodically do food drives), although there was almost always some provided. When the shelter was not flush with food, it still tried to give everyone who came at least a small bag of food.

Pet owners who think about getting free pet food might feel some degree of shame, as do those accessing other free services at the shelter. Although pet owners in or near poverty could clearly benefit from free pet food, perhaps saving as much as $60 a month, asking for a handout can embarrass them. Even worse, the handout is for an animal for which they elected to take responsibility. Shelter workers are aware of this hesitation and want to alleviate it, as one explained: "They're embarrassed to ask for help. But it's our job to make them feel comfortable, so we tell them there's no judgment here and there's no shame to asking for help and that everyone here has also gone through a tough time." Despite such reassurances, some pet owners can still experience shame, especially those coming to the shelter the first time for free food. To cope with this shame, these owners might volunteer why they have come for the food, even though shelter workers do not ask. Medical reasons, such as recent hospitalizations, injuries, or exacerbations of chronic diseases, are common.

Staying with the shelter's Food Bank as an example, pet owners also cope with the shame of accepting free services by distancing themselves from certain people who are present when they visit the shelter. This avoidance can be seen at some pet food banks or pantries around the country when owners walk into a shelter office to register but hesitate to approach the desk or even enter the building if there are people present who are not shelter staff. They might even be neighbors or friends looking to adopt a pet, and because of the tight space at some shelters, pet owners coming to register for free food find it hard to hide from those they fear would negatively judge them. Feeling embarrassed, they may wait outside the building until it is empty to avoid others entirely or enter the building but speak in a lower voice so no one hears them.

Sometimes West Charlotte pet owners distance themselves in other ways when using the Food Bank. One way they do this is to view others getting free pet food as needier or worse off because they are homeless, unemployed, or on welfare. A shelter staff member explained, "Some don't want to admit they need help. Some of our first timers speak in a quiet tone and will say I'm not one of those people. They don't want to be lumped with welfare recipients or food stamp recipients." Or pet owners can distance themselves from others using the Food Bank by simply not going. At the time of our study, there were about 450 people on the Food Bank list eligible for free pet food once a month for up to three dogs. However, only about 125, at best, showed up at the Food Bank on a regular basis. Of course people might not use the Food Bank because their pets have died or run away, they have gotten jobs that allow them to pay for their own pet food, or they have transportation problems or more pressing responsibilities to take care of on Saturday mornings. However, perceived stigma likely explains why at least some pet owners fail to regularly take advantage of this service and no doubt plays some role in their reluctance to use other services as well.

Not all West Charlotte pet owners who perceive stigma cope with it by distancing themselves from other owners or from the shelter itself. Indeed, some owners claim they do not feel at all stigmatized when using the shelter's services. More commonly, others accept such stigma as a reality for someone of color living in a disadvantaged community and take advantage of the shelter's services, despite this awareness. Living with shame is part of their way of life, and they are used to accepting city or state services that also make them feel uncomfortable or ashamed. Predominately white institutions like the shelter also routinely pose another problem for West Charlotte's residents, as we see next.

Distrust

Some pet owners are reluctant to use low- or no-cost veterinary services because they distrust the shelter's intentions. This suspicion is most obvious when shelter workers first meet pet owners during door-to-door neighborhood outreach. Typically, knocks on doors by workers go unanswered, shades or curtains part slightly, as residents peer outside, and doors open a crack for residents to say "no thanks." Some might not even speak to outreach workers and stay inside because they have narcotics or dogfighting activities on their property. The response is somewhat better if Jehovah's Witnesses or similar religious groups are visiting homes ahead of the shelter's outreach workers; as workers say, "animals beat Jesus," meaning that at these times residents will be more likely to open their doors for shelter workers and perhaps talk with them. To residents, the shelter workers are white strangers in predominately black areas of the city who are uninvited and have unknown goals. As one outreach worker said, "The only other white people on these blocks are police officers and bus drivers." So, it is not rare for residents to be blunt and yell at these workers, "What are you doing in my neighborhood?"

There is a different reason why residents distrust shelter workers and are standoffish to them in gentrifying sections of West Charlotte. In these areas of town, some longtime residents are afraid they will be forced to move because neighbors are being pushed out as investors and speculators buy property to develop and resell. Residents then incorrectly assume that outreach workers are coming to their neighborhood to contact and help residents who have moved in with more money, so they will not answer their doors when workers knock.

Residents who talk to outreach workers often question why they are being singled out for this attention and offered something that is heavily discounted or free. "They just don't trust that we're doing it for the reasons we say," observed one worker. That they distrust what shelter workers tell them stems from their general suspicion of predominately white institutions, and most shelter workers are white middle-class females, both paid and volunteer, as well as rescue group volunteers. Moreover, the shelter is a type of health care organization, and African Americans in general distrust the predominately white health care system, whether individual physicians or hospitals (Boulware et al., 2016). Compared to whites in America, African Americans are less likely to ask questions of their physicians and more likely to believe they will expose them to unnecessary risk or not provide them with the best available care (Miller & Kaiser, 2001; Whetten et al., 2006). In addition, when it comes to seeking care for human health problems, there is a strong cultural bias in the

black community, even among younger people, to not listen to what their doctor tells them; they need to have someone they know tell them the same thing
before they listen to their doctor. It seems likely that minority group pet owners would have a similar suspicion of veterinarians, other animal health care
providers, and humane society workers, and a similar reluctance to not listen
to them without confirmation and support from peers.

Given this distrust, residents wonder what if any catch is involved if they
accept the shelter's offer of free or discounted services and will rapidly retreat
from the encounter when they feel pressured to accept these services. For example, if they are told that sterilization costs only $50, a fraction of what pet
owners pay at a regular veterinarian's office, they tend not to believe this and
fear that the surgery will cost them much more. Indeed, there is a type of catch
in at least one Pets for Life program. In Charleston, South Carolina, pet owners
need to take the whole package of services offered by the shelter rather than
making an ala carte selection, as is the practice elsewhere; so if Charleston pet
owners insist on not fixing their animals, they get nothing. At another shelter,
people wanting free pet food get it only if they agree to have their pets vaccinated for rabies within three months of registering for the Food Bank, which
becomes a perceived barrier for some owners even though the cost of the vaccination is only $10. And the West Charlotte shelter recently added steriliza-
tion as a requirement to use its Food Bank, a stipulation that was added to
deal with dwindling supplies of pet food from donors.

The catch perceived by pet owners can involve much more than agreeing to
services that they might not want or paying more than first told. Some fear losing the ability to decide their animals' reproductive fate because they cannot
trust what the shelter tells them about sterilization. This particular concern is
linked to North Carolina's not-so-distant past when it forcibly sterilized African
Americans. The state's prior eugenics law was based on the now-discredited
theory that humanity benefits when people perceived as "defective" are stopped
from reproducing. The law empowered social workers to petition for the sterilization of just about anybody, but was mostly applied as late as the 1970s to
black women who had lower mental capacity, possessed a criminal history, behaved in "sexually delinquent" ways, or were victims of rape or incest (Schoen,
2001). Dehumanized and treated like "animals," people who should not have
been sterilized were uniformed about the nature of this surgery.

The last human sterilization was in 1974, so that racist period in the state's
history is fresh in the minds of some West Charlotte pet owners, especially
among older residents who lived through the horror. But other pet owners too
have heard about this period because of recent news reports of lawsuits over
forced sterilizations, for which the state has offered financial redress to sur-

viving victims (Carmon, 2014; Silver, 2003). Recalling or hearing about this appalling practice has caused a few West Charlotte residents to become very reluctant to sterilize their pets.

Indeed, local pet owners' practice of viewing shelter workers as animal social workers contributes to their distrust of the shelter's offer to sterilize animals because, as we noted, social workers played a key role in applying the state's eugenics policy. Many West Charlotte pet owners conflate shelter and rescue workers with North Carolina state social service workers with whom they routinely deal—child care, elder care, and family social services. Like shelter workers, these social service workers are also predominately white and provide free services. Although the shelter's outreach workers wear bright green T-shirts with HSC emblazoned on them and outreach workers from rescue groups drive cars that clearly label their animal organization (e.g., American Pit Bull Foundation), some West Charlotte pet owners—especially those in the Department of Social Services system—regard and refer to them as "animal social workers." For instance, if the worker makes a home visit and the resident has a friend over, the former will be introduced as an animal (or pet) social worker. Pet owners think that shelter workers, like social workers, visit their homes to check the status of dependent family members, animals in this case, and provide support and services to keep these dependents in the home and well cared for. While on the surface this connection seems harmless and probably is so for many West Charlotte pet owners, others who think of shelter workers as social workers will distrust their intentions because of this fairly recent period in North Carolina's history.

While it is rare for pet owners to directly refer to the state's forced sterilization of humans as the reason why they do not want to sterilize their animals, this memory factors into the decision more quietly as a background reservation in the minds of some pet owners and, if articulated, is expressed in different ways. For example, one West Charlotte dog and cat owner more than once spoke with her outreach worker about how the decades-old forced sterilization policy influenced her thinking to not sterilize. Yet when asked by the shelter's front-desk staff as well as this study's lead author about why she decided to not spay/neuter her animals, she did not mention the forced sterilization of humans. Instead, she claimed to not want the shelter to take away her animals' "freedom" by making the choice (of having a litter or not) for the pets. While anything taking away her animals' autonomy troubled her, fueling this reluctance was how the shelter's urging of sterilization echoed the state's prior forced sterilization policy of black women. Pet owners' concern that sterilizing is wrong because it takes away their animals' reproductive autonomy might also be a projection of their own lack of choice and control over most decisions in their lives, as researchers have documented for working-class Americans in general (Kraus et al., 2009).

Other pet owners fear they will literally lose their animals if they use the shelter's services because they confuse the shelter with the city's animal control department, the former being a private organization, the latter a governmental law enforcement agency. Connecting the shelter to animal control, in the minds of some pet owners, ties it to the city's police department, such that residents think that shelter employees are law enforcement workers.

At some shelters, such as the one in Charleston, workers' outfits contribute to this confusion because of their law enforcement look—cargo pants and military green shirts. In one case, when outreach workers arrived in a Charleston neighborhood, local residents scattered and yelled "Police! Police!" At the West Charlotte shelter, efforts are sometimes taken to minimize this association. For example, plans to distribute fliers about the shelter's services in several local neighborhoods initially included, for safety, the presence of police cars that would follow volunteers as they put fliers in mailboxes. A senior outreach worker heard about the plan and was immediately concerned that doing this was a bad idea because it furthered the unwanted association of the shelter with police. His pushback led to a revision of the plan with police cars parked farther away from the volunteers, although he would have preferred no police presence.

The public's confusion is heightened when a shelter is actually the "pound," such as the one in Charleston, in that it contracts for animal control services, although the latter is run independently by it. Moreover, some of the Charleston shelter's policies can seem less flexible to pet owners and more reminiscent of how they think a governmental department, such as animal control, would operate. For example, to reclaim an unsterilized lost animal from the Charleston shelter, the owner either has to pay $250 to not have it sterilized or the shelter will sterilize it.

The confusion of the shelter with animal control makes people suspicious of shelter workers and distrusting toward them because pet owners think, sometimes correctly, that someone has called animal control to report and confiscate their animals. As one shelter worker recalled, when he started his job and was unknown to local residents, the first thing they would say to him was "Are you here to take my dog?" Or they fear that the shelter will not only confiscate their pets but "kill" them since animal control does euthanize many of its animals.

Turning down or being suspicious of free transportation to the shelter is but one example of pet owners' fear that the shelter will take their animals and perhaps kill them. In West Charlotte, the vast majority of pet owners in need of transportation accept the shelter's offer to provide it, but on rare occasions someone rejects or questions this offer. A few fear that the offer to ster-ilize their pets is an elaborate dog-stealing scam run by the shelter to "steal" their dogs after surgery. Because of this belief, one person simply declined the offer for free pickup and delivery of his dog, another called the shelter to confirm that the volunteer picking up her dog actually worked at the shelter, while another consented to the free transportation only after the driver signed a paper written by the pet owner declaring, "I'm taking Johnny to be neutered. I promise to bring him back." Because of this fear, some owners ask the driver for his or her business card and will take photographs of the van, concerned that their animals will not be returned or that the shelter will charge them to return their pets. Knowing that a few residents fear the shelter will not return their animals after surgery, some workers reassure residents to the contrary. One worker tells residents when pets are being picked up for sterilization, "'I have six dogs at home. Believe me I'm bringing yours back. My husband would divorce me if I bring home another one.' And then they laugh."

The confusion of the shelter with animal control also stirs fears among some pet owners of losing control over personal information about them-selves that they worry will be turned over to law enforcement authorities who might then investigate them. Fearing that the shelter is a law enforcement agency, some pet owners who are illegal aliens or otherwise worried about their immigration status will refuse some or all of the shelter's services be-cause they do not want to give any personal information to organizations they think might deport them. This concern exists even though the shelter asks for only people's name, address, and phone number when they come for free or discounted services, but does not ask for proof, such as driver's licenses, so pet owners can conceal their identity. Concern about not having personal in-formation on record is even stronger with Charlotte animal control since it is housed and affiliated with the police department.

In addition to not giving personal information to the shelter or animal con-trol, there was a particular problem getting immigrant pet owners to agree to microchipping their animals because they thought it was a GPS device that would allow the government to track both their pets and them. However, im-migration officials have never contacted animal control or the shelter, and an-imal control's database is completely separate from the police department's database. Nevertheless, most immigrant pet owners do not know or disbelieve these details, so they may still be uncomfortable going to animal control, al-though perhaps less so with the shelter, for fear they might be turned over to immigration authorities. Indeed, recent immigration stings by the govern-ment in the Charlotte area had a chilling effect on the immigrant community in West Charlotte, exacerbating this fear of microchipping pets.

A similar reluctance—but not about microchipping per se—exists among some pet owners in other Pets for Life cities beside Charlotte, such as Chicago, where pet owners in a section of town heavily populated by Mexicans and Central Americans are concerned about their immigration status because of recent stings that have made them even more uncomfortable accessing the local shelter's services. For example, one pet owner from Honduras had been living in Chicago for three years when his dog escaped and ended up at the city's shelter. But when its owner went to reclaim it, he had to show proof of residency in Illinois with a driver's license or other state ID or present a passport to get past the security desk at the shelter. Even if he had had any of these forms of identification, he would not have shown them for fear that immigration authorities could find him, so he never got his dog. Despite his strong attachment to the dog, the possibility of being investigated and perhaps deported made his decision clear, but not easy.

That some pet owners might isolate themselves from the shelter because they associate it with law enforcement agencies—to the point of turning down free, and desired, veterinary services—is not a response to law enforcement that only pet owners have in disadvantaged communities. Rather, it reflects a wider insecurity among immigrants and minorities in the United States that makes them not trust police. For example, Latinos have been found to avoid police officers after they have been victims of crime because they fear that officers will use the interaction as a chance to inquire into their immigration status (Theodore, 2013). No doubt this deeper distrust of law enforcement furthers the insecurity of some pet owners when dealing with the shelter.

Given this insecurity, it is reasonable, from pet owners' perspective, that they might question the offer of free veterinary services because they fear that using these services must come with a catch or further cost, perhaps greater than losing their animals or their ability to breed them. Doing so, they fear, might lead to their own arrest or deportation if information about them is shared with animal control, the police department, or immigration authorities. In the end, then, some pet owners feel they can potentially lose too much if they have their pets cared for at the shelter compared to the financial gain of using free or cheap services.

Such worry is at odds with the thinking of animal policy makers who approach the problem of getting veterinary care to underserved populations with rational assumptions and sometimes inadequate information about the thoughts and feelings of pet owners in or near poverty. The former might cite the many pet owners who use free or discounted veterinary services as proof that all that must be done to get this population to the shelter is to reduce or eliminate costs and perhaps transportation barriers. However, that free or discounted veterinary services are used by many pet owners in disadvantaged communities does not, on the surface, tell us what the experience is like or explain why a minority of pet owners delay using or refuse these services.

Disaffection

Pet owners who use services like sterilization often feel they have carried out their side of an implied bargain by doing what they think the shelter wants them to do. They become "committed" to the shelter's program or are "turned over," terms vaguely used by shelter workers to describe pet owners who appear to embrace the idea and value of providing veterinary care to further animal welfare by deciding to sterilize their animals as well as use other shelter services. As one shelter worker said, "By the time we see them in spay/neuter, they've obviously made a commitment. They care a little bit because they're doing a wellness treatment." But part of the bargain, from the perspective of these committed pet owners, is that the shelter should then provide their pets with veterinary care beyond just sterilizing, vaccinating, or treating them for the most basic problems. When pet owners feel they cannot count on getting these extra veterinary services, some feel disaffected with the shelter and perhaps even become dismissive of its services.

Although the shelter provides free or low-cost basic veterinary services to West Charlotte pet owners, legal, policy, and liability issues limit the nature and extent of care that can be given to pets at the shelter. Technically and professionally, the shelter's clinic can perform only spay/neuter surgery and some wellness care, which is why the shelter is supposed to send clients to private-practice veterinarians to treat problems that are discovered during or leading up to sterilization surgery.[6] If the shelter veterinarians were to treat the vast majority of these discovered problems, they would violate the jurisdictional separation of veterinary work at the shelter from that of private-practice veterinarians whose toes would be stepped on, in addition to the fact that the shelter is unequipped to handle necessary follow-ups were they to medically intervene in such cases (e.g., the shelter does not have x-ray equipment).

Nevertheless, the shelter's veterinarian could easily handle many problems at a much lower price than pet owners would pay elsewhere, but she usually does not, choosing to refer owners to private-practice veterinarians who are often much more expensive. Treatment for worms, for example, would cost $150 at a private-practice veterinarian versus $10 at the shelter. Restrictions on professional practice mean that the shelter's veterinarians primarily serve in an advisory capacity where they provide diagnostic information to pet owners and referrals to private-practice veterinarians partnered with the shelter who can treat more complicated problems, like heartworm, ruptured bladders, or tumors. Unlike most regular private-practice veterinarians, these veterinary partners often have programs to help pet owners fund treatments and do not give them "a hard time" about "going to a low-cost place like the shelter." But referrals shift financial responsibility back on the pet owner, even if the shelter can occasionally help with the costs. During this study, the shelter had some external funding that enabled it to help some owners with the cost of seeking veterinary care in the community, putting the burden back on the pet owner to pay for private veterinary care not covered by the shelter's funding. One example was a West Charlotte pet owner who had an old dog with a lump of unknown origin that needed to be checked out by a veterinarian. While the shelter paid for the owner's transportation and for a basic veterinary examination, it could not pay $300 for a biopsy or for treatment if the lump turned out to be cancerous.

Despite their advisory role, shelter veterinarians do sometimes perform certain procedures other than sterilization that are acceptable and likely not to be considered professional interloping by most local private-practice veterinarians. Exceptions are made for cases that are easy to justify medically. For example, if the medical problem is thought to be "straightforward" and urgent, like removing an infected uterus or cancerous mass when the animal is under anesthesia, shelter veterinarians can do it. In fact, the shelter veterinarians often get referrals from private-practice veterinarians to do procedures like this because the shelter can do the surgery for a fraction of the price, instead of the latter euthanizing the animal because the client cannot afford the treatment. Hernias can also be repaired because the animal is under anesthesia and the repair is in the same area as the sterilization surgery. (It is considered best practice to do hernia repairs during spay/neuter surgery.) In addition, shelter veterinarians might correct a specific eye problem and occasionally remove a mass. Private-practice veterinarians do not usually have a problem with shelter veterinarians performing these surgeries because they are very important to perform for the animal's welfare and the shelter does not routinely do them.

However, if the shelter tries to correct medical problems other than those noted above or to do anything that is interpreted as more than wellness care, they can get in trouble if local private-practice veterinarians find out.[7] For example, shelter veterinarians have given the prescription drug Drontal to clients whose pets were suspected of having intestinal parasites and did not tell local private-practice veterinarians that they were dispensing it. But the shelter stopped providing this medication to pet owners when its veterinarians became worried about overstepping the limits of their authority and possibly having their licenses challenged by the local veterinary association. In addition, the shelter reversed its policy of not always asking local private-practice veterinarians for permission to provide certain treatments. Anticipating rejection and not wanting to rile local veterinarians, the shelter's veterinarians stopped giving Drontal to pet owners.

Indeed, if for-profit veterinarians find out or suspect that the shelter veterinarians have overstepped their professional limits, they could go to the state veterinary board, which might revoke the latter's veterinary license. An even bigger fear is that the shelter might not be allowed to sterilize animals, so it tries not to draw attention by adopting a conservative strategy about what it will do for clients' pets. For example, if worms are suspected during sterilization surgery, an over-the-counter dewormer medication (for pinworm) will be given , but not a prescription antibiotic, like Drontal, that is needed to kill tapeworms. But even the over-the-counter pinworm medication will not be given to clients for their pets at the Wellness Clinic, despite often being needed, because dispensing it makes the shelter veterinarians look like general practitioners, just as they would not give an antibiotic to a pet for an upper respiratory infection found during a Wellness Clinic checkup—although the antibiotic would be given during sterilization surgery. So the shelter's veterinarians are very cautious about treating clients' pets and are careful not to stretch what they do.

Despite fears of being challenged by some private-practice veterinarians or the veterinary association, the shelter's veterinarians will sometimes treat certain problems that fall in a gray zone because there is ambiguity as to what constitutes "wellness"; some people would say that wellness means treating basic conditions, while others say it means only vaccinating animals. Nor does the state veterinary professional association define what wellness care exactly means or which medications can or cannot be dispensed by shelter veterinarians for certain conditions. The shelter may also be uncertain about clients' ability and motivation to take an injured or sick animal to a private practitioner for immediate care, especially those living in or near poverty.

The result is that the shelter's veterinarians may take some veterinary liberties with unowned animals up for adoption and with Pets for Life animals. With the latter, the shelter worker in charge of the program can sometimes convince the shelter veterinarians to do certain things for clients they might otherwise hesitate to do. For example, they might decide to do entropion surgery for cherry eye on a Pets for Life dog, justifying it by saying that it is inadvisable to put a dog under anesthesia too many times, so it is best to perform the operation while the animal is already under anesthesia for sterilization. But this surgery will not be done for public animals at the shelter because workers cannot do the necessary follow-ups to make sure the procedure heals correctly. For Pets for Life animals getting this surgery, the shelter's outreach workers will go to the clients' homes or call them up to check on their dogs, postoperatively.

Although some gray zone problems are treated, fear of alienating private-practice veterinarians sometimes means that the shelter's veterinarians refuse to treat other problems, putting West Charlotte pet owners and their animals in a difficult situation because they cannot get to or afford a private-practice veterinarian.[8] If the problem could be successfully treated with a single Drontal pill, perhaps costing the shelter one dollar, the only alternative—sending the client's animal to a private-practice veterinarian at the cost of perhaps $150, a fee the client cannot afford—becomes unacceptable. And even if clients can somehow pay for this treatment, they do not always have transportation to the local veterinarian, and the shelter cannot get them there unless pets are in life-threatening situations. These jurisdictional worries and case complexities can prevent needed veterinary treatment and seriously frustrate outreach workers and Pets for Life clients who are trying to do their best for sick or injured pets. At this point, the implied bargain perceived by pet owners for the shelter to provide more veterinary care is cast in doubt, risking their disaffection.

This happened to Steven, a West Charlotte pet owner who cared deeply for his many cats. When he had two of his cats sterilized at the shelter, one of them, Snoopy, had a serious eye problem discovered during the procedure. It most likely had herpes, a common problem presenting as "gunk" around the eyes. Most cats who have this problem just live with it and their immune systems fight it off, but the stress of being transported and Snoopy's weakened immune system caused a flare-up. The shelter veterinarian failed to treat it because the problem was not a surgical complication, and since herpes is a viral infection, antibiotics would have been pointless. Although the outreach worker explained this to Steven, he did not fully grasp or concur with the shelter's rationalization for not treating Snoopy's eye problem. He started to panic because the problem was getting worse and was spreading to his kittens. In his opinion, Snoopy should have had his eye treated when being sterilized or right after, because it came in to the clinic with this medical problem.

The outreach worker suggested to Steven that because Snoopy was now home, he should try a different medication that sometimes helps with herpes by boosting the cat's immune system and treat any possible upper respiratory infection or infection related to sterilization that would make it easier for him to fight the herpes. So he asked the shelter veterinarian for a herpes medication but was denied the request because the veterinarian was worried that treating Steven's cat would fall outside the treatments that the shelter is authorized to provide, potentially getting her into trouble with the veterinary board for dispensing antibiotics when not needed, contributing to antibiotic resistance, and diagnosing the problem improperly. While the shelter veterinarian might have prescribed the medication if Steven had Snoopy first examined by a private-practice veterinarian, doing this was impossible because he could not get to the veterinarian's office or pay for the visit (and the shelter could not afford the $150 office visit). Knowing this, the outreach worker had to tell Steven that he had no medication to give him for his cats and that the shelter could not pay for him to take Snoopy to a private-practice veterinarian. Steven grew more distressed because the shelter and its veterinarians failed to treat his cat's eye problem not only during surgery but also after it was released.

The shelter's failure to help deeply troubled Steven and made him question whether he did the "right thing" by getting his pets sterilized at the shelter. Not helping Snoopy or the kittens seemed contradictory to Steven because, on the one hand, he felt he did what the shelter told him to do by sterilizing his pets, but doing so appeared to create new problems that the shelter veterinarians refused to help with or treat—namely Snoopy's continuing eye infection and its spread to Steven's kittens. Indeed, to Steven, the shelter seemed unconcerned about helping him fix problems that the shelter veterinarians should, in his eyes, have treated during or after Snoopy's sterilization surgery. The shelter's response also frustrated Steven because immovable roadblocks were preventing him from trying to take care of Snoopy and the kittens. Indeed, he started thinking that it would have been better not to have sterilized his cats, and if they had more kittens, he would have been able to find homes for them.

For Steven, the shelter had created an obstacle course that he could neither navigate nor understand. This obstacle course was familiar to Steven and other residents of West Charlotte who routinely have to navigate, often with great frustration and limited success, similar problems in every aspect of their lives when dealing with local organizations and social programs for themselves and their families having nothing to do with animal welfare. In fact, some who reject the shelter's services may do so because they expect to encounter such obstacles if they try to use its services. Instead of using these services, pet owners then tell themselves that even if things are not perfect with their animals, they can deal with what is happening at the moment. But if the shelter gets involved, new factors will be added to their lives that might complicate things to the point where they cannot deal with whatever problems their pets present. So nothing (from the shelter) is better than a (complicated and uncertain) something. Given such disaffection, hesitancy to use the shelter's free or low-cost services makes perfect sense from the pet owner's perspective.

Despite the fact that West Charlotte residents are unable to make choices over many aspects of their lives and are accustomed to being affected by circumstances beyond their control, it would be a mistake to think of them as unthinking and passive recipients of free or discounted veterinary services.

Identifying the hidden "costs" of using low- or no-cost veterinary services highlights the agency of West Charlotte pet owners as decision makers whose knowledge, experiences, and perceptions actively shape whether they use these services and, if they do, what using the services means to them.

What many pet owners bring to their understanding of and experience with the shelter's free or discounted services is an underlying fear of potential loss if they use this veterinary care—whether that involves lost income, lost self-respect, lost pets or the ability to breed them, lost personal freedom, or lost faith in the shelter. And along with these fears, there is an undercurrent of distrust in some pet owners' thinking about the shelter. Will shelter employees or volunteers criticize their pet care or otherwise make them feel like irresponsible owners? Is the shelter connected to law enforcement agencies, and, if so, how might this connection hurt them? Will the shelter help their animals beyond providing them with basic services? What results from these concerns and suspicions is reluctance, or even failure in a few cases, to use the shelter's no- or low-cost services.

Animal advocates hoping to diffuse veterinary services to underserved communities must recognize that pet owners will think differently about these services than will policy makers or authorities from outside these communities. These pet owners experience the shelter's services through a filter of racist treatment in the past and present by white institutions. The fact that the shelter is still predominately white, that its volunteers or novice workers occasionally misspeak or behave in ways that make pet owners feel inadequate, that it sometimes can make pet owners feel like they have to jump through hoops to get help, or that it seems to renege on an implied promise to help their animals all seem reminiscent of the discomfort felt by these pet owners when dealing with any white bureaucracy.

The reality is that most people who choose to work or volunteer at the shelter know little about how pet owners' cultural memories, norms, beliefs, and everyday realities affect their perception and use of free or discounted services. Admittedly, obtaining such inside cultural knowledge is challenging for organizations that, despite their efforts and wishes, have mostly white staff members who are paid very modestly and work very hard to care for the animals in their charge and to provide services to needy pet owners. With few exceptions, they come from a very different social world than that of their clients and have little opportunity when at work to build rapport with pet owners in the community so they could understand their perspective more fully than they now do. In addition, shelter workers might not feel that gaining this cultural knowledge is necessary since most pet owners who are offered low- or no-cost services accept at least some of them, even if not immediately. Given such apparent success, that pet owners might be reluctant to use the shelter's services and think differently about them than do shelter workers is almost beside the point.

Nevertheless, as we see next, the shelter has tried to understand the perspective of West Charlotte's pet owners and why they may be reluctant to use its services for reasons other than cost and logistics. By trying to think like its clients, the shelter can then try at an interpersonal and policy level to address this reluctance to sterilize, vaccinate, and treat animals. Indeed, the ability of the shelter to engage the community rather than distance itself from it may help to explain why its efforts to provide low and no-cost veterinary care have reached so many people.

CHAPTER SIX

"Perfect Is the Enemy of Good"

THINKING DIFFERENTLY ABOUT
LOW-INCOME PET OWNERS

Studies of shelter workers interacting with the public—whether pet owners or those wanting to adopt—often report a strain between the two groups, giving the impression that they are more often at odds with each other than compassionate partners who both want the best for the animals in their charge. Workers can become frustrated or even outraged with owners whose behavior sometimes seems inexplicable to them. When this happens, they become sarcastic if not cutting when talking about "jerks" who appear to casually let the family's dogs or cats have litters so their children can "see the wonder of birth" (Arluke, 2002); they blame owners as a way to avoid feeling guilty about euthanizing surrendered animals (Frommer & Arluke, 1999); and they become puzzled and disturbed by, even "hate," those who surrender their pets or otherwise fail to be responsible and caring for them (DiGiacomo et al., 1998).

To some extent, the antipathy of shelter workers results from pet owners or potential adopters who hide their thinking out of fear the staff will criticize or reject them. By not sharing their concerns, thoughts, and emotions with shelter workers about, for example, problems keeping pets, the latter can easily get the wrong impression that owners are irresponsible or uncaring. But the failure to understand or sympathize with pet owners is also built into the culture and customs of many shelters. For much of the twentieth century, shelters were overwhelmed by many surrendered animals that often had to be euthanized by distressed staff members, a plight that has lessened in recent years (Rossen, 2019). Resentment for having to kill animals that were not sick nor had behavioral problems put an emotional wedge between workers and the public they served that often continued even as adoptions increased and euthanasia declined nationally.

Around the turn of the current century, animal welfare organizations started to recognize this problem and call for less friction and fewer misunderstandings between shelters and the public. For example, the Humane Society of the United States developed a new manual of adoption procedures so shelter workers could adopt a "fresh perspective" to embrace rather than reject community members (HSUS, n.d.-a, p. 2). Such calls were shared by other humane organizations that also mainly focused on modifying how shelter workers dealt with potential adopters and less so with those surrendering them. To wit, the Animal Humane Society (AHS) changed its recommended adoption procedures and policies to stop screening potential adopters and start matching clients and pets "to create a climate of trust, communication, and understanding" (AHS, 1999, p. 6). To do this, the society urged shelter workers to build "comfortable" and respectful relationships with the community by assuming that people are trying to do the "right thing" when they visit the shelter and by abandoning the idea that all animals must live in a "perfect home" (AHS, 1999, pp. 7–8). Nevertheless, the society warned that it can be a "struggle" to get shelter workers to change how they think about and deal with the public (AHS, 1999, p, 9), a concern still valid today.

Reducing strain with the public is all the more challenging when there is a racial, ethnic, and social class divide between shelters and the communities they serve, as there is in West Charlotte, calling for shelter workers to develop "culturally competent" skills to close this divide. Indeed, trying to understand the local culture and consider this when offering basic veterinary care is a cornerstone of the shelter's Pets for Life program and is embraced by the shelter when providing services to other West Charlotte pet owners who are not Pets for Life clients but are eligible for low-cost services. Knowing that the local community is demographically unlike most of those who work or volunteer at the shelter, they are encouraged to develop a deep understanding of the West Charlotte community and the everyday life of its residents, so that veterinary care can be provided in ways that are appropriate for and respect the residents' reality, experiences, customs, and beliefs not just with animals but, more generally, with their way of life as underprivileged minority group members.

However, little is known about how workers in any field—let alone those at animal shelters—learn to be culturally competent and adjust their own behavior accordingly. For example, discussions about how to be culturally competent in fields such as medicine and nursing typically abstract the general features of behaving this way toward clients without describing what that process specifically entails (e.g., Campinha-Bacote, 2002). Understanding what that process is for shelter workers would be invaluable because it is thought to be responsible for the success of Pets for Life programs. For that reason, others wanting to reduce the strain with their local pet-owning communities will want to know how shelter workers adjust their thinking, feeling, and behavior to better understand and work with West Charlotte residents.

Shelter workers face several challenges when adjusting to the local community that can require them to change their expectations of pet owners and their ideals of animal care, while altering, even if only slightly, West Charlotte culture. They need to make available free and low-cost services but not pressure pet owners to use them since that would only exacerbate the long-standing strain between the shelter and disadvantaged pet owners. Nor can they shame people if they decide to bring their animals to the shelter or exclude some who mistreat animals. And they need to accept that local knowledge and customs will sometimes trump their own expertise and value, while lowering their personal standards for how they ideally think pets should be fed and kept as well as how they should be cared for when sick or injured.

Shelter workers trying to be culturally competent also face a different kind of challenge. Evidence from other fields suggests that some of these adjustments to the local culture might be at odds with the humane society's own core beliefs about how animals should be cared for and who should use its free and discounted services. For example, reports have found that when social workers try to be culturally competent, their actions with clients can contradict the basic ideology of social work practice (Johnson & Munch, 2009). That something similar might happen with the shelter workers we studied is implied by the society's own informal motto, "Perfect is the enemy of good." This motto reminds workers and volunteers, especially those new to the job, that being culturally competent will require them to accept, or at least live with, a standard of animal care that can be compromising and leave them with mixed feelings about their efforts to consider the pet owner's perspective.

Although workers learn to accept a standard of care that is adjusted for local knowledge, customs, and practice regarding the treatment of dogs and cats, these animals are likely healthier, and perhaps "happier," than they would be without the benefits of free and low-cost services from the shelter and interacting with its staff. The overall welfare of West Charlotte's pets has been nudged for the better, and that is the point of the shelter's motto. As we see next, by reducing the typical strain found between shelters and the communities they serve, workers change not only the culture of pet keeping but the culture of animal sheltering.

Reducing Shame

The shelter wants low-income pet owners to bring their animals for sterilization, vaccinations, basic exams and treatments, as well as pet food, although
supplies of the latter can be limited. One strategy is to offer free or discounted
services to everyone so the shelter can vaccinate, sterilize, feed, and give basic veterinary treatments to as many of West Charlotte's pets as possible. The
fact that the shelter does not use a means test, ask pet owners to show identification such as a driver's license, or check on the honesty of people wanting
to use discounted or free services stems in part from its belief that financial
hardship is not always the only reason why some people fail to sterilize their
pets or use other services, although financial ability can affect this decision.
The shelter does not want low-income pet owners to have to endure a means
test from yet another large organization, as many West Charlotte residents
have done in other aspects of their lives. Doing so can be demeaning because
it is a public admission of their financial woes, so using a means test could
discourage some owners from coming or make those who use services feel
uncomfortable and ashamed if they have to prove their need. As one worker
said, "We don't make people show any proof of income. All that's going to do is
make those who need it less likely to come."

Other programs providing basic veterinary care are not quite as lax about
eliminating administrative barriers to using their no- or low-cost services. For
instance, one program in Massachusetts asks prospective users of its free services to show a driver's license. In addition to requiring a rabies vaccination
to get services, another program also demands pet owners not acquire any
additional pets while they are using its services because if they cannot afford
to feed their current pets, they should not be taking on more responsibility.
While this stipulation is hard to monitor, if this shelter discovers an offender,
he or she can be disqualified from using future services there. People sometimes admit this, forgetting that they signed an agreement to the contrary.
One woman who is a frequent user of the shelter's Food Bank came in wanting
to adopt another dog. She was told that if she gets another dog, she would no
longer qualify for the pet food program. Since being told this, she has not returned to the Food Bank.

Overall, the shelter's strategy succeeds in making available no- or low-cost
services to many West Charlotte pet owners who need them with as few restrictions as possible. This strategy works for the core—pet owners who become "committed," a term used by some shelter workers to refer to West
Charlotte pet owners who most need and regularly use its free or discounted
services, and who embrace the larger ideal, indirectly espoused by the shel-

ter, that owners follow through with their desire to care and be responsible for their pets. However, there are other West Charlotte pet owners who need free or discounted services but are not committed users. The pride of these owners makes them uncomfortable accepting the shelter's free or low-cost services. Because of shame or even humiliation, they irregularly take advantage of these services only when they are desperate for help.

But the shelter's strategy of opening up its free or low-cost services to as many West Charlotte pet owners who need them with as few barriers as possible is not always perfect. There are a few users of these services who, for different reasons, should not be asking for low-cost sterilization or free pet food, or whose use of animals runs contrary to the shelter's ideals for what constitutes acceptable practices with dogs. Because these faults in the shelter's strategy are very rare, the shelter accepts them as inevitable and often difficult to prevent. The shelter also accepts them, as noted below, because it believes the wider perspective in such cases—reaching the most animals—justifies the strategy's occasional imperfections.

Cheapskates present one such limitation. There are a few people who use some of the shelter's discounted services but should not because they are middle-income pet owners who can easily afford to pay full price for these services at a private veterinarian's practice. Of all the services offered by the shelter, pet owners looking for bargain rates are most likely to bring their dogs and cats to its sterilization clinic and, when interviewed, are forthcoming about their ability to pay more elsewhere but their desire to save money by having the surgery done at the shelter. While never using the shelter's Food Bank, cheapskates will also sometimes take their pets for discounted vaccinations at the shelter's Wellness Clinic, but less often than their use of discounted sterilization.

Although they are rare, gluttons are low-income pet owners who take more pet food and supplies than they are allowed. At one program, a pet owner who regularly used the Food Bank tried to steal pet food and toys after receiving her own allotment, as staff members were occupied with other clients. When one staff member saw what was happening, she told the woman that she was taking donated pet food and toys that were not hers to take. She denied knowing this but was never again seen at the program. Other pet owners who take more than their regular monthly allotment do it by having their children, other family members, or friends stand in line for "seconds," hoping not to be detected by volunteers. And yet other pet owners get more than their share by visiting other pet food banks or human food pantries that distribute pet food, even though the shelter gives each owner about a month's supply of food for each pet they have, unless it is the occasional month when the shelter is low on supplies. Owners do this because they take comfort in stockpiling extra food or they overfeed their pets, even though staff members and volunteers explain to them what constitutes an acceptable portion for the different products they take as well as when and what to feed pets.

Rare imposters who use the shelter's free Food Bank do not own pets or claim they have more pets than they actually do. They then take home the pet food and either resell it on the street for a few dollars or, if the bar codes are not obscured, return it to the store to get cash. For example, before they started their current procedure of punching out each month on a card to indicate that pet food was picked up at the Food Bank, a man would often come and claim that he had more dogs than he had, only to then sell the pet food on the street for $5 a bag, a price well below what stores charge. Because he obviously needed the money, the staff did not criticize or stop him, and they also realized that whoever bought the stolen pet food must have needed it to feed their dogs. At the time of our study, since proof of pet ownership was not required, the program could be scammed this way. However, the shelter subsequently started to require proof of sterilization after a few months of using its Food Bank because of dwindling pet food donations, a measure that should prevent imposters from getting the shelter's food. At other programs, these illegitimate users can get away with this for up to three months, when they finally have to present proof of rabies immunization to continue taking free or discounted services. Shelter workers grudgingly accept imposters because they are so rare and must really need the services they get, and when they resell the food on the streets, it at least ends up in the hands of West Charlotte pet owners who need it.

Outcasts are owners who use their pets in unacceptable ways from the shelter's animal welfare perspective but still take advantage of its no- or low-cost services. For example, breeders will occasionally bring animals to the shelter's discounted sterilization program. Shelter workers and veterinary staff are frustrated when this happens because they disapprove of breeding but do not feel they should turn away anyone willing to sterilize animals, since that is the shelter's mission.[1] Shelter workers recognize these pet owners as breeders because they often openly admit to breeding. They want to make more money by sterilizing pups because buyers will be willing to pay more for animals that have already had this surgical procedure. The amount charged by the breeder for the animal factors into the breeders' cost of paying for sterilization, with an additional profit to cover their costs to the shelter. Even more troubling for the shelter and its animal welfare ideals are rare instances when known dogfighters bring animals to the shelter for low-cost vaccination or sterilization, perhaps because they are selling some puppies they have bred and want to increase their street value. To avoid dealing with the volunteers at the registration desk or employees inside the animal hospital, the dogfighters will send their children with the puppies while they stay some distance away inside their parked cars.

To be clear, these limitations in the shelter's open-use policy are very infrequent and, for the most part, are known by the shelter but tolerated because it wants as many dogs and cats vaccinated, sterilized, and treated for basic health issues as possible, regardless of owners' motivations. Nor should these few cases feed into or be used to support the erroneous stereotype of welfare users who allegedly abuse the use of human social services or are unnecessarily dependent economically on the system (e.g., Goldberg, 1995); the vast majority of West Charlotte pet owners who use the shelter's services genuinely need this help and, given all the limitations they face in their everyday lives, try to do the best for their pets with the shelter's aid.

Empowering Owners

One candidate to be the shelter's new outreach worker stood out from others and was hired largely because of two factors, even though she had no veterinary or shelter experience. The staff members were impressed by a story she related about having taken special interest in one of her clients at a former job who had a pet—a story that revealed the candidate's ability to empathize with people and see their perspective. But an equally important factor in her hiring was the candidate's prior experience as a door-to-door salesman because she and other workers from the shelter need to "sell" sterilization and other basic veterinary care to West Charlotte pet owners who do not know about or have not used these services before. Like salespeople they are getting people to use a new product—in this case sterilization or other basic care—but shelter workers are unlike traditional salespeople who pressure clients to buy something new (Evans, 1963) because they take a soft-selling approach (Okazaki et al., 2010). Rather than hard-selling veterinary care, shelter workers do not want pet owners to feel forced to sterilize, vaccinate, or get basic treatments for their animals.

Workers learn that if they tell pet owners what to do, few would get their animals sterilized, vaccinated, or otherwise treated at the shelter. For example, some humane policies require sterilization and other veterinary services in order for pet owners to qualify for other care. Despite the good intent of many of these programs, some pet owners experience them as coercive and refuse free care. This happened when some West Charlotte pet owners were required to sterilize their animals to qualify for the Beyond Fences' (formerly known as the Coalition to Unchain Dogs) program to build free backyard fences. They complied but then subsequently "shut down" and refused to sterilize dogs they acquired at later times. Other humane policies require sterilization to obtain a pet, but some people bulk at this not because they oppose sterilization per se but because they want to control decisions relating to their pets. This was evident in one case in Charleston where an owner refused to sterilize his pet. He went to reclaim his lost pet and was initially given the county's standard offer—if he agreed to sterilize his dog, he would have to pay only about $50, but if he did not want the dog sterilized it would cost about $250. He agreed to the latter, despite his low income, because allowing the dog to be sterilized to save $200 felt like abdicating control over his pet.

Pressuring owners makes them more reluctant to use services because they feel like their decision-making ability is being taken away, and most West Charlotte residents exercise little decision-making power in their everyday lives. They, like others living in or near poverty (Wallerstein, 1992), do not have much latitude or control over most aspects of their lives; they cannot change their financial situation, job prospects, working conditions, or housing. However, pet keeping can be one of the few things they do or are responsible for where they have decision-making control. West Charlotte pet owners, like others who have a low income or live in poverty, can decide whether or not to have a pet, where it is kept, and how it is fed and otherwise cared for. And unlike with their children, owners do not have to deal with school systems or adolescent peer groups, which they feel powerless to influence. Deciding whether to use the shelter's services can be one of the few areas of their lives where they can determine what will happen, so the shelter does not want its efforts to promote sterilization to make residents feel like they have lost control over yet another aspect of their lives.

Shelter workers take a low-keyed approach to selling sterilization so they can leave the decision to do it in the hands of pet owners. They do this by not "lecturing," "harassing," or being "preachy" or otherwise telling pet owners what they need to do for their pets. Instead, they provide information to pet owners so they can make up their own minds about whether to use the shelter's free or discounted services.[2] Or, as one worker claims, "We don't want them to feel like we forced them into anything, and that we think that our way is better than their way." New workers are coached to use this soft-selling technique. They are told they cannot tell pet owners to "'fix your dog. That's what you should be doing' because the person might say 'I can't afford it' or 'I don't think I should. And now I'm really not going to do it because you're yelling at me.'"[3] So workers let them know that if they want to do something like sterilize an animal, the shelter will do it for free if they are a Pets for Life client or for a reduced charge if they are from the community. In other words, pet owners are given only information and options.

Workers also take a low-key approach by trying harder to develop rapport with pet owners than to sell them basic veterinary care. One senior staff member compared this interactional approach to how the shelter "cultivates" and builds relationships with potential donors rather than just going after financial contributions. Unlike donors, though, there are huge status differences between shelter workers and West Charlotte pet owners that can make it more difficult to form relationships, the former being mostly middle-income, educated white females, while the latter are mostly low-income, poorly educated male and female African Americans. And there is also a knowledge gap because local pet owners often see shelter workers as animal experts.

To reduce these differences and develop some degree of trust, outreach workers entering pet owners' homes and canvasing West Charlotte neighborhoods use methods that, on a smaller scale, echo those used by social scientists to gain access to and acceptance by groups they study. They try to fit in with the "natives" and befriend them with offers of help or even gifts (Adler & Adler, 1987; Alcadipani et al., 2015; Jorgensen, 2015; Randall et al., 2007). When outreach workers first meet pet owners in their homes, they commonly avoid talking about sterilization, especially if pet owners seem reluctant to do this, and instead give them things like dog toys and flea medication, remind them about needed injections, and chat about their animals as well as personal matters unrelated to pets. Outreach workers also might try to fit in by behaving more like pet owners, such as changing how they speak. As one worker said, "When I talk with clients, I start talking differently. It's not like all of a sudden, I start using Ebonics. I know my cadence and everything is different. Even the way I stand is different. I'm not doing it on purpose." And as they talk with pet owners, outreach workers are careful not to talk down to pet owners or judge them so they can feel knowledgeable about caring for their animals and responsible for their welfare. All of these techniques help outreach workers downplay their nonnative status to build rapport, while talking little if at all about sterilization per se.

Despite their soft-selling approach to build rapport and not pressure owners, shelter workers still subtly influence pet owners' decision-making process to use the shelter's free or discounted services, and many ultimately do. As they talk with pet owners, shelter workers embed a rhetoric of individual choice and agency so owners feel they have not been forced to sterilize their animals but rather have elected to do so. In other words, by not telling pet owners what to do, shelter workers can empower them and thereby reduce their reluctance. But more is required to move owners to the point where they consent to sterilize their pets than making this decision appear to be in their hands. Shelter workers need to create a new normal in West Charlotte where owners come to expect animals to be sterilized and view those unsterilized pets as a problem.

Creating a New Normal

While animal advocates have succeeded in making sterilization the new normal for many Americans, they have been less successful in disadvantaged communities. Many West Charlotte residents still expect their pets to bear litters. Parents do not always object to their children's request for the household dog or cat to have puppies or kittens after they see neighbors or hear about friends who have done this. Reproduction is also not regarded as something that is unhealthy for adult animals; in fact, some residents think of it as health promoting. So when shelter workers engage pet owners about the merits and safety of sterilization, they are also trying to change how pet owners generally think about this surgery and its impact on their animals or what the new normal should be when it comes to spaying or neutering one's pet. In other words, what people expect and regard as natural when it comes to the fertility of pets needs to be changed.

Although shelter workers do not frame their attempts to do this as selling sterilization, workers' engagements with owners are not unlike those of others selling medical procedures who also question, as part of their selling, what consumers regard as normal. For example, companies selling cosmetic surgery to women use a strategy where they first pathologize a normal anatomic feature, then normalize the surgery to correct this "problem" or deficiency, and finally minimize the surgery's difficulty, limitations, or complications, while making buyers feel they are making an individual choice to undertake the procedure (Moran & Lee, 2013). As they share information with pet owners, shelter workers use a similar strategy to sell sterilization.

Shelter workers also pathologize a biological feature regarded by many as normal—in this case how West Charlotte residents think about the ability of a pet to reproduce or to be unsterilized as a natural state. Workers do this by framing sterilization as a preventive measure that reduces the likelihood of future untoward medical events in the unsterilized animal. Workers believe that pet owners will be receptive to sterilization if it is explained as part of their animals' larger health package that might prevent serious if not life-threatening diseases and keep them alive longer. So since no one wants their pets to get sick, owners who are reluctant to sterilize their pets are given biological explanations for why sterilization is good for dogs or cats. They are told, for example, that this surgery will prevent problems such as testicular and prostate cancer in male animals, uterine cancer in females, and pyometra (infection of the uterus) in dogs and cats.

They also pathologize a pet's unsterilized state by pointing out the potential problems of having litters for both the owner and the puppies or kittens.

Workers tell owners that having litters can produce harmful or at least undesirable consequences, such as the problem of finding homes for puppies or kittens, the possibility that the puppies or kittens will not be well cared for even
if adopted, and the cost of having litters. In this regard, some shelter workers
take a Socratic approach to dissuade residents from breeding their animals by
asking them "Do you know who will take care of your puppies if you don't?" or
by telling them that "half of the animals we put down are pit bulls. You'll take
good care of the puppies but will you know how they will be cared for once you
give them to somebody else?" A slightly different way to pathologize a pet's
ability to reproduce worked with some West Charlotte residents. Pitching the
value of sterilization as a way to control animal overpopulation in the abstract
usually failed because it was not something that most residents could connect or relate to as their problem, even though their failure to fix pets contributed to this problem. However, for some owners who live in neighborhoods
plagued by a large number of feral or community cats, the offer to sterilize as a
way to control population numbers can be an effective strategy to sell the surgery and thereby prevent or reduce the problems of having too many strays
around residents' homes.

Selling sterilization calls for shelter workers to do more than point out
the dangers or problems of not fixing animals; they also need to change cultural and social perceptions of this surgery as wrong if not harmful. Normalizing sterilization can be challenging for shelter workers, especially with some
West Charlotte males who see the issue of sterilization as more than a biological matter. Resisting the procedure can be a cultural issue (Clark, 2017) for
pet owners who identify with their unneutered pets. Changing owners' minds
about this surgery can be difficult when they are males whose sense of mas-
culinity is closely tied to how they perceive their unsterilized pit bulls' mascu-
linity. Having a tough, intact dog was "cool" because its aggressiveness colored
how an owner saw himself and how he thought others saw him. Castrating
the dog was akin to emasculating its owner within this subculture, a concern
noted in other studies of resistance to sterilization (Urbanik, 2009). Less often
but still a gendered identification with pets were West Charlotte women who
resisted spaying female dogs because they feared that their pets would be "depressed" if they did not have a litter since that was the "womanly thing" to do.

Shelter workers often respond with humor when confronted with cultural
resistance to sterilization. They might remind apprehensive owners that they
are not being neutered—"we don't do humans"—a lighthearted way to poke
fun at the owner's gendered identification with his or her pet. Or humor might
be mixed with information to clarify the nature of sterilization when pet owners are told that sterilization only removes the dog's testicles—"he's still go-

ing to be all man. Everyone is going to know he's a boy." And sometimes shelter workers dropped their attempts at humor and just told owners who feared that sterilization would make their dogs less aggressive or less masculine that unless the surgery were performed on a very young animal, "it won't take away their mating instincts and they're still going to want to protect your home." Despite workers' good intentions to promote sterilization by correcting what they often saw as owners' biological misunderstandings about the surgery, there is no evidence that humor or information changed the thinking of owners tightly identified with the gender of their unsterilized pets. Resistance in this case was not always amenable to biological information because, from the owner's perspective, the issue had deeper cultural significance to them. It was not just a matter of their dog's health or well-being. The surgery had implications for how they saw themselves as well as how their peers saw them.

Since being informative and funny does not always overcome reluctance to sterilize or shift perceptions of what is normal, shelter workers also resort to enlisting other pet owners in the community to help normalize the surgery by endorsing the procedure to peers. Neighbors are far more trusted than are shelter employees or volunteers when it comes to using the shelter's services. Pet owners who agree to sterilize their animals when first visiting the shelter for vaccinations or when being visited at home by outreach workers do so because they usually know someone else who had their pets fixed at the shelter. Indeed, if someone gets a pet sterilized and subsequently tells friends and neighbors with pets that the experience was good and there were no postsurgical problems, the shelter usually gets a flurry of calls requesting sterilization from other West Charlotte pet owners.

Some of these West Charlotte residents exert even more influence on the veterinary decisions of pet-owning neighbors as they step into the informal educational process. They are opinion leaders, or what the shelter calls "community ambassadors," who at their own volition talk to other pet owners in West Charlotte about the shelter and its programs, making them aware of available services while suggesting they get their pets fixed, vaccinated, and/ or treated at the shelter. These community ambassadors play a key role in establishing trust in the shelter's staff and programs because they know their neighbors on a first-name basis and have used its services; when they endorse the shelter's services, other pet owners will more likely use them. As one shelter worker said, "getting in" with community ambassadors had the same impact as getting the endorsement of influential local leaders: "If you can get in with the pastor of a church you're going to get in with the congregation." Conversely, workers "shied away" from people who were not well liked in the neighborhood, although they would still help and provide services to them, and distanced themselves from problematic people whose association with workers could jeopardize their efforts, such as one pet owner who displayed a confederate flag outside his house in a predominately black neighborhood.

For example, one of these leaders who owned four cats appeared to know every household with pets on her block and claimed to have told three neighbors with dogs about the shelter and its services, in one case specifically recommending that they get their dogs "fixed," a term commonly used in the community for sterilization. Another leader, known locally as the "cat man," had a long history of caring for stray or feral cats in the neighborhood and, after contact with the shelter, started doing trap-neuter-release to capture and then sterilize these cats for population control. He started approaching neighbors who fed strays or feral cats, especially during the spring breeding season and found themselves overwhelmed with scores of kittens, to explain why they should let him trap and sterilize the cats to control the population. While these community cat caretakers would listen to the "cat man" because he was a neighbor, they would not have listened to shelter workers talk about the need to sterilize for population control, fearing the shelter would seize these cats and possibly euthanize them.

Pet owners become community ambassadors in different ways. Some long-time animal lovers understand the value of the shelter's services for the welfare of pets without that being explained to them. Not needing encouragement by shelter workers, they tell other pet owners about the shelter's free or low-cost services and why it is a good idea to use them. Other pet owners in the community are financially strapped and very grateful to have received free or low-cost services with no strings attached, so they want to give back in some way. Because they cannot contribute monetarily and know the shelter is nonprofit, they are eager to spread the word. To validate and encourage this type of ambassador, the Chicago Pets for Life program gives them T-shirts with the shelter's name on them and fliers to distribute that describe the shelter's free and low-cost services. And some become ambassadors because an adverse event happened to their pets that makes them suddenly see the major benefits of using the shelter's services—benefits they want other pet owners to also appreciate and seek for their animals. For example, an owner's dog might get a uterine infection that can be cured only by spaying the animal quickly, so fixing the animal saved its life. Such a pet owner may then be especially motivated to encourage pet-owning neighbors to also sterilize their animals. Whatever their pathway to becoming a community ambassador, all of these pet owners complement the shelter's efforts to normalize sterilization and other basic veterinary services.

Selling sterilization entails more than its normalization; workers try to minimize concerns in the community about the surgery's dangers. Some misinformation about sterilization is deeply engrained in the local culture and re-sistant to change. One common concern, often circulated as an urban myth, is that animals, particularly small pets, will not survive the surgery, which could be a recalcitrant belief lingering in the community from decades ago when the mortality rate was higher, reinforced by the fact that very few West Charlotte residents have ever taken a pet to a veterinarian, let alone have surgery per-formed on it.[4] In addition, most of these residents have a general discomfort with any surgery, not realizing how simple and safe sterilization is compared to other procedures. Especially among older pet owners, using the shelter's services seems risky because they may have owned several dogs in the past that were never vaccinated or sterilized but lived long, healthy lives.

Of course, some resistance to shelter workers' information is grounded in real but rare adverse experiences with sterilization when pets died during or right after surgery—something that shelter workers may not recognize when first talking with pet owners who have had such experiences. For example, one pet owner was asked by an outreach worker whether he would consider ster-ilizing his shepherd mix. When he declined without explanation, the mind-set of the outreach worker was that this was just a person who lived in a poor community who did not care about fixing his dog and there was no reason be-hind his objection. However, once they started talking, the owner said he had no family—the dog was his family—and in the prior year he had another dog that got neutered and died on the operating table, although it was unclear if an underlying condition caused the death. Over the following few months, the shelter shared additional information with him and he talked with neighbors who reassured him about the safety of sterilization. He finally consented to the procedure.

Abdicating to Local Knowledge

Reluctance to sterilize also happens when pet owners themselves discuss whether their animals should have this surgery. While many may listen to shelter workers' description of and justification for sterilizing pets, owners si-multaneously gather, use, and defer to their neighborhood's understandings and customs to make final decisions about using veterinary services. This means that the success or failure of the shelter's attempt to be culturally com-petent is partly in the hands of pet owners who rely on their own methods of collecting and trusting information about what the shelter offers them. What results are two systems of knowledge about animal health and welfare—one professional, the other lay—that exist alongside each other, such that the lat-ter may support the shelter's efforts to diffuse services but also allow for po-tential subversion of this goal.

Despite shelter workers' expertise about animal welfare, some people delay sterilizing their pets or using other services because they share "ownership" of community animals and do not want to usurp the decision making of their co-owners, especially if someone else is perceived as more responsible for the animal in question.[5] For example, there are several types of ambiguous ownership of cats in West Charlotte. They can be a resident's cat that is allowed outside so other people may interact with or care for it, a semiferal or friendly stray that someone released and never reclaimed but eats food left outside for it and allows some physical contact, or a feral that avoids contact with people who nevertheless put food out for it.

That was the case with Midnight, a community cat in West Charlotte. Don interacted with Midnight, playing with and feeding her on occasion as well as being mindful of her welfare. Especially after she had two litters, Don was eager to have Midnight sterilized but did not push it with Diane, a co-owner who lived two doors down from Don, because she was the primary person taking care of Midnight and opposed sterilization. But Don no longer cared what Diane thought and refused to further delay Midnight's sterilization after it had a third litter. Don then contacted the shelter to have the cat fixed, only to find that Midnight had gone missing.

West Charlotte pet owners also delay sterilizing their animals or seeking other free or low-cost veterinary care until they get information from other community residents about their experiences with these services. They want to know what it was like to visit the shelter or interact with its staff and, most importantly, what impact sterilization had on their animals. People fear something untoward might happen to their pets during the surgery that could kill them or alter their behavior in undesirable ways. Pet owners trust this information because it is from neighbors or friends rather than from shelter staff members who are strangers working for an organization about which many residents have mixed feelings. In some cases, owners will sterilize their pets only if they see that their neighbor's animal not only has survived the surgery but also has not had its personality changed.

Occasionally the reverse happens when a medical problem could have been averted had the pet been sterilized, and this information is shared in the community. For example, one West Charlotte pet owner brought to the shelter his 10-year-old pit bull with pyometra, or an inflamed uterus, and a mammary tumor. He was told by a staff member that had he sterilized his dog, these medical problems might have been prevented. Hearing this information stunned the dog's owner, according to the staff member, because he never had this information and spaying or neutering was never a priority in his mind. The staff member was certain that if the owner had known, he would have sterilized his dog sooner, but more to the point, the owner returned to his neighborhood and encouraged other pet owners to take their animals to the shelter for this surgery.

If there are no neighbors or community ambassadors to vouch for sterilization or show how their animals managed after being fixed, pet owners empirically "test the water" by looking at their own experiences using the shelter's free or low-cost checkups, vaccinations, and basic treatments. Visiting the organization somewhat demystifies it for people who have never been there, plus they can observe other pet owners and their animals seemingly doing well. As pet owners gradually use these services, their trust usually deepens over time in the shelter's program, enabling owners to slowly work up to consenting to sterilization surgery.

Or owners skeptical or worried about this surgery test its safety, if they have more than one pet, by trying it on only one of their animals to see what happens. Owners who use this in-house method usually choose a lesser valued pet to go first. While dogs might not be sterilized for fear they will die or have their personality and behavior changed, residents worry far less about their cats' survival or change since they tend to value them less than dogs, whether emotionally or economically. Shelter workers usually encounter this approach when they ask a pet owner about sterilization and the owner agrees to fix a cat. Two weeks later when the shelter worker goes to the pet owner's home to check on the cat, the owner says something like, "Oh, I have a Chihuahua too." Not realizing that the owner also had a dog, the shelter worker asks, "Did you just get the dog?" to which the owner replies, "No, we've had him." Test cats can also be outdoor or feral cats that residents have established some connection to by intermittently feeding them. If these "sacrificial cats" live and their behavior does not change, which is almost always the case, then these owners usually fix their dogs.

Testing the water usually builds confidence in the shelter, but there are exceptions that produce the opposite outcome. Surgery invariably goes well, but there are rare occasions when it does not, making owners very reluctant to sterilize any future pets, at least in the short term. For example, one man who had never sterilized an animal decided to fix his only dog—a difficult decision because the two had never been separated before dropping him off at the shelter's clinic—only to have the dog die after a seizure before surgery began. Even though the dog's death was apparently unrelated to the surgery, it deeply shook the owner and made him very frustrated with the shelter, despite being reassured that the dog's death had nothing to do with the procedure. The owner claimed that if he were to adopt another dog, he would probably not sterilize it.

Methods like testing the water and learning from the experiences of neighbors and friends exist apart from the expertise and advice that shelter workers give to pet owners. Both systems of knowledge can influence the pet owner's decision making to delay, use, or reject the shelter's services. However, local knowledge and experience about animals and their veterinary health can sometimes be misinformed and difficult to correct by shelter workers because pet owners may not share what they know and feel with workers, except for the occasional outreach worker who has established close and trusting relationships with them. This might partly explain why the shelter's efforts to educate pet owners about the need for and safety of sterilization and other services do not always lead owners to use them. Lack of knowledge, per se, is not necessarily what prevents West Charlotte pet owners from taking advantage of free or low-cost veterinary services such as sterilization; it is the kind of (local) knowledge they have that is the problem.

All that the shelter can do in the face of these two systems of knowledge is to provide information and reassurance, correct misunderstandings when they become apparent, and cultivate close working relationships with community ambassadors who are in a position to disseminate the shelter's perspective regarding animal health and veterinary care. Perhaps over time the community's experience with and understandings about these matters will align more closely with those of the shelter, but until then the shelter can only abdicate to local knowledge and adjust its own thinking, as we see next.

Changing Expectations

Workers learn to temper their expectations of local pet owners, in light of the everyday struggles they face and the prevailing norms of the West Charlotte community. Taking this approach, workers focus on the big picture of what can reasonably be expected from these pet owners given their limited resources, customary practices, and how they care for and feed their children and themselves. "They are doing the best they can with all they have," observed one shelter worker. Consequently, staff members relax, but do not ignore, many of their pet-keeping ideals except for sterilization, which is clung to as the key feature of veterinary outreach.

One way they modify their thinking is to accept the practice of keeping pets outside. While some dogs in West Charlotte are kept inside homes, many, especially larger breeds like pit bulls, are chained outside in driveways or backyards, so roaming is not an issue as it is elsewhere, such as in the rural small towns of Costa Rica, although it is to some degree with cats. While usually considered to be pets, larger breeds are kept outside because they also serve to protect property. So shelter workers and advocacy organizations (e.g., Beyond Fences) focus on getting dogs off chains and into fenced-in backyards with doghouses rather than to encourage these dogs to be kept inside homes.

When possible, fences are built and doghouses are delivered for West Charlotte pet owners, although shelter workers realize that not all owners can have fences built for them because demand exceeds supply, landlords do not always approve of fences on their property, or owners fail to have their outdoor pets sterilized—a requirement of the coalition.

Shelter workers also come to accept that outdoor dogs in West Charlotte will often be chained. The city's law says no chain can be more than one-tenth of the dog's body weight and has to be 10 feet long, but shelter workers understand that for some dogs this regulation is impractical. For example, a 70-pound aggressive pit bull could break the largest chain legally allowed by the city, so its owner will use a heavier chain, although many people from outside the community would frown on this and using it violates the law.[6] While new workers often flinch when seeing these chains, those with more experience have learned that using a large and heavy chain, from the owner's perspective, is the only way they will feel assured that their dogs will not break them and go missing.

Expectations are also adjusted for how everyday pet owners should feed their animals, even if this falls short of the shelter's ideal. When pet owners come to the Food Bank or the Wellness Clinic, shelter workers strongly encourage them to regularly feed healthier food to their dogs and cats, but recognize the reality many West Charlotte residents face when it comes to feeding family members and themselves as well as their pets. Workers learn that these pet owners often have limited access to food—whether for animals or for themselves—because they live in food deserts (Walker et al., 2010) with few grocery and pet stores near their homes. For example, it would take about five minutes for a West Charlotte pet owner to drive to a grocery or pet store, if they had a car. Without a car, it would take about an hour to reach these stores by bus. Once there, the pet owner could buy only what could easily be carried on the bus, which is usually only enough pet food to fit in a cart the size of a carry-on suitcase. And even if people can afford to buy in bulk to save money, which they usually cannot, they would not be able to get it home on public transportation. The few who would be able to get it home typically have no place to store it.

Without easy access to a pet store, Walmart, or well-stocked grocery store (they are about a mile or more away from most West Charlotte residents), pet owners are left buying poorer grade and unspecialized pet food at a local Dollar Store or gas station where the price is marked up and options are usually limited to products like Alpo, Kibbles 'n Bits, Gravy Train, and Ol' Roy. There is no way, then, for these pet owners to try a different product if their animals have food allergies or if they have to buy or avoid certain nutrients (e.g., a cat with bladder stones needs particular pet foods made for feline urinary problems). And if they cannot afford what is readily available at local stores, they often feed leftovers to their pets, which might be unhealthy for them to eat and could be tomorrow's lunch for a family that is likely struggling to feed itself.

Ultimately, then, shelter workers lower their expectations for how pets are fed in West Charlotte, given owners' everyday realities, plus the fact that the Food Bank is sometimes closed because it has too little food to give away and some pet owners cannot routinely get to the shelter the two Saturdays each month the bank is open. With lowered expectations, workers rationalize less-than-ideal feeding by not dismissing pet owners who feed table scraps or even part of their own meals to pets because this shows they care about their animals, even if this falls short of a proper veterinary diet. And they frown upon outsiders who cannot appreciate the situation faced by most West Charlotte pet owners because they do not give their animals two meals a day with large portions of nutritious pet food when the owners themselves can afford eating only one big meal every other day. As one shelter worker explained, "I could go tell them that it is healthier for their dog to get a meal twice a day in this amount, but if they're still eating one meal every other day and that sustains them, then how can we say they're doing something wrong? Money they spend for pet food, that's money they could use to feed themselves every other day."

The kind of circumstances faced by West Charlotte pet owners also can make it difficult to bring animals to the shelter for basic care, again forcing workers to rethink how owners behave and to focus on the bigger picture to ensure that pets get appropriate veterinary care. For example, staff members did not chastise a local resident who drove his sick pet to the shelter in the back of a pickup truck. They were pleased that he brought in the animal to be treated. "Maybe that's not the best way to get an animal to the shelter because something could happen, but they're doing it," noted a senior shelter employee. Less experienced shelter workers and volunteers sometimes have to be reminded to not be aggressive and unrealistic with local pet owners—an attitude called "rescue brain" at the shelter—and instead make allowances for owners, given their difficult situations. In one case, a pet owner came to Wellness Clinic, which started at 10 o'clock on a Wednesday—a school day—to make sure her pet was properly vaccinated. She brought her two children with her, thinking they would miss only a few hours of school. One of the volunteers at the Food Bank was a social worker and took it upon herself to call the school and report the children as truants, despite being told by a senior staff member to not make the call. She was subsequently let go for doing this. "Some people are very, very black-and-white," explained one staff member familiar with this situation.

Appreciating their often trying circumstances means that shelter workers find themselves accepting less than ideal veterinary results when West Charlotte owners treat their sick or injured pets. Given the shelter's limited funding and staffing, animals may be helped but can have compromised medical outcomes. For example, one pet owner using the Chicago Pets for Life Program had a cat whose paw was so severely injured it could not walk on it. Proper orthopedic surgery would cost between $4,000 and $5,000, far beyond what the Pet for Life program could afford, and certainly beyond the reach of the owner. Unable to pay for such expensive surgery, the program suggested a more modest approach costing far less where the cat might limp but the fracture would still heal and the cat would have a reasonable quality of life. Doing this required splinting the paw and changing bandages every week, things the owner could not do. But taking her cat to the veterinarian for rebandaging each week was also not an option, so the shelter sent one of its staff members to the veterinarian's office to learn how to change the bandages, enabling her to visit the pet owner at home and do the bandaging there. Although it now limps, the fracture otherwise healed.

Providing such home care and offering free or low-cost services not only keeps pets in homes but also prevents them from entering the shelter system, if they are eligible, or going to animal control, where they might be euthanized. This pleases shelter workers, but lowered expectations for veterinary outcomes—as is true of lowered expectations for chaining or feeding pets—create mixed emotions for new shelter workers and volunteers. Their focus on the big picture of getting animals better care and feeding can be dimmed by what is possible, even with the shelter's help.

Working With Objectionable Owners

Finally, workers have learned to tolerate or turn a blind eye to the practices of certain dog owners that are opposed by the shelter. Practices such as dog breeding and dogfighting contradict the organization's mission or can be cruel and illegal. The shelter objects to animal breeding because it contributes to overpopulation, increases demand for free and low-cost veterinary services, and puts more animals at risk of dying or suffering during gestation, birth, or infancy. Dogfighting is strongly opposed by the shelter because dogs are tortured, are disposed of when no longer good fighters, suffer from wounds that go untreated, are bred to be used as bait, and are not always cared for on an everyday basis. As workers try to transcend their objections to these practices by focusing on the bigger picture of promoting animal welfare, they develop strategies to work with breeders and dogfighters so they vaccinate and sterilize at least some of their animals.

To work with local breeders, shelter workers modify their expectations and employ special strategies to deal with them. When encountering breeders who staunchly oppose fixing their animals, workers do not abandon their goal of sterilization but instead build cordial relationships with them and gradually introduce the idea of sterilizing a single animal, hoping that after breeders sterilize one they will subsequently fix more. For example, one pet owner had several terriers and pit bulls that he was breeding for profit. At first, he was adamantly opposed to sterilizing any of his dogs and would not even share his name or phone number with the outreach worker on the case. In response, the worker offered to sterilize his puppies so that their new owners could not breed them and cut into his business. Although the breeder brushed off this offer, he did consent to sterilize one of his favorite dogs that was soon to be retired from breeding after the worker reminded him that fixing the dog would mean it would likely live a longer and healthier life. Although the breeder has not yet sterilized a second dog, the outreach worker on the case continues to build rapport while supporting the welfare of the breeder's dogs, hoping he will agree to fix others in the future. Of course, lowering expectations of breeders to sterilize at least some of their animals does not always work; some never come around to this incremental approach.

West Charlotte breeders are also tolerated and given free or low-cost services for the sake of their animals' health, as noted earlier. The same people visit the shelter with a new set of puppies every few weeks, expecting to get free or low-cost vaccinations before selling their dogs. Shelter workers believe that if they prevent these breeders from getting services like vaccinations, they would probably not take their animals to a regular veterinarian because of the added cost. In turn, these unvaccinated dogs can get life-threatening diseases, something shelter workers occasionally see when very sick dogs come in with diseases like parvo that were bought from a backyard breeder who did not get the animals vaccinated but perhaps lied to the buyer, saying the dogs were vaccinated and giving them doctored vaccination certificates from prior dogs. Because of this reality, shelter workers err on the side of ensuring all dogs are vaccinated rather than risk that some are not.

Shelter workers even come to appreciate some West Charlotte dog breeders when they encourage other pet owners to sterilize and care for their animals. For example, Henry was a local breeder labeled "red" by the shelter (green—yes, yellow—maybe, orange, and red—definitely no) because he, like most breeders, adamantly opposed sterilizing any of his animals. One day an outreach worker was returning a pet owner's dog that had just been fixed and surprisingly bumped into Henry who was sitting on the owner's couch. Not expecting to see Henry, the worker asked why he was there. Henry explained that the pet owner was his mother and that she needed to have her dog fixed, so he told her to call the shelter. "You recommended me to someone?" asked the outreach worker. "Oh yeah, and I also recommended this person and this person and this person," he responded. In fact, Henry recommended about 30 animals to be sterilized in nine months. Even though someone like Henry does not get his own animals fixed, he and other breeders like him may still believe in sterilization as a good thing to do for animals and the community at large.

Shelter workers also try to provide some basic care to animals owned by local residents who are suspected of selling or using dogs for fighting, a process that is largely guesswork. Workers do not automatically conclude that a dog's aggressive behavior means that it is being used for fighting because some local residents have unsocialized dogs chained in their backyards that are not used for fighting but are brought to the shelter wearing muzzles. But occasionally a dog will come in for a vaccination at the Wellness Clinic that looks "busted up" with bites on its legs, scars all over its body, and a terrified look that suggest it might have been injured in a dogfight, although dogs in this condition more often come in to animal control. Or a dog will come in just for the legally required rabies vaccination, but it has cropped ears, does not like anyone to touch it, and is very aggressive toward other dogs at the clinic, requiring the staff to do the vaccination in the owner's car. Or puppies will be brought into the sterilization clinic by the English-speaking children of suspected dogfighters who remain in their parked cars and claim not to speak English to avoid registering and being recognized at the front desk, despite having spoken English at a prior visit.

Despite their strong suspicions, shelter workers do not always feel they have "really good proof" from a 10-minute interaction that these dogs are being used for fighting, so they usually err on the side of providing veterinary services for the good of the animals. In cases of suspected dogfighting, most dogs are given vaccinations, but the staff might subtly acknowledge to the owners that they have this suspicion by saying things like, "Where did he get this gash?" But some are not treated. If the children of dogfighters are sent into clinics in lieu of adults sitting in their cars, they are told only adults can sign up for services like a rabies vaccination, which means the dogs do not get vaccinated unless the owners come forward. Nor does the shelter treat injuries on suspected fighting dogs because it is unequipped to do so, despite owners secretly hoping they will be taken care of at the clinic.

Although providing low-cost veterinary care to these animals, from the perspective of workers, does not endorse their abuse or mistreatment, they can still have some reservations about helping breeders and significant misgivings about helping dogfighters, especially for those new on the job. While never losing sight of their focus on furthering animal welfare, workers can have an uneasy relationship with breeders and sometimes a tense one with dogfighters whose behavior cannot be approved. In the end, workers live with these complications as part of the job and the occasional contradictions it carries.

A cultural, social, and knowledge gap exists between shelters and West Charlotte pet owners. Strain and misunderstandings, so often reported between shelters and local pet owners, should result. But to reduce this tension and increase the use of basic veterinary services, the shelter considers how everyday life in a disadvantaged community and its local culture might affect the willingness and ability of pet owners to vaccinate, sterilize, properly feed, and provide basic treatments to their animals. By adjusting how these services are delivered and the ways workers think about West Charlotte's pets and their owners, the shelter moves closer to thinking like the community it serves. While not eliminating the tension that has long complicated the relationships between shelters and pet owners, these efforts to become community competent have enabled the shelter to lessen it. Rather than strain between workers and pet owners, there is an attempt to understand, offer sympathy, and improve the lot of both animals and people in the community.

Some of these culturally competent approaches stem from formal shelter policy, such as not having a means test to weed out users of services who are middle-income pet owners, but other approaches are more ad hoc and informal and need to be learned by workers and volunteers as part of their socialization into the shelter's culture. Although being culturally competent is part of Pets for Life's mission statement and is embraced by the shelter in general when dealing with any West Charlotte pet owner, learning how to think and behave this way can be challenging for new shelter workers who encounter pet owners, especially when doing outreach. The shelter has no training manual or even informal notes about how exactly to interact with the West Charlotte population, and sometimes an experienced outreach worker quits the shelter before being replaced by someone who is inexperienced. Nor is there a special cultural screening process for job suitability when interviewing candidates to be hired as outreach workers.

New workers who are lucky get to observe more experienced peers who model what to say and how to behave when having face-to-face encounters with pet owners. But others starting to work or volunteer at the shelter have to figure it out for themselves, and some do it better and quicker than others. For example, during door-to-door outreach in West Charlotte, a recently hired outreach worker hesitated before knocking on a pet owner's door and turned to the first author, asking for detailed guidance on how to interact with and approach this and other West Charlotte pet owners regarding their use of the shelter's basic services. She explained that without any "tips" from other outreach workers on how to do this, she did not know the best way to approach these people about potentially sensitive topics like sterilization. She and many shelter workers learn by trial and error on their own how to deal with or over-come some of the racial, ethnic, and class differences between themselves and underserved pet owners.

Even after workers learn how to be culturally competent, the shelter's ef-forts are not perfect. Attempts to empower pet owners by letting them de-cide whether to use basic veterinary care do not always succeed, as is true with other disadvantaged groups that are empowered by those who oversee or govern them (e.g., McKee & Cooper, 2008). Instead of using the shelter's free or low-cost services, some pet owners fall back on long-held misconcep-tions, personal experiences, and residual doubt about what shelter workers tell them, so they disregard or delay acting on information or advice they are given about their animals. Although not every pet in West Charlotte will be vaccinated for every medical risk nor will every pet be sterilized, most pet owners use at least some of the shelter's basic services. Even if this is not opti-mal, the alternative to getting some care is no care—an outcome that is unac-ceptable to staff members who are familiar with the problems faced by West Charlotte residents.

Accepting that cultural competence does not always work is yet one more adjustment by shelter workers. Indeed, the shelter's motto—"Perfect is the enemy of good"—is a constant reminder to workers and volunteers that dif-fusing basic veterinary care means raising the welfare of pets in West Char-lotte, not reproducing or expecting animals to be cared for as they are in less disadvantaged communities. Some pet owners will still use heavy chains to restrain dogs, feed their animals irregularly or with poor-quality food, breed or use them in dogfighting, try to use services they are not entitled to, trans-port their animals to the shelter in unsafe ways, and fail to provide veteri-nary care for sick or injured animals. But after talking with shelter workers, most pet owners decide to sterilize their animals, vaccinate them, and pro-vide veterinary care for many basic medical problems. Workers, then, pur-sue the "good" rather than achieve the "perfect" because this is all they can do, given the resources available at the shelter, the adjustments its staff can make, the realities pet owners face, and the culture that shapes their thinking and behavior.

In the process of becoming culturally competent, shelter workers are not the only ones who adjust their thinking and behavior; so too do pet owners. While some owners do not change how they care for their animals, such as keeping them chained in the backyard, others change their behavior by taking their pets for at least some basic treatments, if not sterilization too, and per-haps by feeding them somewhat better, or at least at a lower cost, than before. Indeed, as we see next, using the shelter's services and coming into contact with its staff can change even more in the lives of West Charlotte pet owners.

CHAPTER SEVEN

Forms of Veterinary Capital

THE UNINTENDED CONSEQUENCES
OF INCREASED ACCESS

The goal of sterilizing dogs and cats is to reduce animal overpopulation and the problems it causes for animals and people. Unwanted dogs and cats may be killed or suffer from malnutrition and various untreated afflictions. Especially in developing countries, they can threaten people, cause disease, and create disorder (Arluke & Atema, 2017). In most modern Western nations, these problems are unusual because pets tend to be not only sterilized but also vaccinated, treated for conditions like worms and mange, and confined indoors or behind fences or secured with a leash, chain, or rope. Animals are healthier and people are rarely threatened or disturbed by them. However, this may not be true in many disadvantaged communities, which is why programs provide veterinary interventions at little or no cost to underserved pet owners. If effective, these programs can improve animal health and welfare while reducing whatever disorder the pets might cause if loose on the street.

However, diffusing basic veterinary services and animal care to underserved communities can do more than reduce animal overpopulation and its attendant problems—the intended goals of this policy. Using them might also impact pet owners themselves in personal ways because social policy applications can have unintended consequences (Merton, 1936) that were not conceived of in advance or intended by policy makers (Perri 6, 2012). While these unexpected outcomes can sometimes be unwelcome or benign, they can also be welcome surprises (Hirschman, 1991).

One surprise of providing basic animal care is that it can promote greater interconnectedness, sometimes an unintended consequence of other social policies too (Margetts et al., 2012). Using the shelter's free and low-cost services can lead to closer ties between pet owners and shelter workers as well as with their own dogs and cats, or what we call veterinary capital. Although these services are not primarily delivered to benefit pet owners' lives by heightening their social connections and animal bonds, the fact that they do so is no less important when assessing their full impact on underserved communities.

The concept of veterinary capital stems from social capital theory, which argues that relationships develop from mutual acquaintance, recognition, and obligation, which in turn lead to feelings of gratitude, respect, and friendship along with access to other resources available through the contacts or connections networks bring. Nor do these social ties have to be profound or long-lasting to have such impact. For example, through "weak ties" (Granovetter, 1973) and "friends of friends" (Boissevain, 1974), network members can gain privileged access to useful information and opportunities. In addition, people can acquire a new social status or desired reputation because they have these contacts, although gains in status resulting from new associations have been reported only in elite organizations where membership is relatively restricted (D'Aveni & Kesner, 1993); nevertheless, it seems equally likely that similar gains can occur in everyday life when lower-status individuals associate with those having higher social status in the community. As with social capital, then, veterinary capital looks at how pet owners form ties, even if weak, with other people and develop new statuses in the process.

Veterinary capital is also similar to yet different from another concept, animal capital—when pets lead to greater cooperation and trust in the community by increasing their owners' social ties with neighbors and friends as well as their sense of having shared values and understandings. Pets can encourage and strengthen interpersonal connections among humans by making people appear to be less threatening, by giving them something to talk about with a joint focus, and by becoming a source of resource sharing and support (Arkow, 2013; Wood et al., 2005), whether that interaction occurs in dog parks or on neighborhood streets (Graham & Glover, 2014).

With veterinary capital, it is the delivery of services for animals rather than informal interaction with owners and their pets that is responsible for deepening social connections and cooperation, and this interaction may be with not only neighbors but also shelter workers and veterinary staff members. Moreover, veterinary capital, unlike animal capital, can strengthen social ties between people and their pets as the shelter services they use draw them closer to their animals, while creating new statuses for owners that can change their identities. These new ties and identities result from inclusionary and exclusionary cultural capital as well as bridging and bonding capital.

Inclusionary Capital

People express their social status or standing in society relative to other groups by drawing on cultural capital. This capital can be embodied within individuals in the form of knowledge, skills, and behaviors or objectified externally through owned objects that signal to other people what kind of and how much cultural capital someone possesses (Bourdieu, 2011). However, class, race, ethnicity, and other demographic factors influence the resources available for people to demonstrate where they fit in society as well as present them with different issues as to how or whether they should fit in.

For minority or low-status group members, cultural capital allows them to express in- and out-group affiliations. Those who are cultural mainstreamers (Carter, 2003) accept the ideology that minority group members should be socially, economically, and politically assimilated with society's dominant group and use their available cultural capital to project this position, while those who are cultural straddlers draw on their cultural capital to identify with both their respective ethnoracial community as well as the mainstream.

Many West Charlotte pet owners who use some or all of the shelter's basic services are cultural straddlers. They affiliate with society at large by providing a level of veterinary concern and care that is more in line with mainstream pet care than is traditional in West Charlotte, while affiliating with the black community by interacting with their pets in ethnoracially unique ways. Pet keeping and caring can facilitate such straddling because pets are tangible objects that can also serve as symbols to gain social status and construct identity for anyone regardless of demographic background (Tipper, 2011). Dogs in particular have been shown to be used as props to frame certain kinds of identities, such as gender (Ramirez, 2006) and family (Tannen, 2010).[1]

But what animals specifically say about their owners and to whom will vary from group to group because animals, much like inanimate objects, can signal certain meanings between different groups and project or signal sought-after identities to people outside one's community, just as scholars have observed in other contexts (Veevers, 1985). To affiliate with mainstream pet keeping, some West Charlotte pet owners use animals and the basic veterinary services they receive to signal normalcy to people not from their part of town. They do this by telling stories about their affection and caring for pets to situate themselves in the larger societal narrative about pets being members of the family (Tovares, 2010). Motivation for such signaling stems from West Charlotte pet owners' awareness of a general bias against them that assumes people living in poverty or having very low income must not be very good pet owners because of their alleged irresponsibility and lack of attachment to pets.

To counter this negative image, having a pet dog in a poor family can symbolize that the family, by its outward appearance, is like any middle- or upper-class family, just as pets in family photographs normalize black and LGBT families (Matthews, 2003), or at least that the family is different from other families in their community, especially if they take good care of their animals. Indeed, many West Charlotte residents want the shelter staff to see their pet ownership as a signal that they care about their animals like any middle-class white pet owner, unlike those West Charlotte pet owners who do not and happen to be African Americans in or near poverty. To separate themselves from these other West Charlotte pet owners, they will declare, "I'm not like other people around here," regarding the quality of their pet care or name and criticize local pet owners who allegedly do not take good care of their animals, even though the latter may be very caring and responsible pet owners. This fear (of a negative perception) explains, at least in part, why so many pet owners interviewed for this book strongly emphasized how well they took care of their pets and how much they "loved" them, even though they were not asked directly about this. But because the interviewer was a white outsider to West Charlotte, pet owners likely assumed that he might question their ability to be responsible and caring owners.

Signaling they are good pet owners by using the shelter's free and discounted veterinary services conveys a different cultural message in West Charlotte. Some people in the community view their pets as a form of personal property, and having the shelter examine and treat them is thought to be a type of conscientious property maintenance, which they would do with any possession that gives them pride. They are proud to take care of their homes, their cars, and their yards and will often point out how well they have taken care of these things when shelter workers visit their homes. By saying in so many words "See how well I do this," the pet owners are telling shelter workers that they take good care of all their important possessions—including but not limited to their pets—unlike some neighbors.

While differentiating themselves from other West Charlotte pet owners, these owners simultaneously affiliate with the local African American community by distinguishing their pet keeping from that of middle-class whites. They accomplish the latter by using their pets to assert collective black identity more generally—a type of identity not of individuals but of a group whose meaning is partially defined by what (or who) the group is not. However, collective black identity means different things to different segments of the black community (Demo & Hughes, 1990). How low-income and poor black pet owners in West Charlotte viewed and treated their animals enabled them to define their identity as neither white nor middle class to people inside and outside their community, just as many African Americans avoid "acting white" as part of their collective black identity (Ogbu, 2004) by not behaving in certain ways.

Some West Charlotte pet owners who used the shelter's basic services signaled their collective black identity by saying they interacted differently with pets than did white owners. By racially distinguishing their animal relationships, these owners communicate their black identity to themselves, neighbors, friends, and strangers, just as they do with other behaviors, such as rejecting academic success (Fordham & Ogbu, 1986). For example, many black West Charlotte pet owners are aware that they restrict their pets' movement inside homes more than do most middle-class white owners. When kept inside, dogs rarely have the run of the entire home. Bedrooms are almost always off limits, so dogs will not sleep with their owners. Often, if there are two floors in the home, pets will be excluded from the entire second floor because bedrooms are there. Commonly, pets are also excluded from living rooms, or if allowed there, they cannot sit on the furniture. Instead, inside dogs are most likely kept in kitchens or family rooms, where they might have a small bed or pillow to sleep on, or perhaps they are kept in a cage at night. In addition to restricting pets from certain rooms or floors, West Charlotte pet owners also occasionally joke about how only white people let dogs lick their faces or call them their "kids," a finding consistent with Anderson (1990), who reported that some blacks were perplexed by whites' or middle-class blacks' friendly relations with dogs, where, for example, they would let them run free inside homes or display physical affection toward them. However, Anderson acknowledges that antipathy for the presumed middle-class treatment of pets may also exist among working-class white pet owners.

West Charlotte pet owners justified their distancing from pets. Some feared overly rambunctious pets in the home would destroy their furniture or floors. One resident said that her dog would damage or soil the carpet, so she kept her pet in the kitchen, which was the only uncarpeted room. Others simply kept larger dogs outside after first trying them out inside. When they first acquire large dogs, West Charlotte families often keep them inside until they start destroying furniture and rugs, at which point they are put outside on a chain or behind a fence. Other owners just think that "big dogs don't belong in the house" and "naturally" want to be outside, compared with smaller dogs, which are usually kept inside, tightly woven into the family's routines and interior spaces. Others think dogs are "smelly" or "dirty," so they should not freely roam inside homes. Perceiving dogs as smelly or dirty sometimes stemmed from a specific event, such as seeing the pet roll in the dirt or carry a dead animal in its mouth. At these times, they were seen as somewhat less humanized companions, although still clearly loved in most cases, just as such dirty or smelly pets might be seen by middle-class white pet owners (Borthwick,

2006). But at other times, dogs—especially larger ones kept outside—were just seen as inherently dirty creatures, even if they never covered themselves with dirt, played in leaves, or trolled through garbage cans. This subcultural frame in West Charlotte sees most dogs and cats as less pure and more ritually polluted or unclean than humans, hence they are best kept at a distance—a belief and practice remotely similar to those held in Islam and Rabbinic Judaism (Menache, 1997).

Collective black identity can also be signaled through the names of pets when cultural straddlers use the shelter's free and low-cost services. Just as racial differences exist on a wide range of cultural dimensions, including the choice of human names (Fryer & Levitt, 2004), the choice of pet names can also function as identity markers. Of course many pets in West Charlotte had names that did not signal group identity, nor would we expect that. People choose different ways to signal identities that are important to them, and pet naming is but one way. That only some people did so is still socially significant because pet names carry into an owner's interactions with other people as friends, neighbors, strangers, and shelter staff members hear or are told the pet's name and respond accordingly. So any one pet may be introduced, and potentially signal black identity, to dozens of people inside and outside the pet owner's neighborhood.

Some West Charlotte residents named family pets after iconic figures in black popular culture to extend these symbolic connections, such as the hip-hop star Pettidee. Other racially identified names, such as Gangsta, playfully drew on stereotypical images of the black underclass that conjured drugs, weapons, and other antisocial behavior. And yet other names, such as White Devil, reinforced intergroup differences between blacks and whites. Although often chosen in jest, these names nevertheless poked fun at what to many residents seemed like a huge racial divide. With equal parts of humor and seriousness, one resident felt that her pet's name disqualified her or made some neighbors question her community identity. She said, "I can't be a good representative [of black identity] because I have a terrier named Oliver—what kind of name is that? It's old English."

When West Charlotte residents think their pets' names might racially offend some people, they may choose not to use them or make up a fake name, although not all name switching is intended to avoid racial or intergroup awkwardness; it can also be to avoid embarrassment when pets have obscene or very derogatory names. For example, West Charlotte pet owners visiting the shelter for services will sometimes hesitate to register their pets with the pets' actual names because they are embarrassed and instead make up names on the spot that they think would be more palatable to white shelter workers. That happened with the owner of White Devil, who changed the pet's name to Toby when she registered for free vaccinations at the shelter's Wellness Clinic. Yet such name changing was rare; pet names that signaled black identity were typically used in interactions with others, just as any pet name would be. Such awkwardness is yet one more reminder of their cultural straddling, as these West Charlotte residents negotiated the use of pet names to work both at home in the community and with strangers not from their community at the shelter.

Exclusionary Capital

Cultural capital can also be used as a tool of social exclusion by which individuals and their communities become polarized and socially differentiated (Barry, 1998) as groups bar others from membership or access (Waldinger, 1995) and make them feel as though they do not belong (Wessels & Miedema, 2002). Although exclusionary capital is a tool or skill, when the members of any group signal their social separation from others they usually do it unconsciously because the process is learned through socialization and incorporated into cultural codes as habit and custom (Bourdieu, 1977; Lamont & Lareau, 1988). As part of the unconscious cultural codes of some groups, animals can become such tools to demarcate social boundaries. For example, the process of taking care of pigeons enabled Turkish men living in Berlin to reinforce their Turkish ethnicity and culture in opposition to the surrounding German society where they lived (Jerolmack, 2007).

West Charlotte pet owners also use animals to exclude perceived outsiders to their community, while straddling culture by agreeing to have their animals sterilized, vaccinated, and treated at the shelter as well as fed through the shelter's Food Bank. As a tool of social exclusion, these pets are not so much symbolic devices to tie residents into their ethnoracial identity as they are a way to signal an identity that is in contrast or opposition to that held by another group in close proximity. This signaling is displayed effortlessly and naturally to create racial boundaries from others, especially in some parts of the city that are undergoing gentrification, causing discomfort and even friction between longtime residents and newcomers.

In these contested neighborhoods, black and Hispanic residents often have tense relationships with developers and new people moving into their neighborhoods who are often white and in search of affordable housing. Prior residents face the dilemma of staying put or selling their homes to developers and making it less likely that future generations can live in these traditionally black low-income neighborhoods (Clasen-Kelly, 2017). These groups, which have different stakes in maintaining or changing the neighborhood, are suddenly face-to-face and must negotiate the meaning of public space that is now shared.

Some West Charlotte residents who used the shelter's basic services had dogs, especially pit bulls, that served as living boundary markers to separate themselves as longtime black or Hispanic residents from newcomers.[2] For longtime residents in these sections of town, owning a stereotypical large and threatening dog helped to maintain racial boundaries by visibly showing and reminding newcomers that their new neighborhood is not theirs. To many people from outside the community, the presence of "dangerous" dogs like pit bulls in urban areas characterizes their owners as aggressive "thugs" (Harding, 2013; Weaver, 2013) and can be perceived as a threat to normative whiteness (Tarver, 2014).[3] As one West Charlotte resident explained, newcomers on his block would be threatened by his pit-bull-owning neighbor: "Just by looking at him [the dog], people out of his neighborhood were threatened." Even if they are not threatened by these dogs, the mere fact that former residents far more commonly own pit bulls or similar large dogs than do newcomers is itself a way to mark intergroup boundaries.

For their part, newcomers can also use dogs to signal intergroup differences and demarcate social and physical boundaries, in this case with longtime residents. While owning dogs facilitated neighborly relationships and built friendships for newcomers, they were usually with other newcomers, most of whom were white, a finding reported in other cites also having diverse populations (Mayorga-Gallo, 2018). In that respect, dogs become tools to form cliques that establish group boundaries (Bueker, 2013). In addition, the type of dogs owned by newcomers helped to maintain racial boundaries because they were very different from pit bulls or similarly stereotyped breeds. Like upper-middle-class whites in other towns who are suddenly living in black working-class neighborhoods (Tissot, 2011), they choose small or "elegant" dog breeds rather than those that show strength or aggressiveness associated with working-class dogs, so they can assert their own class-specific values and display their wealth.

Newcomers in these contested parts of West Charlotte can also signal intergroup differences by claiming that a neighbor's dog is dangerous or threatening. Tensions between old and new residents, some of whom used the shelter's services, could spill over and be expressed through dog complaints typically leveled against the pit bulls of black neighbors who had lived in West Charlotte for years. In one case, a black husband and wife, who were longtime residents and users of the shelter's basic services, had a newer white neighbor who filed a complaint to animal control against their pit bull, Sailor, who they said escaped from its kennel and barked at a cable company repairman, allegedly causing him to have a heart attack and leading animal control to designate the dog as "dangerous" and needing to be euthanized. Shelter workers familiar with the dog and its owners knew it was not dangerous and inter-

vened to prevent Sailor's death and to gain its release. After Sailor was returned to his owners, the neighbor continued to allege to animal control that
this dog was a danger and that he kept escaping, even though he had not. Ultimately, animal control considered this to be a case of harassment by the com-
plainant and no longer investigated it.

However, there was more sociologically to the tensions over Sailor than
mere bickering between neighbors over whether he did or did not behave in
certain ways. Clearly, the newcomers used a racial logic to maintain boundaries by stereotypically interpreting nonwhite dog ownership as irresponsible and dangerous (Mayorga-Gallo, 2018). And the pit bull owners understood
that these complaints about their dogs' allegedly dangerous behavior communicated, in so many words, that they—both people and animals—were deval-
ued and unwelcome in the neighborhood.

Whether the cultural capital of pets is used to separate groups as we have
just seen or to identify with an ethnoracial community as described earlier in
this chapter, people using the shelter's services are cultural straddlers. They
understand the cultural code of dog ownership and use it to change their status position accordingly to draw boundaries from outsiders viewed as interlopers or connect with their own group's identity, while maintaining a link to
mainstream society every time they visit the shelter, talk with its staff, and
have their pets cared for there.

Of course, using dogs as inclusionary or exclusionary capital is just one
small part of a collection of many other behaviors, most of which have nothing to do with pets or their care, that people draw upon to tell themselves and
others who they are and to draw ethnoracial boundaries from groups that are
culturally different. Nevertheless, when combined with other forms of veterinary capital, such signaling through pet ownership and the use of the shelter's
basic services becomes a significant means to create and communicate self-
and group identities.

Bridging Capital

Weak social ties can form among people who differ on key personal characteristics or who normally do not come together, or what is known as bridging
capital. These ties have the potential to create a flow of information, obliga-
tions, expectations, sympathy, trust, and the ability to work together to solve
problems (Bhandari & Yasunobu, 2009). Because relationships can develop
that link people across social cleavages usually dividing groups from each
other, such as race or class, bridging capital is crucial for mobilizing resources
to solve community problems (van Oorschot et al., 2006).

Bridging capital can form inadvertently in West Charlotte when its residents interact with shelter workers who talk with them about using free or low-cost veterinary services and the needs of their pets. Opportunities to form loose social ties can occur when outreach workers visit their homes, when residents bring their pets to the shelter for its Wellness Clinic or sterilization surgery, or when residents cannot bring their animals to the shelter and call workers to discuss their pets' issues on the phone.

Social ties are most likely to emerge between outreach workers and community ambassadors, or pet owners who strongly endorse the shelter and its programs to others in the community. Knowing that their recommendations can carry special weight with neighborhood peers, shelter workers work hard to build relationships with them so that they will continue to recommend the shelter's services to peers. To secure relationships with potential ambassadors, outreach workers pay extra visits, often monthly, to their homes to chat about their animals or perhaps to drop off some extra pet food and toys. The visits are very warm and informal, with ambassadors sharing personal information about their family, work, and health. After several visits, many ambassadors start to view outreach workers as both animal "social workers" and friends.

Bridging capital can also develop between shelter workers and everyday pet owners in West Charlotte, especially when workers help them with their animal problems, whether that is to provide access to services, veterinary information, pet supplies, or pet-keeping skills. For example, pet owners might call outreach workers to report that they think their animals look sick and to ask if they could make a house call to examine them, which workers will sometimes do. Or owners may just ask questions about their pets' health when the outreach workers have their next "touch" (i.e., speaking contact) with them. Sometimes the help is unsolicited when the outreach worker sees an animal-related problem and intervenes to help. A case in point, during one home visit a worker saw that the pet owner's dog was emaciated to the point where some people would call animal control but instead got the owner a large bag of dog food, along with a bowl and scoop. In addition to food, outreach workers will give owners pet collars, toys, and medication for fleas and ticks or worms, while owners going to the bimonthly Food Bank also come away with unexpected free collars and toys in addition to the food. Occasionally, pet owners also get free doghouses or even have their backyard fenced in.

Outreach workers show interest in pet owners' animals and their personal lives to help them but also to establish rapport and trust.[4] For example, workers might play with the animals and allow owners to talk about their human-animal ties, or they might show interest in and concern for the personal problems of pet owners. During these conversations, workers may offer emotional support if pets are not faring well or if owners have their own personal, human problems. For example, one pet owner was dying of cancer and had no family and few friends to visit her in the hospital and provide support. The outreach worker on this case had grown close to this pet owner and was her main contact when hospitalized, visiting several times.

Showing interest and helping pet owners is a form of gift giving, and the giving of gifts can spark the formation of friendships not only because of the implied reciprocity but because the offer of a gift is an invitation to associate and cooperate (Sherry, 1983). However, the partnership between shelter workers and West Charlotte pet owners is unequal or imbalanced.[5] Making contact and providing presents, products, help with problems, and veterinary services are primarily instrumental behaviors done by shelter workers to get pet owners to alter their animals and, more generally, to increase the pets' quality of life. But to pet owners these acts can make them feel socially tied to shelter workers, especially those doing outreach. Normally weak social ties between shelter workers and pet owners can then be converted to stronger ties (Wilson, 1998). Indeed, there are times when a pet owner approaches a shelter worker and the former clearly appears to know and like the latter—behaving warmly and referring to the worker by his or her first name—only for the latter to not recognize the pet owner. At the end of one such imbalanced encounter, the pet owner walked off saying "I love you" to the shelter worker, who politely responded in kind without still knowing the pet owner's identity.

Further imbalance to the shelter worker–pet owner friendship stems from the exchange sparked by gift giving where the recipient feels indebted to return something of equal worth to the gift giver (Mauss, 1990). Because recipients have few or no material resources to reciprocate the gifts, if nothing else they can respond with affection for the gift giver. Pet owners often repay shelter workers for their gifts with affection, whose ties with shelter workers can become quite affective and meaningful. For example, one pet owner calls her outreach worker "my favorite white person," another tells his outreach worker that he "loves" him, and another hugs the outreach worker at first sight and when she leaves. In one case, the outreach worker gets a text every Mother's Day from a "kid I kinda got close to," but with whom she no longer works, who continues to wish her a happy holiday even though he knows she is childless.

Another way to repay the gifts of outreach workers is for pet owners to support the shelter's goal of helping the underserved care for and keep their animals. For example, owners may ask workers, with whom they have some ties, to intervene on behalf of neighbors or friends who need help with their pets. In one case, a pet owner asked an outreach worker if she could help a friend whose dog was being held at animal control because she could not afford the

fee to have it released. As the worker recalled, "I was able to negotiate to reduce the fee so the owner could pay to get this dog out of animal control. The
only way I was able to help was that someone I built a fence for is still in touch
with me. She texted me about a problem a neighbor was having with her dog."

Pet owners also try to repay shelter workers for their gifts by protecting
workers and keeping them safe when visiting West Charlotte. For example,
one day when the shelter transport was dropping off a dog at a resident's
home after being fixed, a drive-by shooting occurred. The worker recounted
what happened: "I was standing on the lady's porch explaining spay/neu-
ter after-care to her. Twelve shots went off and she grabbed me by the shirt
and pulled me into the house. She freaked out, not for herself, but because
she wanted me to get out of the house before the police shut down the road."
These protective efforts are also sometimes done to prevent shelter workers
from "buying into stereotypes" of life in low-income black neighborhoods. To
wit, the worker above speculated, "She was also embarrassed that I had seen
that. They are afraid of our perception of them. They don't want stuff to happen that would make us buy into stereotypes of the area."

Sometimes pet owners' protective efforts enable shelter workers to avoid
or remove themselves from uncomfortable or tense situations. Even if workers are not attuned to possible danger, the neighborhood will be and someone
will warn them. One worker was doing outreach and stopped on the sidewalk
to take some notes about 20 feet from a parked car with someone in it. Because the worker was new on the job, she did not know that the person in the
car was stationed there all day to deal drugs—an aspect of everyday street life
in West Charlotte that workers eventually learn. The drug dealer became increasingly uncomfortable as the outreach worker continued to stand so close
to him and write in her notebook. A pet owner living nearby saw this tense
scene unfolding, knew the worker had no idea that her presence could make
the dealer so uncomfortable, and told her to move on.

Outreach workers with more experience know that on certain West Charlotte blocks they routinely visit residents will give them a "pass" (i.e., allowed
to be present without being threatened) because they are recognized and distribute free pet toys, flea powder, medication, doghouses, and pet food to pet
owners. An outreach worker describes the reaction he got before and after residents on one street recognized him: "I went to see this guy and pulled up at his
house. Walked up to this group of 10 guys that were hanging out in front of his
house and said 'Hey guys, do you know where this guy lives?' And they started
yelling at me. 'What are you doing here?' It was scary but I just kept walking towards them. 'Oh no it's the dog guy.' And all of a sudden five guys said, 'It's the
dog guy' and started asking me for dewormer and flea and tick medicine."

Such social reciprocation by pet owners reflects the successful efforts of outreach workers to build bridging capital with the community, but weaker ties can also form among pet owners themselves when using the shelter's free and discounted services. Fleeting and weak connections form among pet owners when they visit the shelter for its Wellness Clinic or Food Bank, although these ties are spontaneous and fleeting. Brief informal communication sometimes occurs as pet owners wait for veterinary services or pet food at the shelter because they are all there with their pets waiting for similar services but with nothing to do other than to sit idly or chat with each other. However, most pet owners waiting together in the parking lot adjoining the Wellness and Spay/ Neuter Clinics, or right outside of them, do not interact with each other, and when they do, their conversation is usually limited to talking about the "cuteness" of the pets rather than their veterinary care and the use of shelter services. But even if they do not talk among themselves, they see other pet owners—sometimes numbering over 100—also coming to the shelter for free or low-cost services. This observation can validate the importance of pet care in the minds of West Charlotte residents who, prior to the visit, might not have regarded themselves as animal caregivers or even "guardians," in the loosest sense of the term. And, if nothing else, they see themselves as a part of a community of pet owners united, however briefly, through their shelter visits.

The formation of such bridging capital—whether with shelter workers or other pet owners—suggests that providing free or low-cost veterinary services can change more than animal health and welfare for the better. As the shelter delivers this care, pet owners' social world expands too as they are brought together with people in ways that would not have otherwise occurred. Although passing ties with other pet owners while waiting at the shelter are very weak social connections, they can sometimes reinforce what is often a nascent identity as pet owner and reaffirm the value of the shelter's basic services, if not more advanced veterinary care.

Certainly, the ties between pet owners and outreach workers can be more significant to owners as their reliance on, rapport, and friendship develop over time. For some, these connections were not superficial when they started to view particular shelter workers as friends or confidants.

A different kind of capital, but no less important, can also result from providing veterinary services. These interventions can lead to deep and meaningful connections with animals when they generate bonding capital. This form of social capital in human interaction (Putnam, 2000) strengthens existing ties and develops affection among people who are known to each other and have some shared history and identity together (Marshall and Stolle, 2004) as a closed network of family and friends (Sabatini, 2005). As a form of veterinary capital pet owners' contacts with shelter workers and use of the shelter's basic services can create bonding capital for people and their animals. As we see below, receiving these services enables pet owners to enjoy more-meaningful interactions with their animals and to see them as having inner lives and subjective experiences, or what Irvine (2004) calls animal selves.

Bonding Capital

An unintended consequence of using the shelter's basic services is the production of bonding capital between people and animals. Developing or deepening owners' commitment to and connection with their pets begins when owners are informed by shelter workers, volunteers, and veterinarians about sterilizing, vaccinating, or otherwise caring for their animals and subsequently undertake some or all of these measures. At these times, people are exposed to information that can undo lifelong beliefs about what constitutes proper animal care, including information about how to care for and interact with their pets as well as what veterinary treatments and other interventions are available and should be considered.

Some bonding capital can result from advice or information that shelter workers give to West Charlotte pet owners about caring for their animals in ways that can draw them closer. Some advice, if carried out, can alter a pet's behavior and, in turn, the owner's sentiment toward it. For example, some West Charlotte residents believe that the best way to stop a chained dog from knocking over its food bowl is to not feed it. Outreach workers will suggest to these owners that instead of feeding their dogs 10 cups of food every third day, a common practice in this area, they should feed them half a cup of food twice a day. If owners take this advice, their dogs will be less likely to go hungry for days, even if they knock over an occasional bowl, and if not hungry, the dogs may become friendlier and more docile, while owners will become less frustrated and more likely to feel positively toward them and to engage their pets.

Some advice is less about the practicalities of pet keeping than about the joys of having pets. If followed by West Charlotte residents, bonds with pets may be enhanced. In turn, these positive interactions might spur pet owners' interest in promoting their animals' welfare because deepening attachment can increase empathy for pets and willingness to seek veterinary care, while maintaining veterinary health helps to ensure that owners can continue having rewarding interactions with their animals.

Some of this informal teaching is intended to verbally point out what pet owners could be experiencing with their animals—whether that is a positive experience that the owner has but is not aware of and cannot articulate or one that they could have if so desired. If not pointing out the benefits of engaging pets, shelter staff members also role modeled ways to engage them, although the modeling was often done unconsciously. For example, during outreach visits, workers routinely interacted with owners' pets in very affectionate and playful ways, in part because they enjoyed the animals and liked such engagement, but also because their engaging behavior would be seen by all family members present as well as any neighbors who might be observing them.

Bonding capital can also result from the impact of using the shelter's free or discounted services on both pets and owners. If pets are chained in backyards all day, unsterilized, untreated for basic veterinary problems, and fed irregularly with innutritious food, owners may be reluctant to touch, pet, groom, play with, or even approach them because they consider their appearance to be unappealing. Pets look better after they are regularly fed more nutritious food, given basic treatments for problems like fleas, worms, or mange, and released from their chains. Owners, in turn, may behave with and feel differently toward them.

This happened with one West Charlotte resident whose dog suffered from a type of mange whose mites made it lose hair and look unsightly. Outreach workers knew that this skin problem was likely due to a poor immune system caused by the owner feeding her dog only Gravy Train, a pet food without nutritional value. They gave the owner a bag of Blue Buffalo pet food that was donated to the shelter and suggested that she mix it with the Gravy Train to combat the dog's skin problem. After the new diet eliminated the mange and the dog's appearance improved, the owner was seen petting and grooming her dog.

Behavior toward pets can also change when owners see pets acting differently after interventions by shelter workers. Pets become more approachable because their constant barking stops, as does their unruly jumping on owners, so they spend more time playing with and walking them. Fence building often produced dramatic changes in the behavior of pets and subsequently how their owners behaved with them. For example, one owner's pit bull, Whitey, was "crazy" when chained in her backyard, but after a fence was built and Whitey was unchained, its personality mellowed and it allegedly became "less crazy." Another West Charlotte resident kept her dog outside on a very short chain. The dog, a small chow, was not very friendly or approachable when outreach workers first met it. After they built a fence for it, the dog allegedly "opened up." They saw this changed behavior when they came to put up tarps for shade and found the dog to be very friendly. Days later, one of the outreach workers saw the dog's owner walking it on a leash down the street, something she never did with it prior to installing the fence. Outreach workers believed that interactions changed between this owner and her pet because chaining it caused the dog to always jump on her when approached, which in turn forced the owner to avoid interacting with the dog, making it impossible for her to get to know its personality.

Indeed, some interventions by outreach workers more fully integrated pets into the personal spaces and lives of their owners. Having a fence built and getting outdoor dogs off their chains can transform guard dogs into family pets inside homes. Charlie was a 60-year-old West Charlotte resident who agreed to have a fence built for his pit bull, Blue, who had always been chained in the backyard. Before the fence was built, Charlie did not incorporate Blue into his life, but weeks after unchaining Blue, outreach workers noticed that he was rarely outside in his fenced-in yard. Once unchained, Blue stopped barking as much and appeared less aggressive, so Charlie started to play with and spend more time with him, eventually keeping Blue inside his house. Because the behavior of pets becomes more interactive and their appearance more appealing to owners after some interventions, some dogs are allowed not just inside homes, as with Blue, but inside cars—a space that many West Charlotte pet owners typically avoid with dogs when they are seen as dirty and not close family members. One worker said that change happened with a person who drove to the clinic with her dog—recently treated at the shelter for unsightly mange—in the front seat of her car, something she never would have done in the past because the dog's skin condition made her avoid getting near it.

Use of the shelter's basic services can also directly impact the behavior of owners as well as their pets. For example, receiving services like free monthly pet food sometimes reduced West Charlotte pet owners' stress about feeding their animals, which led to closer bonds. Worry over feeding and caring for them on an everyday basis seemed to slowly corrode human-animal relationships in West Charlotte. Owners struggling with these issues often spoke about having less "energy" for or interest in engaging their pets in affective or playful ways, and their pets seemed to follow suit. The stress of worrying about the cost of veterinary services or pet food can be contagious to pets because they can empathize with human emotions (Sümegi et al., 2014). Many owners claimed that receiving free pet food, along with other veterinary services, significantly reduced their anxiety over caring for their animals since they had one less thing to worry about buying. With a reduction in their owners' stress, presumably pets' stress declined as well as they reflected the improved morale of their owners. As stress dissipated for both humans and animals, the behavior and demeanor of pets became more amiable while owners became more engaging, in turn drawing both closer.

Using the shelter's services can help to preserve bonding capital rather than merely create it. Some owners have problems managing pets that make it difficult to keep them and raise the possibility of their surrender. An inter-vention like building a fence can prevent an outdoor dog from frequently es-caping and make all the difference between surrendering the animal to the shelter and keeping it. In one case, a West Charlotte pet owner had a pit bull that kept breaking off its chain and escaping. The owner was frustrated and grew tired of dealing with the escapes because she could not prevent them from repeatedly happening, so she decided to surrender the dog despite her fondness for it. Also weighing on her were the cost of pet food as well as the difficulty of going to a store to buy it because of recent unemployment and dis-ability. To remedy these problems and make it easier for her to keep the dog, the shelter built a fence to retain the unruly pet and provided needed pet food, although the shelter could bring the food only occasionally. These steps en-abled the owner to not only keep her dog but also spend more time with it, un-til a tree fell on her house, severely damaging it and forcing her to move out. Since she could not take her dog with her but now did not want to surrender it, a shelter worker stepped in and convinced animal control to board it for 10 weeks until she could return home with her dog.[6]

By creating and preserving bonding capital between people and their pets, the shelter's basic care and other interventions often accomplished more so-ciologically; they changed how pet owners regarded themselves. The steps that West Charlotte residents take to promote the health and welfare of their animals can encourage people to see themselves as caring and responsible pet owners because changing an individuals' behavior can change their self-concept (e.g., Schlenker & Trudeau, 1990). That is, they come to regard them-selves as having the traits implied by their overt behavior, especially when the new behavior is performed publicly rather than privately (Tice, 1992). Pet own-ers who take animals to the shelter for free or discounted services do so in a public setting: Wellness Care can draw over 60 pet owners together at one time in a small parking lot adjacent to the shelter's clinic, with approximately six shelter volunteers in the midst and more volunteers and veterinary staff inside the clinic; the Food Bank draws dozens of pet owners who stand in line with each other and interact with about four shelter volunteers.

West Charlotte residents' new identity as responsible and caring pet own-ers is also encouraged by significant others, or those who wield influence over them, when they attribute motivations to people using the shelter's services (Laurent-Simpson, 2017). Each time pet owners take their animals to be exam-ined, vaccinated, sterilized, or given basic treatments at the shelter, workers and volunteers—who are relatively high-status professionals—view and treat them as responsible and caring owners. This perception—along with having an audience that sees them behaving in apparently responsible ways—en-courages them to enact and perhaps embrace a role with their animals that approximates the role of an adult parent who is expected to act on behalf of his or her child's health by seeking medical care to prevent and treat illness.

In prior chapters we focused on why some pet owners were reluctant to use free or low-cost veterinary services and what the two shelters did to change this behavior. When we think of who benefits from using free or low-cost basic veterinary services, our minds go first to the pets themselves. It is likely that the welfare of these animals is enhanced—they live healthier and perhaps longer lives. But using these services can also impact people, whether pet owners, their neighbors, or the local community, by providing them with different forms of social capital.

Indeed, just having a pet, especially a dog, can enable people to craft their identities, define their group membership, and create boundaries from other groups. For West Charlotte pet owners, this animal-related cultural capital gives them the ability to express and shape racial and class identities by affirming where they see themselves and outsiders in their social world. Not just pet ownership but also how owners care for their pets by using the shelter's free or low-cost basic veterinary services provide cultural capital, although in this case people are distinguishing themselves from other pet owners in West Charlotte.

Use of other shelter services can also increase pet owners' social connections to people through bridging capital. What changes people are their informal exchanges with those who provide veterinary services. While the shelter in Costa Rica tried to change the norms for how villages and individual pet owners interacted with dogs, the program in West Charlotte focused more on changing how its staff think about and behave with pet owners. The shelter is effective in getting pet owners to use its free or low-cost services not only because it removes cost barriers per se but because it addresses larger social and cultural issues involved when dealing with pet owners living in or near poverty. Exposure to and use of some free or low-cost veterinary services involves repeated contact with specific shelter workers as well as other pet owners. Increasing social ties and friendships not only changes owners' behavior but can also heighten commitment to providing subsequent veterinary care by affirming in a public space their new social role as care provider.

Finally, bonding capital from using these services appears to enhance pet owners' emotional investment and attachment to their animals. Whether it is pets' improved health and appearance or their changed behavior, sterilizing, vaccinating, medically treating, feeding, and unchaining animals encourage more touching, grooming, or playing with them than typically happens. In short, some West Charlotte animals become more pet-like and more integrated into the personal if not community lives of their owners following basic veterinary care.

While these findings are very encouraging for animal advocates who may need to convince local authorities, funding agencies, and pet owners of the merits of providing low- or no-cost basic veterinary services, it is impossible to definitely attribute these behavioral changes to the activities of the West Charlotte shelter. However, we have seen positive changes in human behavior after the initiation of dog sterilization programs elsewhere in the world and regard the West Charlotte findings as bolstering anecdotal reports from Bhutan, the Philippines, and India that also suggest human behavior changes as a result of veterinary interventions.[7] These changes—fewer street dogs, better relationships with dogs, higher demand for veterinary services, and better care and treatment for animals—augur well for the social capital changes we observed in West Charlotte.

Increasing Access to Veterinary Care

PROBLEMS, PARTERNSHIPS, AND PARADOXES

We started our research by asking what then seemed to be a simple question: what barriers prevent people in underserved communities from using low- or no-cost basic veterinary services, and what bridges help to overcome these obstacles? To answer this question, we looked at how humane and veterinary organizations provided these services in two cultures where the programs differed in operation and scope, as did the impact of class, race, and ethnicity on how people interacted with and cared for dogs and cats. As with many important questions, the answer was not so simple. Answering it required us to ask other questions about people with pets or those caring for street animals, the basic veterinary services they use, and the providers of these services. What started at one level as a seemingly straightforward goal of identifying barriers and bridges to using affordable veterinary care soon revealed themes that turned out to be richer and more complicated.

Parallels

What kind of relationship do people in or near poverty have with dogs and cats, and why are they sometimes reluctant to use free or low-cost veterinary services? At a general level, the answer is the same, whether in the underserved villages of rural Costa Rica or the disadvantaged neighborhoods of West Charlotte. Culture, in the fullest sense of the term, made underdogs of both owners and animals, suggesting that class may have more influence on these human-animal relationships than race or ethnicity (Caron-Sheppard,

1995; Dolin, 1988). People and their pets or street animals were underdogs because the same structural disadvantages weighed on them both—compromising what they could do, mediating how well they could live, and limiting their prospects for a healthy life.

While there is almost no literature in anthrozoology on social class and pet keeping, we could fall back on a large and established literature in psychology and sociology on how social class affects parent-child relations. This literature underscores the importance of social class, arguably more than any other single demographic variable, on child-rearing practices and the resulting mental and physical health of children (Conger & Conger, 2008). We thought that comparing our findings to this social science research was reasonable because, at least in the United States, and increasingly among young, educated Costa Ricans, pets are regarded as childlike and treated as part of the family, although not quite like they are in affluent American homes. This is not surprising because we increasingly view pets as family members and pretend children (Cain, 2016; Cohen, 2002; Hickrod & Schmitt, 1982), not just in modern Western societies but elsewhere too (Siddiq & Habib, 2016).

Indeed, class influences even the decision to have a child or pet. Low-income pregnancies are often unplanned (McCormick et al., 1987) and occur far more often among low-income than upper-income women (Guttmacher Institute, 2019). In the communities we studied, most dogs and cats were not planned additions to households. Residents often acquired them randomly, with little planning or forethought. Most commonly, animals drifted into the lives of residents, whether literally wandering onto their property, being abandoned near or at their home by strangers, or being left to residents by friends and family who could no longer care for them because they were evicted, fell into ill health, became suddenly unemployed, or went to prison. When they acquired their pets intentionally, residents did not do so through authorized breeders in West Charlotte but rather through local residents breeding illicitly. When the people we studied in Costa Rica had pets, they never bought them at a pet store, instead usually getting those that were "donated" from another owner or were found on the street, as is the case in rural Mexico (Ortega-Pacheco et al., 2007), or very rarely buying one outside the local market being sold by a neighbor because one of their pets or a street animal near their home had a litter.

We saw that relations between people and pets were remarkably similar in many ways to the relations between low-income parents and their children. Low-income parents have different conceptions of children and draw stronger boundaries between adults and children than do middle-class parents (Lareau, 2002). The pet owners we studied also drew clear boundaries between humans and animals, more so among the poor in Costa Rica than in West

Charlotte because of their fundamental view of what it means to be an animal. Costa Rican pet owners—again, they did not own animals or were not regarded as irresponsible if they let animals roam compared to pet owners in Charlotte—often made it clear that dogs and cats were *animalitos* that should be kept separate from the family's space, so they were rarely inside homes and rarely touched or groomed. Pets were given much more independence and separation from humans compared to West Charlotte, where pets were more likely to be incorporated into the family's interior space, although usually with limitations as to where they could go and how they could be touched, such as not kissing them.

At the same time that low-income parents draw boundaries between themselves and their children, they expect children, like adults, to contribute in some way to running the household, helping with chores, and sustaining the family (Cassells & Evans, 2017; Kohn et al., 1979). We often saw a similar expectation among poor Costa Ricans and many residents of West Charlotte. People in poor villages and towns in Costa Rica might have affection for dogs and cats, even viewing them as companions, but still expect them to fulfill many household jobs, whether to protect families from rats, snakes, and other unwelcomed animals and reptiles or to provide security as well as serve other roles in the community. Pet owners in West Charlotte often expected their dogs, whether kept outside or inside the home, to serve as guards or alarms, while cats were sometimes expected to control rodents.

In low-income families, especially among racial and ethnic minorities, children contribute to the family income (Falicov, 2001; Orellana, 2001; Song, 1997). Pooling labor and resources is a key household economic strategy for survival or to cover household expenses. In both locations, although we observed this practice more in West Charlotte, owners expected their dogs to be yet one more source of family income by breeding and selling their puppies. Families commonly bred their dogs for extra income with the expectation that pets, as members of the family, were obliged to help the household stay afloat financially. By contrast, in Costa Rica pets were less likely to be considered family members in this way and there was not much market to sell puppies, although we did observe a few instances of this.

Indeed, low-income relationships with pets and street dogs were complicated and ambiguous, defying simple classifications. They could serve multiple roles for multiple families and communities not typically experienced by white middle-class owners who see pets primarily as friends or family members (Walsh, 2009) that are well controlled and made into good citizens (Perin, 1990). Pets were not just outdoor or indoor, family member or guard, a part of only one family or even one neighborhood, instrumental or affective, stabilizers of families in turmoil or burdens on them, status conferring or unimportant to an individual's identity. They could, at one time or the other, be all of these or none to an individual, a family, a neighborhood, a community.

Conceptions of a child's nature also influence how parents care for them. White and black working-class and poor adults focus their efforts on providing their children with basic needs such as love, food, and safety (Lareau, 2002). But material shortages can make it difficult to provide even for these basic needs. The pet owners we studied also provided for the needs of animals according to how they perceived their nature and how they thought these animals fared best. In Costa Rica, people defined their own role less as a caretaker of pets and more as an uninvolved host—given that the animals often adopted them and they were presumed to be capable of foraging for themselves. So providing food or water on a regular basis was unnecessary and veterinary care for injury or disease was extremely rare. In West Charlotte, caretaking generally meant giving water and some kind of human or pet food of whatever quality to their animals on a somewhat regular basis (e.g., feeding every other day), without necessarily making up for spilled bowls. Veterinary care for injured or very sick animals was somewhat more likely than in Costa Rica, but still far from routine.

Different beliefs about the impact of parenting are also class related and affected child-rearing methods. For example, poorer parents resort more often to disciplining children for inappropriate behavior or using punishment to modify their actions because they believe that parenting has little effect on outcomes (Pinderhughes et al., 2000). We observed this practice in both locations when people tried to control animal behaviors that were unwelcomed, deemed to be inappropriate, or were not understandable. For example, if a pet spills its food bowl, it might not be fed again to punish it and "teach it a lesson." Indoor pets that accidentally defecate or throw up on the floor or furniture will be cast outside. And dogs that bite (even if playfully done) or cats that scratch (even if in self-defense) might be swatted.

How parents in poverty care for their children's basic needs is also affected by what the family is accustomed to. In both locations we studied, the poor diets and lack of veterinary care for dogs and cats are not different from what many people in or near poverty are accustomed to for their children and themselves. While middle- and high-income parents can afford foods high in nutrients and provide medical care for children, lower income parents struggle to do so (Conger & Conger, 2008). We saw this struggle too with pet owners or those caring for street animals, although it was more profound in rural Costa Rica, where dogs were often fed scraps or were left to roam for their own food and almost never received any veterinary care, practices that were even more common with cats.

In poverty, material shortages in the home and poor environmental conditions also severely affect the extent to which low-income parents participate with their children (Wilson, 1974). For example, poorer parents spend less time playing or in close contact with their children, in part because most families have very few or no toys. The parallel to this was most apparent in rural Costa Rica, where dogs and cats were rarely in the home and sometimes not even on the homeowner's property, while in West Charlotte cats and larger dogs were usually kept outside or were regarded as dirty; even smaller dogs kept inside were often restricted to certain rooms and were not permitted on furniture, let alone on beds. Pet toys were also rare in rural Costa Rica and West Charlotte, except when shelter workers offered them for free during outreach or at the Food Bank. Two-thirds of poorer parents never take their children out for an activity (Wilson, 1974). Poor Costa Ricans never walked their pets, although a few took them to work, while in West Charlotte walking dogs and taking them in the car did sometimes occur. In addition, in the milieu of poverty, families suffer from poor diet, lack of sleep, polluted air, untreated conditions of ill health, and chronic stress that produces apathy and depression and deters parents' participation with their children (Wilson, 1974), which also might account for the lack of participation with pets that we observed in Costa Rica and West Charlotte.

The burdens of class make it challenging for low-income parents to be close to and responsible for their children, who can sometimes appear to fare poorly when compared to the children of middle-class parents. However, social class differences in terms of being responsible for children largely stem not from differences in parents' desire to help their children but from differences in parents' access to a wide range of resources, including money and the social capital to learn about and gain access to programs for their children (Chin & Phillips, 2004). But within time and financial constraints idiosyncratic to being poor and relying on welfare, these low-income parents try to make time for and give meaning to their engagements and relationships with their children during daily activities, such as talking, play, or meals (Tubbs et al., 2005).

The burdens of class also make for complicated pet relationships, sometimes impairing owners' ability to be attached to and responsible for animals, while at other times encouraging them. People in underserved communities had a harder time maintaining their pet relationships, not because of lapses in attachment but because of the vicissitudes of life in or near poverty that often resulted in unemployment, evictions, unmanageable health problems, prison time, family emergencies, and suddenly uninhabitable homes. And there were also times when, rather than deterring attachment or responsibility, the burdens of having a pet became the bedrock of relationships with them. "Love" for pets may exist across social classes, but despite or perhaps because of the challenges of keeping them, attachment can sometimes be stronger in disadvantaged communities, as noted in survey studies (Johnson et al., 1992; Lago et al., 1988), than in more affluent ones.

If not stronger, attachment to and responsibility for children by low-income parents can take a different form than that of more affluent parents. For example, both black and white American families sometimes share child-rearing responsibilities with others, but black families are more likely to share these responsibilities with and get practical support from extended family members and people from outside the household, perhaps due to the fact that black caregivers are more often single-parent families (Kesselring et al., 2016). In Costa Rica, pet-keeping responsibilities were sometimes shared by the neighborhood if not community, while in West Charlotte pets were often shared, although often just temporarily, with extended family members living elsewhere or with friends a bus or car ride from the household. Because pet-caring responsibilities were often shared by people outside the home, it may be worthwhile to broaden the definition of pet caretaker to include other friends and family members involved in the care, as has been suggested for immigrant parents caring for their children who also get substantial practical support from outside the household (Jones et al., 2007).

These parallels between low-income parenting and low-income pet keeping underscore the powerful influence of social class on individual development, life opportunities, and well-being of both humans and nonhumans. Because of these comparable long-term consequences, humane educators, animal behaviorists, and scholars would do well in the future to explore child-rearing research to better understand the nature and consequences of pet keeping in disadvantaged communities. Of greater relevance to *Underdogs*, this connection is a stark reminder of the significant impact that class has not just on pet keeping but also on the delivery of affordable veterinary care in underserved communities. Indeed, the process of providing low-income children, or their family members, with health and social services is hindered by tensions and conflicts that, as we see below, strongly resemble those faced by people with pets and the groups trying to provide them with basic veterinary services in Costa Rica and West Charlotte.

Problems

Providers and policy makers of health, social, and educational services for the children of low-income parents often assume that cost of and access to services are the chief reasons for not using this care. However, personal, social, and cultural barriers are more often reported by parents (Mansour et al., 2000). When examined together, these barriers share in common an underlying distrust or suspicion of professionals and their institutions, just as they underlie many social interactions in everyday life (Kee & Knox, 1970). This sentiment becomes a social class pitfall blocking or preventing low-income parents from using services for their children. For example, distrust is the major barrier, beyond cost and access, that makes poor parents anxious or hesitant to deal with their children's teachers, school officials, or child care workers because parents fear their parenting skills will be judged (Fothergill, 2013; Lareau, 2002; Verzaro-Lawrence, 1981).

Because of this distrust, low-income parents sometimes rely on their own experience and knowledge about their child's health and welfare, which prevents them from using health or social services for their children. This happens when these parents underutilize dental services for their children not because of access or cost but because they trust their own perceived ability to diagnose and manage their children's oral health (Muirhead et al., 2013). Or if not relying on their own knowledge, they rely on that of their peers to decide whether to use social and health care services for their children or themselves. In one such case, advice given by providers to low-income parents about reducing the obesity of their children often conflicted with the advice mothers received from relatives or friends (Chamberlin et al., 2002). These findings suggest that a body of lay knowledge exists in disadvantaged communities that is contrary to what professionals would advise and is drawn upon by parents as just as legitimate or authoritative, if not more so, than the knowledge of health care practitioners.

Here too the experience of low-income parents is remarkably similar to what we saw among low-income pet owners and those caring for street animals. Lay knowledge became a barrier to using affordable care in both Costa Rica and West Charlotte, leading some people to doubt information and advice from shelter workers. For the most part, shelter workers were unaware of this doubt or at least its depth and frequency. Instead, they typically expected people in the community to understand and respond to information they were given. If told that sterilization would prevent cancer, this was expected to motivate owners to consent to sterilization, but it did not always, and even if they consented, it may not have been because of this information. Workers placed too much weight on cognitive and not enough on cultural influences, which easily trumped the former. Because of this doubt, people did not take an incremental and stepwise progression to using available free or low-cost veterinary services after being given information about them, such that they gradually used most if not all of them. Instead, they were often leery and opportunistic about using services, taking months to decide which if any services to get for their pets.

Laggards and nonadopters of free or low-cost veterinary services were reluctant to change because they embraced fundamentally different definitions of messages communicated by the shelters, NGOs, and governmental groups that tried to diffuse new ways of thinking and acting about animals. They saw value in their own cultural knowledge and customs, while trying to abide by new expectations for pet ownership that they did not passively obey. This local knowledge, experience, and understanding meant that they assessed the need for and safety of various veterinary procedures alongside or in spite of information given to them by shelters or other humane groups, such that two systems of veterinary knowledge existed—one professional the other lay—and at times these systems conflicted with each other and subsequently made pet owners or those caring for street animals question the value, safety, or need for basic veterinary services. Far greater trust was placed on knowledge gained from making firsthand observations of neighbors' animals that survived sterilization surgery or on the advice of a friend or family member about pet care than what people were told by shelter workers.

Low-income parents also hesitate to use health or social services for their children, or themselves, when they cannot trust that interactions with providers or organizations will go smoothly and respectfully. Based on their experiences or those of friends and family, they expect interactions with professionals and service organizations to be trade-offs; the benefits of getting services can be outweighed by the psychological or emotional costs of accessing them. To obtain services they have to undergo what they perceive as unnecessary requirements, adopt the value system of others, accept services that result in a loss of control over their surroundings, or face the unwelcome judgments of intrusive staff members (Silverstein et al., 2008).

We also found that how pet owners or those caring for street dogs interpreted low- or no-cost basic services could create reluctance to use them. Anticipating a negative experience, whether or not based on prior contact, they too, like their low-income parental counterparts, experienced or expected the use of affordable care to be a trade-off. This made them ambivalent about going to the shelter or sterilization clinics, although the nature of this trade-off was different in the two settings we studied. In West Charlotte, the trade-off could be getting free or discounted animal care at the cost of feeling guilt or shame from taking handouts they could not pay for, revealing personal information that might get them into trouble with authorities, hearing negative comments by the staff that made them feel like they were irresponsible pet owners, or more generally being unable to trust advice from a white institution, just as knowledge of the Tuskegee syphilis experiment leads African American males in particular to resist health promotion programs (Green et al., 1997). Although the trade-offs were different in Costa Rica, they also made pet owners or those caring for street animals ambivalent about trusting advice to use the shelter's basic services. For them, getting cheaper basic care came at the expense of possibly feeling anxious about sneaking a male dog to the shelter for sterilization against another family member's wishes or, more commonly, about taking an animal for surgery that some pet owners feared would likely kill it. Most pet owners being offered low-cost sterilization, especially those in rural or coastal villages, had never taken animals to veterinarians for any kind of care; indeed, in many cases they never or very rarely used professional health care for themselves or family members. Not knowing what to expect of the encounter and fearing untoward results from sterilization surgery led many to think twice about using this service and gave them great caution when they did.

Distrust can also be a problem among the groups providing services to low-income people. Health and social service organizations trying to deliver care to poor parents have to contend with distrust from other stakeholders who work with the same clients, making it difficult to collaborate and more effectively deliver these services. Similarly, intergroup distrust can affect whether, how much, and by whom basic veterinary care is ultimately provided to pet owners and people dealing with street animals. That such tension and conflict existed struck stakeholders as unfortunate and ironic because they all realized that everyone wanted the best for animals and that, in theory, everyone could be a partner in promoting animal welfare. Yet their reality spoke otherwise.[1]

Although intergroup tension existed in both Costa Rica and West Charlotte, its nature and intensity differed. Intergroup tension was greater in Costa Rica because of competition for scarce resources. Groups with some resources (like El Refugio) were looked upon with suspicion and envy. In the United States real income for animal care groups has increased fivefold since the early 1960s. Nevertheless, some groups still complain about a lack of money, but most have sufficient resources to fund their programs, apart from small groups trying to provide low-cost veterinary services or free pet food that have relatively little funding by comparison.

Stakeholders' distrust also varied in the two settings because each shelter had to manage relationships with different sets of stakeholders. Different groups presented different challenges to the shelters' hopes to diffuse affordable care. Apart from pet owners being one kind of stakeholder, El Refugio faced such tension with other shelters, rescue groups, sanctuaries, fosterers, NGOs, private-practice veterinarians, and, to some extent, underserved towns and villages, while the Humane Society of Charlotte did so with shelters, low-cost spay/neuter clinics, rescue groups, animal control, private-practice veterinarians, veterinary hospital chains, and potentially groups whose mission is not promoting animal welfare, such as the state's housing department or organizations for homeless people.[2]

For one, distrust could occur when groups disagreed as to how to best manage perceived animal problems. In Costa Rica, this manifested in charges of incompetence or mismanagement, bickering and backstabbing among groups, and the weary dependencies that formed among them. Tensions stemmed from allegations by mainstream humane organizations that other groups were treating their charges inhumanely, whether this involved institutional hoarding by sanctuaries, shelters, casa cunas, or sterilization-only groups, or were conducting business unethically. Unlike intergroup relations in West Charlotte, there always seemed to be questions in the air about which animal organizations were legitimate or "official" and which were suspect and perhaps should be investigated and perhaps shuttered by the Colegio Veterinarios or SENASA when necessary to protect animals.

Distrust from disagreements over animal care were rarer in West Charlotte and, when they occurred, less disruptive to group cooperation. Most notably, while the shelter has had a cordial relationship with the local animal control office, there has been some tension involving actions taken by its officers that seem to be prejudicial against low-income pet owners. The shelter claims that, despite its efforts, it has been unable to get animal control to be sensitive to the nature of pet keeping in West Charlotte; they remove and potentially euthanize animals they view as problematic strays that many local residents consider to be unproblematic community pets or tolerate as just part of the neighborhood landscape. Outdoor cats commonly fall into such an ambiguous zone, where animal control officers see them as nuisances to be disposed of, even though local residents have not filed a complaint with the department and consider them to be shared community pets.

Intergroup distrust was greatest when there were competitive disputes over the right to provide certain treatments to certain clients, especially sterilization surgery. Suspicions bred from perceived competition more commonly surfaced in Costa Rica because this surgery was a far more important market for some groups there than in greater West Charlotte, where there was much less competition, if any, for spay/neuter clients among the latter's groups. In Costa Rica, some of this competitive friction over doing this surgery has come from upstart groups that have become emboldened to pursue this business, despite the current informal policy, honored by larger and more established groups, to respect a "gentlemen's agreement" to either notify each other of forthcoming clinics or check online to see the locations and dates of clinics run by other programs. While this agreement prevents the overlap of services in certain areas, it is not always honored by new outreach or rescue groups seeking to compete with established programs for sterilization clients, exacerbating tension.

In the past even more pressure on shelters, especially in Costa Rica, came from veterinary associations over limiting what treatments, including but not limited to sterilization, could be performed by shelter veterinarians. The for-profit veterinary industry saw efforts to provide affordable care as economically threatening and cast doubt on the quality of care provided by shelter veterinarians, whose work with low-income pet owners was monitored and controlled to differing degrees. As pet owners increase their demand for using veterinary services in Costa Rica, there may even be increased friction if not conflict with private-practice veterinarians economically threatened by the growth of programs. Distrust, then, may grow and become an even more formidable barrier to getting basic care to underserved communities in Costa Rica, especially between private practitioners and less established sterilization-only groups. Although El Refugio has had periodic complaints about poor veterinary skills from the Colegio, those complaints have diminished and the relationship between the Colegio and El Refugio is now less confrontational. It is possible that the Colegio is coming to recognize that the shelters are helping to increase veterinary demand overall.

By comparison, in West Charlotte and the United States more generally there is typically less concern by veterinary associations over shelters offering veterinary services to low-income clients, but private practitioners are always on the lookout for upper-income pet owners using low-cost services. The Alabama Veterinary Medical Association recently tried to pass a law banning shelters from offering veterinary services, and South Carolina has also been entertaining a similar move. Typically, however, shelter clinics constitute about 2 to 4% of the total veterinary market in a state. Nevertheless, concern remains. In Mississippi after Hurricane Katrina, the state veterinary school received funds to offer outreach clinics (Mississippi Board of Animal Health, n.d.), but the Mississippi Veterinary Medical Association was very concerned and permitted the veterinary school to proceed with the project only if clients were provided with vouchers to get follow-up care from private practices. Within a couple of years the veterinary association decided it did not want the clients the veterinary school was serving and dropped the demand for vouchers.

Whether this distrust or conflict exists between groups providing basic veterinary care or between the shelters and the people who might use their free or low-cost services, the sentiment and its consequences are the same. Either individuals or organizations perceive certain behaviors to be undesirable, medically risky, or morally doubtful, and these perceptions can complicate if not derail the delivery of basic veterinary care and its use by people in underserved communities. Facing this situation, the shelters in Costa Rica and West

Charlotte hoped to create more collaboration and trust to replace competition and distrust with individuals and other groups, but they took different approaches to reducing this tension and achieved different outcomes.

Partnerships

How the shelters dealt with this conflict is remarkably similar to the ways that human and social service providers dealt with the distrust of clients whose lower class background most strongly predicted their distrust of providers, regardless of race (Whetten et al., 2006). These providers, like the shelter workers we studied, found that getting disadvantaged clients to use services could require more than merely making free or low-cost services available to them or providing information alone, since clients often trusted advice from family and friends that contradicted professional advice.

To make these changes, providers had to first develop rapport with parents and better understand their social situations, although they felt uncomfortable doing so because they had so little time with parents and were not trained in "social work." Then they had to try to change the attitudes and behavior of low-income clients and get more of them to use services for their children by changing, albeit in small steps, parents' perceptions of and behavior with their children and altering their child-rearing skills to some degree (Chamberlin et al., 2002). In so doing, relationships could sometimes be nudged to become less hierarchical between providers and clients and more collaborative with groups.

As with health and social service providers who work with low-income parents, the shelter workers we studied did more than merely make these services available and convey information about them to get underserved pet owners or those caring for street animals to use basic and affordable veterinary care. They also tried to alter their relationships with these people to reduce distrust and increase use of basic services. Like their health and social service counterparts, shelter workers tried to change the thinking and behavior of people to create partnerships in place of resistance and trust in place of doubt. They became, in effect, community change agents (Eng & Young, 1992) whose friendship, support, education, and counseling could alter people's perceptions of and behaviors with their animals to some degree.

The workers at the two shelters behaved differently in this role and produced different changes. In Costa Rica, the shelter tried to convince underserved villages or towns of the value of hosting sterilization clinics and then by having its veterinarians normalize the idea of veterinary care by continuing to visit the same places every few months. When possible, they also mobilized local volunteer rescue groups whose members knew the town's pet owners and could encourage them to sterilize their animals and help them get to the clinic. Then, when interacting with people trying to help street animals, shelter workers subtly encouraged them to become more emotionally invested in their animals, so they would see them as pets for whom they accepted some responsibility. To the extent their efforts were successful, these "passive" pet owners (Alie et al., 2007) started to handle and play with their animals for the first time.

Becoming a community change agent took a different form in West Charlotte, in part because shelter workers had an opportunity to make home visits but also because the social gap was wider between the shelter's outreach team and the pet owners they served. Although developing rapport was more of a challenge for outreach workers, they nevertheless sought to break down barriers of class, race, and expertise by befriending pet owners when possible. This gap called for shelter workers to work on being culturally competent as they delivered affordable care, building rapport as they spoke about veterinary interventions. They also mobilized community ambassadors to alleviate the distrust of neighbors and friends who owned pets in the community. In their contacts with pet owners, shelter workers in West Charlotte took steps that changed how people viewed and ultimately interacted with their animals. What was being altered was not just the biology of dogs and cats but their relationships with owners in the process.

To be effective community change agents, both shelters used other strategies, but with less success, to break down distrust and create more of a sense of partnership with people having pets or street animals, although to be fair, neither organization had staff members with the time or training to do so. For one, the programs sought to make inroads into underserved communities by trying to widen the message they communicated. Instead of just telling people about the value of using basic veterinary care for their animals' health and welfare, they told them how they, along with their animals and their communities, could benefit from these services since animal and human welfare are closely connected (Molento, 2014). In other words, they hoped that people might begin to see that providing at least a basic level of animal care can benefit their pets, themselves, and their neighbors.

The shelters also tried to create a partnership—or were at least open to this idea—by somewhat reducing their own authority and expertise while acknowledging more in pet owners. Although a similar change has been called for in the work of professionals who deal with low-income parents, it rarely occurs because a rigid hierarchy of expertise is typically followed. For example, workers providing education in poor communities in the United States expect low-income parents targeted for change to take their advice, while not exploring the local contexts and the everyday interpretations of the people who inhabit these communities that influence the process of implementation and participation (Nielsen, 1996). The result is that parents' expertise about their children remains unrecognized (Cheatham & Otrosky, 2011).[3]

Many shelter workers understood that pet owners or those caring for street dogs often had some emotional stake in their animals and drew on folk or local knowledge about animal care and behavior. This understanding stopped them from lapsing into the role of information givers who expected everyone to comply with their advice, instead allowing people to play more of a part in making decisions about their animals' veterinary care. Workers did this in both locations by acknowledging the bonds that people in underserved communities could have with their animals, the realities of their life in or near poverty, and the powerful influences of local culture on their thinking and behavior with animals.

Understanding and then acceding to this folk knowledge was easier in Costa Rica because shelter workers often lived in the same communities they served, or at least lived in similar communities, so they understood the perspective toward dogs and cats found in shantytowns, small villages, and poor sections of cities. Because of this similarity, workers accepted some elements of local knowledge and practice about pet keeping as inevitable or intractable. By comparison, almost none of the shelter workers in West Charlotte lived there or in similar communities. So the local culture and pet owners' knowledge about animals operated more independently from whatever changes in owners' behavior were hoped for by the shelter.

Based on this understanding, shelter workers in both locations changed their own thinking and lowered their expectations for how much or what kind of animal care low-income people could provide. To do so has parallels with health care providers who see patients living with long-term illnesses as partners in decision making about their care because they have developed expertise and wisdom about their welfare (Wilson, 1999). In the long run, establishing partnerships that recognize this desire and knowledge might increase trust in shelters by pet owners or those caring for street animals, give them more control over their lives, and get them more committed to using veterinary services in the future.

A final approach to lessen distrust was for the shelters to mobilize community support for providing basic veterinary care. Local institutions might be strong and successful advocates for basic veterinary care because they can be important to pet owners and influence their thinking and behavior (Rowland & Isaac-Savage, 2014). To this end the shelter in West Charlotte hopes that churches, schools, shelters for homeless people, and food pantries, if viewed as partners in lifting the level of animal welfare, might become sites to disseminate information about affordable care and encourage if not endorse the shelter's goals. Establishing community partnerships took a different shape in Costa Rica. Efforts by El Refugio to ensconce its outreach clinics in under-served towns and villages speak to this aim.

Suspicions and conflicts with stakeholders could also become formidable barriers to the shelters' efforts to improve animal welfare in underserved communities. To deal with these problems, the shelters tried to form more collaborative or working relationships with stakeholders, much like health care providers who have tried to build working relationships, if not consensus, legitimacy, and mutual commitment, with other organizations that can potentially influence the problems faced by low-income children in different ways (Chamberlin et al., 2002). Attempts by these providers to create collaborative rather than competitive relationships have succeeded when partners had mutual trust (Mizrahi & Rosenthal, 1996), believed that benefits could result for all partners, and valued skills each brought to the alliance (Kanter, 1994).

The shelters, in different ways, also sought to create at least some collaboration and a modicum of consensus where none had existed. Resource sharing was one strategy. El Refugio shared its resources to help rescue groups overrun with animals by housing, feeding, and trying to get them adopted at the shelter. Doing so created some goodwill between these groups when little existed before. The Humane Society of Charlotte also shared resources to further intergroup cooperation. For example, to reduce the high rate of cat euthanasia at the county's animal care and control department, the shelter created a program to move cats that were not adoption candidates (i.e., stray/living outside and unsocial) from animal control into situations they might thrive in. The shelter uses its own resources to spay/neuter, microchip, and vaccinate them and then advertise these "urban barn cats," line up homes for them, and coach adopters on how best to get these cats established. Putting labor and money into this program relieved the euthanasia burden at animal control and likely improved its public image.

Another strategy to build consensus was to change how other groups conducted animal care to bring it more in line with what the shelters saw as best practices. For example, the West Charlotte shelter has attempted to stop the city's animal control officers from seizing neighborhood cats as ownerless strays instead of seeing them as valued pets that should not be taken and most likely euthanized, a practice objected to by the shelter and one that taints what is otherwise a supportive and cordial relationship between the organizations. Efforts by the shelter to ear-tip outdoor cats so they can easily be identified as quasi-owned and not collected and euthanized by animal control have been only partially successful because there are so many outdoor cats in West Charlotte. To ensure that more of them are not seized, the shelter has considered asking animal control for permission to instruct its officers about how local residents view these cats as their pets.

The shelters also promoted consensus by trying to change stakeholders' perceptions of their efforts to provide affordable care, especially when there were charges of unfair competition or substandard veterinary care, by more positively framing their concerns. To replace these negative perceptions, the shelters tried to convince stakeholders that they could benefit rather than be harmed by their efforts to help pets in underserved communities. Both shelters took this approach and tried to reassure private-practice veterinarians that they should not be threatened by low-cost veterinary services because using these services could encourage pet owners to seek veterinary care for their animals in the future, thus helping rather than hurting their business.

The West Charlotte shelter has taken this framing one step further, in anticipation of veterinary resistance to its plan to build a new facility that could do diagnostic testing at little or no cost with state-of-the-art equipment, such as the latest radiological imaging technology.[4] Since the shelter would only be diagnosing rather than treating medical problems, it does not believe that the planned facility would compete with or hurt the practice of local veterinarians in Charlotte (none of whom practice in West Charlotte). Nevertheless, some of these veterinarians might still feel threatened by the new facility's diagnostic services because diagnostic tests are a source of income for private clinics—more so than spay/neuter surgeries—so the shelter is trying to frame their plan by describing scenarios that show how it can help rather than hurt their practices. For example, if an owner took her dog with a broken leg to a private-practice veterinarian, she would spend $200 for x-rays but then not be able to afford treatment for the problem, resulting in the dog being euthanized. But if the same person came to the shelter's new facility for free x-rays, she could afford to take the injured dog to the veterinarian for treatment, where she would spend the $200 to fix the dog and not have it euthanized. In addition, the veterinarian will probably get a future client in this scenario. A euthanized dog is no future client.

Although it is doubtful that many veterinarians will be convinced by this framing since they might assume that poor pet owners cannot afford much care beyond the basics, at least in Costa Rica, they may accept that growing demand for veterinary medicine is partially due to the shelter's efforts to disseminate basic veterinary services.[5] Through these efforts, the shelter has started to change how people regard their animals, seeing more value in them as companions and potentially wanting to spend more for their welfare. Prior resistance by the Colegio Veterinarios to the shelter's program, and others like it, may subside if the Colegio acknowledges that the shelter's program can help to increase demand for private-practice veterinarians rather than compete with it.

The humane society in Charlotte has taken a more collaborative approach to easing competitive tensions with private-practice veterinarians. In recent years the shelter has groomed specific partner veterinarians from the nearby community who sympathize with the plight of low-income pet owners and who agree to work with the shelter on a referral basis with such owners to provide more affordable veterinary care—an approach that was easier to arrange when the shelter had a large external grant that enabled it to pay for some of the costs of reduced veterinary care provided by these partners. As the number of veterinary partners has grown, the shelter has considered trying to change the sentiments of more threatened veterinarians by organizing social activities where they would meet the partner veterinarians and have an opportunity to share their concerns in a collegial setting. Overall, these veterinary collaborations have not only neutralized some resistance to free and discounted services but also enabled the shelter's approach to helping low-income pet owners get veterinary care and promoting animal welfare. For example, some of these partnering veterinarians have started to refer clients to shelters that offer discounted veterinary care and to help pet owners get less expensive medications by no longer demanding that their prescriptions be filled and purchased from their practices.[6]

A final strategy to lessen intergroup friction was more passive in that alliances were not formed, resources were not shared, and perceptions were not altered. When change seemed unlikely, the shelters chose to coexist with other groups by trying to respect professional guidelines for what its veterinarians should or should not do clinically. At these times, shelter veterinarians were reluctant to broaden their clinical functions, fearing this might come at the expense of their core responsibility of providing basic care and encouraging owners to take a more active role in caring for their animals. By laying low when providing services in outlying communities and trying to limit the nature and frequency of surgical interventions performed during sterilization on a case-by-case basis, the shelters could continue their efforts to diffuse affordable care with the fewest impingements possible.

Of course, some stakeholder conflict might subside in the future for reasons having nothing to do with efforts by the shelters to create more collaborative relations. For example, in Charlotte some local veterinarians may have shifted their opposition to free or low-cost veterinary services from the shelter to veterinarians operating mobile vans in low-income neighborhoods who offer relatively inexpensive services like vaccinations. These low-cost mobile veterinarians are worrisome to private-practice veterinarians because they are perceived as stealing clients, much like the shelter was blamed in the past.

In the end, the shelters were able to widely diffuse affordable care because they did not just think about changing animal welfare and limit their efforts to reducing cost and increasing access to care. They also thought about changing their fundamental relationships with people and organizations to become more collaborative than conflictive, more trusting than doubting. To the extent these efforts succeed, new norms of trust can emerge among these groups, as perceptions of competition and conflict are slowly replaced by more accurate understandings of each other's priorities, skills, and resources. If mutual learning and adaption can occur, humane and veterinary groups vying for clients in the same organizational space can indeed change (Vaaland & Håkansson, 2003). As collaborators rather than competitors, these groups should have even more collective impact on the behavior of low-income pet owners and, ultimately, the welfare of their animals. But how much can these people be expected to change? The answer presents a paradox for animal advocates who want to make a sea change in the level of care provided to dogs and cats in underserved communities.

The Paradox of Affordable Care

Everyday thinking about responsible behaviors by people living in or near poverty assumes they do not want to accept responsibility for anything including but not limited to their children, but the standards by which parents are often judged and found to be insufficiently responsible are those of white middle-class families and do not necessarily apply to parents living in more challenging circumstances or whose cultural norms differ from those of this group (Katz et al., 2007). On the contrary, low-income parents have demonstrated remarkable resilience and parenting capacity. Nevertheless, policy planners' thinking continues to be heavily influenced by this assumption and has led, since the mid-1990s, to rapid growth in programs designed to promote "responsible" parenting in low-income families (Lewin Group, 1997) by encouraging parents to provide more emotional support to children, be more involved with their education, be more engaged with their leisure activities, and feel closer in their relations with them (Anderson et al., 2002).

Again, there are close parallels between how social policy makers think about low-income parents and the thinking underlying programs trying to provide affordable veterinary care to underserved communities. Although these programs and the policy makers behind them do not set out to make people more responsible—Pets for Life specifically denies this—they do end up changing their behavior in ways that could be considered more responsible. They feed their animals more and with higher quality food, they vaccinate them from disease and prevent suffering, they sterilize them and reduce the overpopulation problem, and they give them basic treatments and ward off problems like worms or mange. The welfare of these animals is improved.

Indeed, we saw that the use of services like sterilization, vaccination, sup-

plemental pet food, basic veterinary treatments, and fence building, combined with pet owners' interactions with shelter workers, had effects beyond
improving animal welfare. These services could have these effects because
they are much more than simple medical or animal welfare interventions;
they are interpersonal and subjective experiences for pet owners that can
change their perceptions of animals and themselves in far more substantial
and complicated ways than reported in surveys that find respondents display-
ing, for example, more positive attitudes toward dogs after being vaccinated
against rabies (Knobel, Laurenson, Kazwala, & Cleaveland, 2008).

By offering these services and interacting with pet owners in culturally
competent ways, programs nudge people to take steps to care for their animals in ways they never did and begin to rethink what their roles should entail as caretakers. Attempts to diffuse affordable care are then a form of moral
entrepreneurship, or a process by which groups try to influence individuals to
adopt a norm by labeling a particular behavior as problematic and then recommending a new behavior to replace it. Efforts to provide affordable care label the failure to provide basic veterinary services as a problem and then try
to change how low-income pet owners or others trying to care for animals
think about providing these services to their charges. If successful, these efforts change people's perceptions of the worth of animals and the value of veterinary care.[7]

However, the shelters we studied deny that these changes are the goal of
their work, claiming they are only in the business of providing free or low-
cost services to people who, on their own, decide whether to use them or not.
Nevertheless, by definition affordable care programs assume that people in
low-income communities should care for their animals more like affluent pet
owners do. In other words, for whatever reason people have not provided basic veterinary care in the past, the shelters are making a moral judgment that
it would be preferable they do so now. Improved animal welfare is the desired
outcome, and low-income pet owners should behave accordingly, a moral
position also taken by organizations offering welfare or family counseling to
low-income clients who, in the process of providing these services, confer a
moral judgment about the nature of their problems and the hoped-for outcomes of using these services (Hasenfeld, 2000).

This moral assumption sometimes became explicit in both settings we
studied. In Costa Rica, judgments about lapsed responsibility for animals
were apparent when shelter workers and outreach veterinary staff members
offered unsolicited explanations about why rural or poor people allowed their
animals to roam or failed to feed, water, or medically treat them. While they
understood the cultural reasons for these behaviors and tried to have realistic
expectations, they also blamed individuals for being neglectful or irresponsi-

ble in general or being fearful of change. In Charlotte, such moral judgments were rarer and were usually made only by new staff members or volunteers who were overly zealous about local pet owners providing a level of care closer to their own standards.

Most of the more experienced shelter workers we studied accepted a different reality and did not brand people as "irresponsible" for not sterilizing, vaccinating, or treating basic medical problems. They know that individuals living in or near poverty do their best to care for their animals, given severely limited resources, adverse conditions, and unpredictable crises that constantly test their ability to have a residence to live in, food to survive, utilities for comfort and health, and medical care for all members of the family, whether human or animal. In other words, the level of care they provide reflects not their intent but the structural limitations of living in or near poverty.

From a structuralist perspective, the problem with the vague notion of "responsibility" for animals is that attempts to define and apply it will be culture bound and limited by the assumptions or biases of those who expect the residents of low-income communities to behave like pet owners who have the resources, experience, prior socialization, and social support to feed, care for, train, and tend to their pets in certain ways. In this sense, notions of responsibility for animals will have a middle-class bias toward how much veterinary care can be realistically expected of people who have trouble taking care of their own children let alone their pets and who follow subcultural norms about human-animal relationships that are different from white middle-class norms. If responsibility is defined only in terms of feeding animals regularly, keeping pets indoors most if not all the time, having pet sitters when away or keeping pets in day care, and providing veterinary care for serious medical problems, then most of the low-income respondents we studied will fail by comparison with affluent pet owners. But these are all outcome measures of responsibility rather than measures of effort to be responsible, especially in the face of unpredictable problems where the unfortunate pet owner has little or no social support to fall back on or resources to draw on to manage the problems. If responsibility is defined as the attempt to find solutions to problems at hand and the degree to which people are willing to sacrifice or compromise their own quality of everyday living to manage these problems, then our findings suggest that people in or near poverty can be more responsible than their wealthier counterparts when it comes to animal care.

People unfamiliar with the way of life of people in or near poverty will not see this. They will be unaware of indigenous ways of caring for street animals or pets that exist in shantytowns in Costa Rica or the neighborhoods of West Charlotte that are unique cultural assets enabling people to behave responsibly in their situation, given whatever limited resources they have. For example, we saw that access to an informal network of friends was particularly relevant to pet owners living in or near poverty as a resource to deal with problems that unexpectedly emerged in their lives, such as facing eviction from their homes, being forced to serve jail time, experiencing frequent job layoffs, or having cars that are unreliable. These sorts of problems made it difficult to use low- or no-cost veterinary services; indeed, these problems forced some people to relinquish their pets to shelters or animal control departments. Yet research on social networks among the disadvantaged (Belle, 1983) suggests that unexpected or novel solutions can emerge to help people living in poverty adapt to problems they face. These natural helping networks among poor pet owners helped them cope with animal-related problems. They wanted to act responsibly and expressed this intent in culturally specific ways.

Given that most of our respondents already have a sense of responsibility, they do not need to be made into more responsible people. They want to be responsible but face barriers; however, with the help of affordable veterinary care programs, they can care for their animals in ways they would like to. They are nudged in the general direction of what the wider culture thinks of when it speaks of responsible guardianship, although use of the term outside of the United States or in developing countries is often limited to having cats and dogs sterilized, vaccinated for problems like rabies, given basic exams, and treated for problems like parasites, as well as limiting their access to public areas and collecting feces (Domingues et al., 2015), while in the United States the welfarist agenda (Irvine, 2003) usually suggests more, such as not having pets if owners are gone for long hours or travel a lot (Nakaya, 2005).

If responsible pet guardianship as a goal to pursue in underserved communities is not only vague but also inappropriate and unfair, then what should be the appropriate and realistic measure for assessing the care of pets and street animals in these communities? This an ethical and definitional question about what expectations humane societies and veterinarians can or should have of low-income people, given the difficulty in changing their behavior because they have limited resources to spend on animal care, lack social support, follow subcultural norms for pet keeping, and face everyday priorities and problems that they cannot easily manage. For example, can we expect all low-income pet owners to sterilize their pets? No, because some need the small amount of money they make from breeding their dogs. Can we expect all low-income pet owners to feed their pets daily relatively nutritious pet food? No, because their children are poorly or underfed and they are at least giving their pets occasional table scraps or low-quality cheap pet food once in a while. Can we expect all low-income people to take injured or very sick dogs and cats to veterinarians for animal care? No, because they lack health care for themselves or their family or, if they do have it, the cost of using private-practice veterinarians means sacrificing food for themselves or not paying for utilities or an over-due credit card bill. Can we expect all low-income pet owners to take their out-door dogs off their heavy chains and give them at least a doghouse to use? No, because chaining them is itself a type of responsibility they are taking to not let their pets become strays, and they cannot afford a doghouse and their land-lord will not allow them or a group like Beyond Fences to erect a fence on the property.

Given these limits on what people living in or near poverty can do for their animals, some animal advocates will say that perhaps the underserved should not have pets if they cannot be responsible guardians in ways that resemble pet keeping and caring in affluent white communities. We do not concur, nor do others who have looked closely at the problem of unequal access to veter-inary care. One such study (Access to Veterinary Care Coalition, 2018), led by a veterinarian, noted that "while it may be logical that someone should not have a pet if they cannot provide veterinary care, it is difficult to defend deny-ing companionship with pets." Since families in or near poverty will continue to live with dogs and cats, they deserve to enjoy their companionship and all of the benefits that come through these relationships.

Perhaps a better and more culturally informed goal would be to talk about "reasonable" rather than "responsible" guardianship. Instead of imposing an external standard of behavior on people in underserved communities, most of whom will subsequently be found to be deficient, it is more useful to ask how the surrounding culture shapes their thinking about and acting toward dogs and cats in ways that make some behaviors reasonable, despite falling short of the middle-class standard of pet keeping, and how living in or near pov-erty constrains or limits the behavior of individuals such that they cannot be-have like middle-class pet owners, despite wanting to. Providing affordable care will advance animal welfare but perhaps not always as fast or far as some would like.

If animal advocates and policy planners behind affordable care programs modify what they can expect of low-income pet owners when diffusing these services, this should not be considered a failure. Becoming realistic about how much change can be made in caretaking behaviors is no small achievement in the quest to improve the health and welfare of dogs and cats in underserved communities. Some programs providing low- or no-cost services will see what they are now doing as enough and will be grateful for any basic care they can bring to these communities. Indeed, many programs struggle to provide much less care than does Pets for Life. Trying to catch up with the level of pet care found in more affluent neighborhoods will be challenging if programs pro-vide only free or low-cost services like sterilization, vaccination, treatments for problems like worms, and physical examinations.

But the ultimate goal for some animal advocates is getting even more veterinary care and caretaking skills to underserved pet owners than does Pets for Life. To come close to this goal, programs will need to provide even more resources to people in poor neighborhoods than they currently do, in the same way that health policy planners speak of providing equal access to quality medical care or educators speak of creating equal access to education. Policy makers would then need to think about making structural changes that would affect low-income pet owners' opportunities, lifestyle, and socioeconomic status. If successful, doing this will inevitably change human-animal relationships, an outcome that some people will criticize as yet one more unfortunate impact that modernization can have on traditional identity and social interaction, while others will cheer the advance as a form of trans-species social justice.

Whether affordable care programs pursue realistic ownership or responsible guardianship, in the end they will be changing both animals and humans for the better because these programs are much more than what meets the eye. Low or no-cost sterilization, vaccination, pet food, fences, and basic treatments go a long way toward changing the quality of life for dogs and cats and the people who want to care for them. In this regard, what we saw in Costa Rica and North Carolina should encourage animal advocates elsewhere to also try to overcome the challenges of providing veterinary services in underserved communities.

NOTES

Introduction. Pets, Poverty, and the Problem of Access to Veterinary Care

1. When existing problems are resolved or reduced, organizations dealing with these social problems move on to new problems. To wit, after the problem of street animals lessened, unwanted pets became the new problem (Irvine, 2003).

2. In 2018, approximately 38 million people, or 12% of the U.S. population, lived in poverty. The poverty line for an individual was $12,784. For each additional person, the line is incrementally higher. For example, $25,701 is the cutoff for a family of four. Another 30% of the population live close to poverty (U.S. Census Bureau, 2019). Families with annual incomes between 100% and 200% of the poverty line (i.e., between $25,701 and approximately $49,000) are vulnerable to difficulties associated with economic strain and are often considered "near poor" (Huston & Bentley, 2010).

3. We decided to forgo use of the terms "guardian" and "guardianship" because they were not used in the communities we studied, in favor of the commonly used language of "owner" and "ownership." We also concur with the AVMA's recommendation to not use "guardian" when referring to pet owners (AVMA, 2005).

4. Out of simplicity we use the term "animal" to refer to nonhuman animals, while supporting those who call for a nonspeciesist language (e.g., Freeman, 2010).

5. A few researchers have also studied how social class influences the contemporary pet owner's choice of breeds, indicating that choice of breed and function of pets vary by class (Lian & Mathis, 2016).

6. However, lower income people in Great Britain are more likely to own pets than those with higher incomes (Marsa-Sambola et al., 2016), suggesting that some social class differences in pet ownership might reflect different research sample sizes and makeup.

7. These zip codes include 28206, 28208, 28214, 28216, and 28217. Other parts of West Charlotte are demographically mixed or are being gentrified because property is inexpensive and close to downtown and locations like Bank of America Stadium.

8. Most other Pets for Life cities have similar demographic profiles; the St. Louis program, for example, serves part of the city where about 97% of the targeted residents are African American, about 40% of whom live below the poverty line, and the median household income is about $23,000; and the Milwaukee Pets for Life program focuses on a neighborhood with about 9,500 households where 98% of the population is African American, 50% lives below the poverty line, and another 33% are close to that line.

9. Lack of private-practice veterinary services in disadvantaged communities is not unique to West Charlotte. When the HSUS took over a spay/neuter clinic in South Dallas (in the early 2000s), there were 59 veterinary practices in North Dallas (the rich side of town) and 13 in South Dallas, but 11 of these were on the boundary between the city of Dallas and neighboring suburbs. Only two were in South Dallas, and one was close to North Dallas. The other was a small (1.5 veterinarians) practice along with the HSUS spay/neuter clinic. When clients' zip codes were examined, it was determined that fewer than 10% came from the zip codes around the clinic.

10. The percentage of pet owners who never used veterinary services is even higher in other Pets for Life cities, such as Milwaukee, where the rate is approximately 80%, or Chicago, where the rate is closer to 85%.

11. In relation to spaying or neutering a pet, shelter workers often used the vernacular terms "fix" and, less often, "alter." We use both the veterinary and vernacular terms since our study considered both perspectives.

12. Pseudonyms are used when referring to pet owners and their pets to ensure confidentiality.

13. About 10% already have altered pets that were vaccinated; blocks are revisited until about 85% of the pet owners have been met.

Chapter 1. Liminal Pets and Their People

1. For simplicity, throughout *Underdogs* we at times use the terms "owner" and "pet" even though many of the Costa Ricans we studied did not consider themselves to be owners and were not viewed as such, and they did not view the dogs and cats with which they interacted as pets in the modern sense.

2. We prefer the term "street animals" to "stray." "Stray" incorrectly suggests the lack of an owner or someone particularly associated with a dog or cat. Research in developing countries (Morters et al., 2014) has found that approximately 95% of dogs roaming the streets are owned and return to their owners at night. "Street" rather than "stray dogs" is a more accurate term.

3. Of course more Westernized forms of pet keeping can occur in less developed nations among upper-class residents who own pedigree dogs as status symbols (Savvides, 2013).

4. In some cultures becoming a street animal is so normal it is almost a rite of passage, as people keep puppies as family pets but abandon them when they mature, an act that is rarely punished by law (Hsu, 2007a).

5. Even people with low levels of attachment to dogs and cats still usually provide at least some rudimentary everyday care. Shore et al. (2005) and Knobel, Laurenson, Kazwala, and Cleaveland (2008) found that pet owners with low attachment provide beneficial care and attention to their pets, deemed as either "essential" or "standard" (i.e., providing for little more than the basic physical needs of the animal), at which level they found minimal differences in frequency of behavior based on the reported degree of attachment.

6. Dump dogs may be less tolerated because they can become more of a nuisance from scattering trash or a potential danger if they are threatened by people using the dump.

7. Attempts to rehome these dogs invariably fail because they escape and return to their former locations or packs.

8. Refusing to sterilize some animals means that outreach workers will overestimate the success of their spay/neuter campaigns. People bringing animals to these low-cost clinics may bring only some of their animals for sterilization, but outreach workers usually do not ask if there are more animals at home.

9. Ironically, this view may exist because spay/neuter campaigns have been successful. Not only are there fewer dogs on the streets, they are healthier and less threatening, as reports suggest in other developing countries (Jackman & Rowan, 2007) where street dogs appear to be more content and robust than they used to be.

Chapter 2. Who Speaks for the Underserved?

1. Traditionally, there has also been a lack of regulation or monitoring of rescue and foster care organizations in the United States. By not subjecting these groups to inspections or even a mandated minimum set of standards of care, rescuers and fosterers function on an honor system (Pariser, 2014).

2. Indeed, clients gained by private practice veterinarians are likely to purchase more animal health care services than just the surgery, based on the Humane Society of the United States' experience of providing low-cost sterilization in Puerto Rico.

3. A group known as Vida charges a fee to veterinary students to get experience performing sterilization surgery, while El Refugio takes student volunteers for free.

4. Research in U.S. shelters found guilt to be common among pet owners surrendering their animals (DiGiacomo et al., 1998).

5. If outreach groups cannot find volunteers to help, staff members do this preparatory work, although once a clinic is held in a community they usually do not have to put up any advance publicity for future clinics.

Chapter 3. Sterilization as an Agent of Social Change

1. Costa Ricans may ask neighbors to donate money to pay for sterilization and, if needed, a taxi, when the sterilization is to control a very local animal problem. (Even with the added expense of a round-trip taxi ride, the cost of sterilizing an animal at an outreach clinic is significantly less than at a private veterinary practice, if there were one in the area.)

2. Small rescue groups and El Refugio ask for symbolic payments for services other than sterilization to also further responsibility for animals. In the past, the latter adopted out animals for free but now more commonly charges a small fee to enhance the perceived worth of animals and to encourage adopters to take more responsibility for their pets. The shelter also asks people who want to drop off their animals or need veterinary care to pay for these services rather than get them for free. As the manager said, "I always try to get money out of them so they have some responsibility—not everything is for nothing. For example, a lady comes to me with a dog that had broken legs. It costs 500,000 colones to do the operation. We lowered the price but she said she still couldn't afford it. We settled for both legs for 150,000 colones and she found the money."

3. Modeling with the same intention also happens at El Refugio. Some who visit the shelter do not know how to behave around dogs or cats and appear to be uncomfortable or awkward doing so. Knowing this, the shelter manager sometimes deliberately interacted with the one of the mascots, Pepito, to set an example of what visitors could do with animals at home or on the street. Every day when she arrived at work Pepito greeted her at the gate, and she would pick him up and kiss him, aware that visitors watched and were curious about what she was doing with Pepito, especially since the dog was old and sick, perhaps then thinking, "maybe it's not so bad" to be so affectionate with a dog, even when it is an unappealing stray.

Chapter 4. Underdogs and Their People

1. A lack of resources is not the only reason for making sacrifices for pets. Domestically abused women who are vulnerable sometimes forsake the safety of a shelter to stay with their pets, despite the danger of doing so (Faver & Strand, 2003).

2. If the shooting is reported to the police, an animal control officer will likely show up to ensure that the owner takes his or her injured pet to a veterinarian for necessary care; otherwise animal control will euthanize it. Conversely, in the unlikely event that a pet is shot in a middle- or upper-income neighborhood, an animal control officer will not automatically be called to ensure that the owner's pet receives veterinary care because it is assumed that the owner can afford it and will want to use a veterinarian to help the injured animal.

3. Even in the absence of spotting a dog in someone's backyard, chewed up tires indicate a dog with a "serious jaw" likely lives on that property and should be avoided.

4. Occasionally, if outreach workers are aware of these situations, they will offer to take dying pets to be euthanized by veterinarians, so the animals do not needlessly suffer.

5. Where veterinary deserts exist, more remote private-practice veterinarians probably do not feel like the shelter's free or discounted services pull from their clientele.

6. Although shelter workers prefer that pet owners see their animals as sentient creatures and not objects, even if they see animals as property, they may be willing to maintain them as well as they do their machines. "This is a thing I've got to maintain," as one shelter coordinator paraphrased the thinking of these car-valuing pet owners.

7. Some animal activists argue that landlords have no right to exclude any pet, regardless of breed, because under the law pets are property and apartment owners have no legal basis to forbid various kinds of property. Despite such arguments, pet restrictions and exclusions are commonplace in Charlotte.

8. However, children are more likely to cause property damage, but any attempt to impose special fees on people with children would cause an uproar. In addition, studies have shown that people with pets do not surrender their security payments at greater rates than those without pets, suggesting that damage from pets is no more likely than that from adults or children.

9. The Section 8 Program, known as the Housing Choice Voucher (HCV) Program, enables low-income families in the Charlotte area to rent safe, affordable housing in the private market through funds provided by the U.S. Department of Housing and Urban Development. Those who enroll in the program receive a voucher that allows a portion of their rent to be paid directly to the property manager or owner by the Charlotte Housing Authority.

10. Landlords can also complicate or prevent efforts to further pet welfare. For example, some oppose the building of a fence on their rental property—a service provided by the shelter and Beyond Fences, whose fences allow dogs to not be constantly chained outside. Sometimes they do not like how the fences look or that they enclose the entire backyard. Since any fixture on the landlord's property becomes theirs, they have the right to prevent fence building or to take a fence down at any time. Outreach workers explain that fences need not be permanent and can be taken down when the renters leave or that it is much safer to have a fenced-in dog than not, but these arguments do not always change the landlord's mind.

Chapter 5. The "Costs" of Care

1. This rate compares to 99% in rural Montana, 74% in Atlanta, 60% to 70% in Milwaukee, and 25% in the Charleston. This variation is partially due to differences in the number of towns or zip codes covered as well as distance from the shelter served by each program. For example, the rural Montana Pets for Life program has the most pressing need to provide transportation because of the great distance between pet owners and the nearest shelter; this need is still pressing but less so in Atlanta because the zip codes it covers span about 80 miles from the shelter.

2. The shelter and Charlotte animal control have succeeded in sterilizing about 80% of the West Charlotte pet population, compared to about 85% to 90% of pets sterilized nationally.

3. While larger dogs like pit bulls are commonly kept outside in West Charlotte all or most of the time, this is not the case for some urban Pets for Life programs, such as the one in Chicago, where winter weather is harsher and fewer pet owners have yards.

4. In addition, some patients do not seek health care because they are ashamed of their medical condition (e.g., Nadeem et al., 2007) or are reaching outside the family for help (Abrams et al., 2009); we found no evidence for these sources of stigma among West Charlotte's pet owners.

5. The estimated average yearly cost of feeding is $224 for a cat and between $150 and $500 for a dog, depending on its breed and size (Rauktis et al., 2017).

6. This restriction stems from the fact that in North Carolina veterinarians have to own and operate spay/neuter clinics. Technically, nonprofits such as the shelter are not allowed to own veterinary practices, but the West Charlotte shelter's spay/neuter clinic was grandfathered into this law and owns the clinic because it provides contractual services to Charlotte's Animal Care and Control office and has a medical director who does all the medical protocols there.

7. A few pet owners first visit the shelter but then see a private-practice veterinarian if something goes wrong after the shelter veterinarian treats the pet. When the private-practice veterinarian examines the animal, he or she might ask the pet owner, "Where did you get this medication? It almost killed your pet."

8. In addition to being afraid of breaking the rules about what they are allowed to do, the shelter veterinarians also worry that their work will be held to higher standards than that of other veterinarians if private-practice veterinarians assume that low cost means low quality.

Chapter 6. "Perfect Is the Enemy of Good"

1. Some within the sheltering community vehemently oppose breeding. As one outspoken critic said, "The breeding of companion animals, including pure breeds, must be made to carry no less stigma than wearing fur, as those who breed for any reason are complicit in perpetuating the confinement and killing of precious beings" (Duvan, 1989).

2. It is common for residents in low-income neighborhoods to be functionally illiterate, or reading at a third-grade level, so the shelter cannot reliably communicate with them through email, assuming they have internet access.

3. Only some are comfortable bringing up this issue, while others feel that it is "confrontational" and will not say anything about topics perceived as sensitive, including but not limited to sterilization.

4. A few people initially consent to sterilization because they think it involves only an injection rather than a surgical procedure.

5. According to city law, a stray or feral cat can technically be defined as someone's pet if that person has fed the animal a few times.

6. Indeed, animal advocates often decry the chaining of dogs as inhumane. For example, the adoption guidelines recommended by the Humane Society of the United States state that "regardless of local law, no dog should be released for adoption unless the adopter can provide an adequately fenced yard in which the dog can exercise, unless it is determined that the adopter will provide the dog with adequate exercise under humane control. (Simply chaining the dog in the yard for extended periods would provide neither adequate exercise nor humane control.)" (HSUS, 1998, p. 4).

Chapter 7. Forms of Veterinary Capital

1. Cats are less likely to serve this straddling function because families are more likely to project onto their dogs (Albert & Bulcroft, 1988). Also, in culture at large, cats are not seen as part of the ideal family, while dogs are more commonly viewed as part of the nuclear family equation. Commercials show children opening boxes with puppies under the Christmas tree, stories of young boys often feature their strong companionship with dogs, and family sitcoms commonly have dogs as background characters. None of that happens with cats. Cats do not have quite the same normalizing effect as do dogs (except within the population of people who own cats).

2. To most outsiders these dogs are generic "pits," but in West Charlotte many owners use more precise labels referring to specific types of pit bulls, with some types conferring more status than others. While pit bulls of whatever type are commonly owned in West Charlotte, many residents do not set out to acquire them but do so because that is all they could find. Only some residents deliberately seek out locally known backyard breeders of pit bulls.

3. That pit bulls can be used to signal boundaries between former and new community members is somewhat surprising because they are increasingly owned by people who are neither minorities nor disadvantaged, and who consciously present these dogs as unthreatening (Twining et al., 2000). Nevertheless, they still can be perceived by outsiders as threatening because of stereotypes that link low-income minorities with dogs that are assumed to be dangerous.

4. These steps taken by outreach workers to build rapport with pet owners are similar to what social-science ethnographers do to lessen the social distance between themselves and their field subjects by befriending people when they interact with and help them (e.g., Heuser, 2012). While ethnographers might hope that their befriending leads to a quid pro quo, such that their subjects might be more forthcoming and willing to be interviewed, shelter workers do not want pet owners to feel that their kindness or concern for them is quid pro quo for them to sterilize their pets.

5. The depth and significance of the friendship are often asymmetrical between ethnographers and their subjects too. To ethnographers, rapport-building efforts are meant to win trust not friends, but field subjects may misinterpret these efforts as creating friendship (Glesne, 1989). Thus, field subjects may feel more attachment—sometimes even profoundly—to ethnographers than the reverse.

6. Charlotte animal control provides disaster boarding of pets for up to six weeks. In other cases, where more temporary boarding is needed for owners to not surrender their pets (e.g., the owner is hospitalized or has an out-of-town emergency), the shelter can sometimes offer two weeks of free boarding at a cooperating kennel. Despite these efforts, the number of owners who retain their pets after boarding is very small because many are evicted or homeless and cannot find places to live.

7. Of course, there are benefits to animal health, with reports of lower incidence of mange and other diseases (Yoak et al., 2014).

Conclusion. Increasing Access to Veterinary Care

1. The challenge of creating stakeholder engagement and agreement is not unique to shelters. Other animal advocacy groups wanting more collaboration among stakeholders have experienced similar problems, such as policy makers in the one health movement (Mazet et al., 2014).

2. From the perspective of veterinarians in North Carolina, the range of stakeholders is relatively narrow, limited to pet owners, veterinary care providers, people in academia and industry, regulatory agencies, and licensing boards (Stull et al., 2018).

3. This hierarchy of expertise is not inevitable. A more negotiated form of expertise has also been reported in some cases where teachers in Sweden saw themselves as experts when it came to educational matters but saw parents as experts in child-rearing issues (Forsberg, 2007).

4. It would be cost-saving and convenient for the shelter to operate this facility. For example, if it looks like a pet owner's dog has a broken leg, the shelter can pay to have it x-rayed at its facility and then send the owner, the dog, and the x-rays to a veterinarian.

5. Along with a dramatic increase in the number of new members joining the Colegio de Medicos Veterinarios (the Costa Rican Veterinary Medical Association) in the last ten years, the number of private veterinary clinics has also increased substantially this century. From 2014 to 2016, the number of veterinary clinics in the country increased from 575 to 618 (a 7.5% increase).

6. If clients buy prescribed medications directly from their local veterinarians they often pay more for them than if they purchase them elsewhere. For example, a thyroid medicine can cost three times more if purchased directly from the veterinarian compared to a pharmacy; or a ten-day supply of a particular antibiotic could cost $50 from the private-practice veterinarian, while a three-week supply of the same pill can be purchased elsewhere for $3.

7. The efforts of animal advocates, as moral entrepreneurs, to persuade underserved pet owners to use basic services resemble the efforts of social movement protesters in general (Jasper, 2008) who engage in moral work about what ought to be rather than what is. Given the growth in the number of programs to provide affordable veterinary care to underserved pet owners, their collective efforts could be considered an incipient social movement seeking to make a sea change not only in the level of animal welfare in disadvantaged communities but also in the extent to which pet owners become invested in their animals as companions.

BIBLIOGRAPHY

Abrams, L., Dornig, K., & Curran, L. 2009. "Barriers to Service Use for Postpartum Depression Symptoms Among Low-income Ethnic Minority Mothers in the United States." *Qualitative Health Research, 19*(4), 535–551.

Access to Veterinary Care Coalition. 2018. *Access to Veterinary Care: Barriers, Current Practices, and Public Policy.* Knoxville: University of Tennessee College of Social Work.

Ackerman, L., ed. 2013. *Blackwell's Five-minute Veterinary Practice Management Consult.* Hoboken, N.J.: John Wiley.

Adeola, F. 2005. "Racial and Class Divergence in Public Attitudes and Perceptions about Poverty in USA: An Empirical Study." *Race, Gender & Class, 12,* 53–80.

Adler, P., & Adler, P. 1987. *Membership Roles in Field Research.* Newbury Park, Calif.: Sage.

Agoramoorthy, G. 2007, January 31. "Avoid Using Caste Names for India's Beasts." *Down to Earth.*

Ahmed, S., Lemkau, J., Nealeigh, N., & Mann, B. 2001. "Barriers to Healthcare Access in a Non-elderly Urban Poor American Population." *Health & Social Care in the Community, 9*(6), 445–453.

Albert, A., & Bulcroft, K. 1988. "Pets, Families, and the Life Course." *Journal of Marriage and the Family, 1,* 543–552.

Alcadipani, R., Westwood, R., & Rosa, A. 2015. "The Politics of Identity in Organizational Ethnographic Research: Ethnicity and Tropicalist Intrusions." *Human Relations, 68,* 79–106.

Al-Fayez, G., Arikawa, H., Awadalla, A., & Templer, D. 2003. "Companion Animal Attitude and Its Family Pattern in Kuwait." *Society & Animals, 11*(1), 17–28.

Alie, K., Davis, B., Fielding, W., & Maldonado, F. 2007. "Attitudes towards Dogs and Other 'Pets' in Roseau, Dominica." *Anthrozoös, 20*(2), 143–154.

Alkan, A. 2016. "Deportation as an Urban Stray Dogs Management Policy: Forest Dogs of Istanbul." *Lex Localis, 14*(3), 615–638.

Anderson, E. 1990. *Streetwise: Race, Class, and Change in an Urban Community*. Chicago: University of Chicago Press.

Anderson, E., Kohler, J., & Letiecq, B. 2002. "Low-income Fathers and 'Responsible Fatherhood' Programs: A Qualitative Investigation of Participants' Experiences." *Family Relations, 51*(2), 148–155.

Anderson, L. 2016. "The Pet in the Military Family at Transfer Time: It's No Small Matter." *Marriage & Family Review, 8*(3–4), 205–222.

Animal Humane Society. n.d. "Alternatives to Surrendering Your Pet." Retrieved from www.animalhumanesociety.org/surrender/alternatives-surrendering-your-pet.

———. 1999. "AHA Adoption Forum." Retrieved from www.animalhumanesociety.org.

Arkow, P. 2013. "The Impact of Companion Animals on Social Capital and Community Violence: Setting Research, Policy and Programs Agendas." *Journal of Sociology and Social Welfare, 40*, 33.

Arluke, A. 2002. "Managing Emotions in an Animal Shelter." In A. Manning & J. Serpell (Eds.), *Animals and Human Society* (pp. 183–203). New York: Routledge.

———. 2003. "The No-kill Controversy: Manifest and Latent Sources of Tension." In D. Salem & A. Rowan (Eds.), *The State of the Animals II* (pp. 67–83). Washington, D.C.: Humane Society Press.

———. 2010. "Animal-assisted Activity as a Social Experience." In A. Fine (Ed.), *Handbook on Animal-assisted Therapy: Theoretical Foundations and Guidelines for Practice* (3rd ed., pp.401–420). Cambridge, Mass.: Academic Press.

Arluke, A., & Atema, K. 2017. "Roaming Dogs." In L. Kalof (Ed.), *The Oxford Handbook of Animal Studies* (pp. 113–134). New York: Oxford University Press.

Arrington, A., & Markarian, M. 2017. "Serving Pets in Poverty: A New Frontier for the Animal Welfare Movement." *Sustainable Development Law & Policy, 18*(1), 40–43.

AVMA (American Veterinary Medical Association). n.d.-a. "Mandatory Spay/Neuter Laws." Retrieved from www.avma.org/Advocacy/StateAndLocal/Pages/sr-spay-neuter-laws.aspx.

———. n.d.-b. "Spaying and Neutering." Retrieved from www.avma.org/public/PetCare/Pages/spay-neuter.aspx.

———. 2005. "State Advocacy Issue: Ownership versus Guardianship." Retrieved from www.avma.org/Advocacy/StateAndLocal/Pages/ownership-vs-guardianship.aspx.

———. 2007. *U.S. Pet Ownership & Demographics Sourcebook*. Schaumburg, Ill.: American Veterinary Medical Association.

———. 2012. *U.S. Pet Ownership & Demographics Sourcebook*. Schaumburg, Ill.: American Veterinary Medical Association.

Baker, O. 2001. *A Dog's Life: Homeless People and Their Pets*. Oxford: Blue Cross.

Balcom, S., & Arluke, A. 2001. "Animal Adoption as Negotiated Order: A Comparison of Open Versus Traditional Shelter Approaches." *Anthrozoös, 14*(3), 135–150.

Barba, B. 1995. "A Critical Review of Research on the Human/Companion Animal Relationship: 1988 to 1993." *Anthrozoos, 8*(1), 9–19.

Barry, B. 1998. *Social Isolation and the Distribution of Income*. London: London School of Economics.

Beck, A. 2002. *The Ecology of Stray Dogs: A Study of Free-Ranging Urban Animals*. West Lafayette, Ind.: Purdue University Press.

Belk, R. 1996. "Metaphoric Relationships with Pets." *Society and Animals, 4*, 121–144.

Belle, D. 1983. "The Impact of Poverty on Social Networks and Supports." *Marriage & Family Review, 5*(4), 89–103.

Benford, S. 1993. "Frame Disputes Within the Nuclear Disarmament Movement." *Social Forces, 71*(3), 677–701.

Bhandari, H., & Yasunobu, K. 2009. "What Is Social Capital? A Comprehensive Review of the Concept." *Asian Journal of Social Science, 37*(3), 480–510.

Billock, J. 2018, March 6. "This Costa Rican Paradise Shelters Over 1000 Stray Dogs." *Smithsonian*. Retrieved from www.smithsonianmag.com/travel/these-photos -transport-you-dogs-central-american-paradise-180968018/.

Blouin, D. 2008. "All in the Family? Understanding the Meaning of Dogs and Cats in the Lives of American Pet Owners." Doctoral dissertation, Indiana University, Bloomington.

———. 2013. "Are Dogs Children, Companions, or Just Animals? Understanding Variations in People's Orientations toward Animals." *Anthrozoös, 26*(2), 279–294.

———. 2017, December 7. Personal communication.

Boglio Martínez, R. 2008. "Grassroots Support Organizations and Transformative Practices." *Journal of Community Practice, 16*(3), 339–358.

Boissevain, J. 1974. *Friends of Friends: Networks, Manipulators and Coalitions*. New York: St. Martin's.

Borthwick, F. 2006. "Noisy, Smelly, Dirty Dogs: A Sensorial Autoethnography of Living with Dogs." Paper presented at the ASCPRI Social Science Methodology Conference, Australian Consortium for Social and Political Research, Sydney.

Boulware, L., Cooper, L., Ratner, L., LaVeist, T., & Powe, N. 2016. "Race and Trust in the Health Care System." *Public Health Reports, 118*, 358–365.

Bourdieu, P. 1977. "Cultural Reproduction and Social Reproduction." In J. Karabel & A. Halsey (Eds.), *Power and Ideology in Education* (pp. 487–511). New York: Oxford University Press.

———. 2011. "The Forms of Capital." In I. Szeman & T. Kaposy (Eds.), *Cultural Theory: An Anthology* (pp. 81–93). New York: Wiley-Blackwell.

Boyko, A., Boyko, R., Boyko, C., Parker, H., Castelhano, M., Corey, L., Degenhardt, J., Auton, A., Hedimbi, M., Kityo, R., & Ostrander, E. 2009. "Complex Population Structure in African Village Dogs and Its Implications for Inferring Dog Domestication History." *Proceedings of the National Academy of Sciences, 106*(33), 13903–13908.

Bradshaw, J. 2017. *Animals Amongst Us*. New York: Basic.

Bretzlaff-Holstein, C. 2018. "The Case for Humane Education in Social Work Education." *Social Work Education, 37*(7), 924–935.

Brooks, A., & Hesse-Biber, S. 2007. "An Invitation to Feminist Research." In S. Hesse-Biber (Ed.), *Feminist Research Practice: A Primer* (pp. 1–24). Thousand Oaks, Calif.: Sage.

Brown, S. 2002. "Ethnic Variations in Pet Attachment Among Students at an American School of Veterinary Medicine." *Society & Animals, 10*(3), 249–266.

Brulliard, K. 2019, October 11. "The Growing Debate Over Spaying and Neutering Dogs." *Washington Post.*

Bueker, C. 2013. "Leads to Expanded Social Networks, Increased Civic Engagement and Divisions Within a Community: The Role of Dogs." *Journal of Society & Social Welfare, 40*(4), 211–236.

Burns, K. 2008, June 19. "Human Animal Bond Boosts Spending on Veterinary Care." *JAVMA News.*

Burton, C. 1992. *The Poverty Debate: Politics and the Poor in America.* Westport, Conn.: Praeger.

Cain, A. 1985. "Pets as Family Members." *Marriage & Family Review, 8*(3–4), 5–10.

———. 2016. "Pets as Family Members." In M. Sussman (Ed.), *Pets and the Family* (pp. 5–10). New York: Routledge.

Campinha-Bacote, J. 2002. "The Process of Cultural Competence in the Delivery of Healthcare Services: A Model of Care." *Journal of Transcultural Nursing, 13*(3), 181–184.

Carmon, I. 2014, June 27. "For Eugenic Sterilization Victims, Belated Justice." MSNBC.

Caron-Sheppard, J. 1995. "The Black-White Environmental Concern Gap: An Examination of Environmental Paradigms." *Journal of Environmental Education, 26*(2), 24–35.

Carter, P. 2003. "'Black' Cultural Capital, Status Positioning, and Schooling Conflicts for Low-income African American Youth." *Social Problems, 50*(1), 136–155.

Cassells, R., & Evans, G. 2017. "Ethnic Variation in Poverty and Parenting Stress." In K. Deater-Deckard & R. Panneton, *Parental Stress and Early Child Development* (pp. 15–46). Dordrecht: Springer.

Chamberlin, L., Sherman, S., Jain, A., Powers, S., & Whitaker, R. 2002. "The Challenge of Preventing and Treating Obesity in Low-income, Preschool Children: Perceptions of WIC Health Care Professionals." *Archives of Pediatrics & Adolescent Medicine, 156*(7), 662–668.

Charles, K., Hurst, E., & Roussanov, N. 2009. "Conspicuous Consumption and Race." *Quarterly Journal of Economics, 124*(2), 425–467.

Cheatham, G., & Otrosky, M. 2011. "Whose Expertise? An Analysis of Advice Giving in Early Childhood Parent-teacher Conferences." *Journal of Research in Childhood Education, 25*(1), 24–44.

Chetty, R., Hendren, N., Kline, P., & Saez, E. 2014. "Where Is the Land of Opportunity? The Geography of Intergenerational Mobility in the United States." *Quarterly Journal of Economics, 129*(4), 1553–1623.

Chin, T., & Phillips, M. 2004. "Social Reproduction and Child-rearing Practices: Social class, Children's Agency, and the Summer Activity Gap." *Sociology of Education, 77*(3), 185–210.

Clancy, E., & Rowan, A. 2003. "Companion Animal Demographics in the United States:

A Historical Perspective." In D. Salem & A. Rowan (Eds.), *The State of the Animals II* (pp. 9–26). Washington, D.C.: Humane Society Press.

Clark, M. 2017. "Considering the Canine: Human Discourses of Gender, Race, and Power in Interspecies Entanglements." Doctoral dissertation, Arizona State University, Tempe.

Clasen-Kelly, F. 2017, June 30. "'We Can't Be Bought,' Can This Neighborhood Stop Investors from Moving In?" *Charlotte Observer.*

Clifton, M. 2010. "How Not to Fight a Rabies Epidemic: A History in Bali." *Asian Biomedicine, 4*(4), 663–670.

Cohen, S. 2002. "Can Pets Function as Family Members?" *Western Journal of Nursing Research, 24*(6), 621–638.

Conger, R., & Conger, K. 2008. "Understanding the Process Through Which Economic Hardship Influences Families and Children." In T. B. Heaton (Ed.), *Handbook of Families and Poverty* (pp. 64–81). Thousand Oaks, Calif.: Sage.

Coppinger, R., & Coppinger, L. 2016. *What Is a Dog?* Chicago: University of Chicago Press.

Crawley, L., Payne, R., Bolden, J., Payne, T., Washington, P., & Williams, S. 2000. "Palliative and End-of-life Care in the African American Community." *JAMA, 284*(19), 2518–2521.

Cuadraz, G., & Uttal, L. 1999. "Intersectionality and In-depth Interviews: Methodological Strategies for Analyzing Race, Class, and Gender." *Race, Gender & Class, 6*(3), 156–186.

D'Aveni, R., & Kesner, I. 1993. "Top Managerial Prestige, Power and Tender Offer Response: A Study of Elite Social Networks and Target Firm Cooperation During Takeovers." *Organization Science, 4*(2), 123–151.

Dearing, J. 2009. "Applying Diffusion of Innovation Theory to Intervention Development." *Research on Social Work Practice, 19*(5), 503–518.

Deckha, M. 2012. "Toward a Postcolonial, Posthumanist Feminist Theory: Centralizing Race and Culture in Feminist Work on Nonhuman Animals." *Hypatia, 27*(3), 527–545.

DeMello, M. 2012. *Animals and Society: An Introduction to Human-Animal Studies.* New York: Columbia University Press.

Demo, D., & Hughes, M. 1990. "Socialization and Racial Identity Among Black Americans." *Social Psychology Quarterly, 53,* 364–374.

DiGiacomo, N., Arluke, A., & Patronek, G. 1998. "Surrendering Pets to Shelters: The Relinquisher's Perspective." *Anthrozoös, 11*(1), 41–51.

Djerassi, C., Israel, A., & Jochle, W. 1973, January. "Planned Parenthood for Pets." *Bulletin of the Atomic Scientists,* 10–19.

Doane, M., & Sarenbo, S. 2019. "A Modified Combined C-BARQ and QoL for Both Companion Dog and Its Owner: An Embryo to a Companion Dog Welfare Assessment?" *Applied Animal Behaviour Science, 213,* 91–106.

Dobbie, D., & Richards-Schuster, K. 2008. "Building Solidarity Through Difference: A Practice Model for Critical Multicultural Organizing." *Journal of Community Practice, 16*(3), 317–337.

Doi, K., & Pettier, J. 2018. "The Ambiguous Status of Companion Animals in Rapidly

Changing Societies." In I. Amelung, M. Balz, H. Holbig, M. Schumann, & C. Storz (Eds.), *Protecting the Weak in East Asia: Framing, Mobilisation and Institutionalisation* (pp. 196–223). New York: Routledge.

Dolin, E. 1988. "Black Americans Attitudes toward Wildlife." *Journal of Environmental Education, 20,* 17–21.

Domingues, L., Cesar, J., Fassa, A., & Domingues, M. 2015. "Responsible Pet Animal Guardianship in the Urban Area of the Municipality of Pelotas in the State of Rio Grande do Sul, Brazil." *Ciencia & Saude Coletiva, 20*(1), 185–192.

Donovan, J. 2007. "Attention to Suffering." In J. Donovan & C. Adams (Eds.), *The Feminist Care Tradition in Animal Ethics* (pp. 174–197). Cambridge, Mass.: Harvard University Press.

Drews, C. 2001. "Wild Animals and Other Pets Kept in Costa Rican Households: Incidence, Species and Numbers." *Society & Animals, 9*(2), 107–126.

———. 2002. "Attitudes, Knowledge and Wild Animals as Pets in Costa Rica." *Anthrozoös, 15*(2), 119–138.

———. 2003. "The State of Wild Animals in the Minds and Households of a Neotropical Society: The Costa Rican Case Study." In D. Salem & A. Rowan (Eds.), *The State of the Animals II* (pp. 193–205). Washington, D.C.: Humane Society Press.

Duvan, E. 1989. "In the Name of Mercy." *Animalines.* Reprint, Best Friends Animals Society, www.bestfriends.org.

Edvardsson, B., & Roos, I. 2001. "Critical Incident Techniques: Towards a Framework for Analysing the Criticality of Critical Incidents." *International Journal of Service Industry Management, 12*(3), 251–268.

Eng, E., & Young, R. 1992. "Lay Health Advisors as Community Change Agents." *Family & Community Health, 15*(1), 24–40.

Eraut, M. 2004. "Informal Learning in the Workplace." *Studies in Continuing Education, 26*(2), 247–273.

Evans, F. 1963. "Selling as a Dyadic Relationship—A New Approach." *American Behavioral Scientist, 6*(9), 76–79.

Falicov, C. 2001. "The Cultural Meanings of Money: The Case of Latinos and Anglo-Americans." *American Behavioral Scientist, 45*(2), 313–328.

Farnworth, M., Blaszak, K., Hiby, E., & Waran, N. 2012. "Incidence of Dog Bites and Public Attitudes Towards Dog Care and Management in Samoa." *Animal Welfare, 21,* 477–486.

Faver, C., & Strand, E. 2003. "To Leave or to Stay? Battered Women's Concern for Vulnerable Pets." *Journal of Interpersonal Violence, 18*(12), 1367–1377.

Fazio, R. 1986. "How Do Attitudes Guide Behavior." In R. Sorrentino & E. Higgins (Eds.), *The Handbook of Motivation and Cognition: Foundations of Social Behavior* (pp. 204–243). New York: Guilford.

Feldman, B. 1974. "The Problem of Urban Dogs." *Science, 185,* 931.

Fielding, W. 2010. "Dog Breeding in New Providence, the Bahamas, and Its Potential Impact on the Roaming Dog Population I: Planned and Accidental." *Journal of Applied Animal Welfare Science, 13*(3), 250–260.

Fielding, W., Samuels, D., & Mather, J. 2002. "Attitudes and Actions of West Indian

Dog Owners towards Neutering Their Animals: A Gender Issue?" *Anthrozoös, 15*(3), 206–226.

Fink, T. 2015. "Combatting the Food Crisis: Issues of Trans-species Food Insecurity." Doctoral dissertation, Humboldt State University, Arcata, Calif.

Flanagan, J. 1954. "The Critical Incident Technique." *Psychological Bulletin, 51*(4), 327–358.

Flores, G., Abreu, M., Olivar, M., & Kastner, B. 1998. "Access Barriers to Health Care for Latino Children." *Archives of Pediatrics & Adolescent Medicine, 152*(11), 1119–1125.

Fordham, S., & Ogbu, J. 1986. "Black Students' School Success: Coping with the Burden of 'Acting White.'" *Urban Review, 18*(3), 176–206.

Forsberg, L. 2007. "Involving Parents Through School Letters: Mothers, Fathers and Teachers Negotiating Children's Education and Rearing." *Ethnography and Education, 2*(3), 273–288.

Fothergill, A. 2013. "Managing Childcare: The Experiences of Mothers and Childcare Workers." *Sociological Inquiry, 83*(3), 421–447.

Fox, R. 2008. "Animal Behaviours, Post-human Lives: Everyday Negotiations of the Animal-human Divide in Pet-keeping." *Social & Cultural Geography, 7*(4), 525–537.

Freeman, C. 2010. "Embracing Humanimality: Deconstructing the Human/animal Dichotomy." In G. Goodale & J. Black (Eds.), *Arguments About Animal Ethics* (pp. 11–30). Lanham, Md.: Lexington Books.

Freeman, L. 2002. "America's Affordable Housing Crisis: A Contract Unfulfilled." *American Journal of Public Health, 92*(5), 709–712.

Freidson, E. 1975. *Doctoring Together: A Study of Professional Social Control.* New York: Elsevier.

Friedman, E. 1994. "Money Isn't Everything: Nonfinancial Barriers to Access." *JAMA, 271*(19), 1535–1538.

Friestad, M., & Wright, P. 1994. "The Persuasion Knowledge Model: How People Cope with Persuasion Attempts." *Journal of Consumer Research, 21*(1), 1–31.

Frommer, S., & Arluke, A. 1999. "Loving Them to Death: Blame-displacing Strategies of Animal Shelter Workers and Surrenderers." *Society & Animals, 7*(1), 1–16.

Fryer, R., Jr., & Levitt, S. 2004. "The Causes and Consequences of Distinctively Black Names." *Quarterly Journal of Economics, 119*(3), 767–805.

Fujii, L. 2004. "Transforming the Moral Landscape: The Diffusion of a Genocidal Norm in Rwanda." *Journal of Genocide Research, 6*(1), 99–114.

Gaard, G. 2011. "Ecofeminism Revisited: Rejecting Essentialism and Re-placing Species in a Material Feminist Environmentalism." *Feminist Formations, 23*(2), 26–53.

Gaarder, E. 2011. *Women and the Animal Rights Movement.* New Brunswick, N.J.: Rutgers University Press.

Gans, H. 2014. "Studying the Bottom of American Society." *DuBois Review: Social Science Research on Race, 11*(2), 195–204.

Garner, S. 1998. *Political Animals: Animal Protection Politics in Britain and the United States.* London: Palgrave Macmillan.

Gecas, V., & Schwalbe, M. 1983. "Beyond the Looking-glass Self: Social Structure and Efficacy-based Self-esteem." *Social Psychology Quarterly, 46*(2), 77–88.

Gilardi, F. 2012. "Transnational Diffusion: Norms, Ideas, and Policies." In W. Carlsnaes, T. Risse, & B. Simmons (Eds.), *Handbook of International Relations* (pp.453–477). Thousand Oaks, Calif.: Sage.

Gilgun, J. 1999. "CASPARS: New Tools for Assessing Client Risks and Strengths." *Families in Society, 80*(5), 450–459.

Gillespie, K., & Lawson, V. 2017. "'My Dog Is My Home': Multispecies Care and Poverty Politics in Los Angles, California and Austin, Texas." *Gender, Place & Culture, 24*(6), 774–793.

Gilligan, C. 1982. *In a Different Voice: Psychological Theory and Women's Development.* Cambridge, Mass.: Harvard University Press.

Glesne, C. 1989. "Rapport and Friendship in Ethnographic Research." *International Journal of Qualitative Studies in Education, 2*(1), 45–54.

Goffman, E. 1974. *Frame Analysis: An Essay on the Organization of Experience.* New York: Harper & Row.

Goldberg, M. 1995. "Substance-abusing Women: False Stereotypes and Real Needs." *Social Work, 40*(6), 789–798.

Graham, T., & Glover, T. 2014. "On the Fence: Dog Parks in the (Un)Leashing of Community and Social Capital." *Leisure Sciences, 36*(3), 217–234.

Grandin, T. (Ed.). 2015. *Improving Animal Welfare: A Practical Approach.* Boston: Cabi.

Granovetter, M. 1973. "The Strength of Weak Ties." *American Journal of Sociology, 78*(6), 1360–1380.

Green, B., Maisiak, R., Wang, M., Britt, M., & Ebeling, N. 1997. "Participation in Health Education, Health Promotion, and Health Research by African Americans: Effects of the Tuskegee Syphilis Experiment." *Journal of Health Education, 28*(4), 196–201.

Greenbaum, S. 2015. *Blaming the Poor: The Long Shadow of the Moynihan Report on Cruel Images about Poverty.* New Brunswick, N.J.: Rutgers University Press.

Greenebaum, J. 2009. "'I'm Not an Activist!' Animal Rights vs. Animal Welfare in the Purebred Dog Rescue Movement." *Society & Animals, 17*(4), 289–304.

Greenhalgh, T., Steven, G., Macfarlane, F., Bate, P., & Kyriakidou, O. 2004. "Diffusion of Innovations in Service Organizations: Systematic Review and Recommendations." *Milbank Quarterly, 82*(4), 581–629.

Greenhill, B. 2012. "Norm Diffusion in IGO Networks: The Case of Gay Rights and Women's Rights." Paper presented at the Globalization Colloquium, New York University.

Grimm, D. 2014. *Citizen Canine: Our Evolving Relationship with Cats and Dogs.* New York: Public Affairs.

Gronskaya, N., & Makarychev, A. 2014. "The 2014 Sochi Olympics and Sovereign Power: A Political Linguistic Perspective." *Problems of Post-Communism, 61*(1), 41–51.

Grossmann, I., & Huynh, A. 2013. "Where Is the Culture in Social Class?" *Psychological Inquiry, 24*(2), 112–119.

Guenther, K. 2017. "Volunteers' Power and Resistance in the Struggle for Shelter Animal Survival." *Sociological Forum, 32*(4), 770–792.

Guttmacher Institute. 2019. "Unintended Pregnancy in the United States." Guttmacher Center for Population Research Innovation and Dissemination. Retrieved from www.guttmacher.org/fact-sheet/unintended-pregnancy-united-states.

Hamilton, F. 2010. "Leading and Organizing Social Change for Companion Animals." *Anthrozoös, 23*(3), 277–292.

Haraway, D. 2013. *When Species Meet*. Minneapolis: University of Minnesota Press.

Harding, S. 2013. "'Bling with Bite'—Rise of Status and Weapon Dogs." *Veterinary Record, 173*(11), 261–263.

Harper, D. 1987. *Working Knowledge: Skill and Community in a Small Shop*. Chicago: University of Chicago Press.

Hart, B., Hart, L., Thigpen, A., & Willits, N. 2014. "Long-Term Health Effects of Neutering Dogs: Comparison of Labrador Retrievers with Golden Retrievers." *PLOS ONE, 9*(7), e102241. Retrieved from https://doi.org/10.1371/journal.pone.0102241.

———. 2016. "Neutering of German Shepherd Dogs: Associated Joint Disorders, Cancers and Urinary Incontinence." *Veterinary Medicine & Science, 2*, 191–199.

Hasenfeld, Y. 2000. "Organizational Forms as Moral Practices: The Case of Welfare Departments." *Social Service Review, 74*(3), 329–351.

Hasler, B., Neville, G., Bennani, H., Onono, J., & Rushton, J. 2011. *Evaluation of Rabies Control in Colombo City, Sri Lanka*. London: Royal Veterinary College.

Heller, P., del Carmen Rivera-Worley, M., & Chalfant, H. 1979. "The Stable Poor and Criticism of Poverty Area Agencies." *Journal of Sociology and Social Welfare, 6*(3), 385–399.

Hens, K. 2009. "Ethical Responsibilities towards Dogs: An Inquiry into the Dog-human Relationship." *Journal of Agricultural and Environmental Ethics, 22*(1), 3–14.

Herzog, H. 2007. "Gender Differences in Human-animal Interactions: A Review." *Anthrozoös, 20*(1), 7–21.

———. 2010. *Some We Love, Some We Hate, Some We Eat: Why It's So Hard to Think Straight About Animals*. New York: Harper.

Heuser, E. 2012. "Befriending the Field: Culture and Friendships in Development Worlds." *Third World Quarterly, 33*(8), 1423–1437.

Hickrod, L., & Schmitt, R. 1982. "A Naturalistic Study of Interaction and Frame: The Pet as Family Member." *Urban Life, 11*(1), 55–77.

Hill, S. 2001. "Class, Race, and Gender Dimensions of Child Rearing in African American Families." *Journal of Black Studies, 31*(4), 494–508.

Hirschman, A. 1991. *The Rhetoric of Reaction*. Cambridge, Mass.: Harvard University Press.

Holodynski, M., & Friedlmeier, W. 2006. *Development of Emotions and Emotion Regulation* (Vol. 8). Dordrecht: Springer.

Horowitz, A. 2019. *Our Dogs, Ourselves: The Story of a Singular Bond*. New York: Scribner.

Hosey, G., & Melfi, V. 2019. *Anthrozoology: Human-Animal Interactions in Domesticated and Wild Animals*. New York: Oxford.

Hoy-Gerlach, J., Delgado, M., Sloane, H., & Arkow, P. 2018. "Rediscovering Connections Between Animal Welfare and Human Welfare: Creating Social Work Internships at a Humane Society." *Journal of Social Work, 19*(2), 216–232.

Hsu, M. 2007a. "Taiwan: Animal Welfare Law." In M. Bekoff (Ed.), *Encyclopedia of Human-Animal Relationships* (Vol. 3, pp. 1015–1016). Westport, Conn.: Greenwood.

———. 2007b. "Taiwan and Companion Animals." In M. Bekoff (Ed.), *Encyclopedia of Human-Animal Relationships* (Vol. 2, pp. 613–615). Westport, Conn.: Greenwood.

HSUS (Humane Society of the United States). n.d.-a. "Adopters Welcome Manual." Retrieved from www.animalsheltering.org/page/adopters-welcome-manual.

———. n.d.-b. "Promoting Social Justice Through Spay/neuter." Retrieved from www
.animalsheltering.org/social-justice-spay-neuter.

———. 1998. "HSUS_Guidelines_Adoption_1998." HIS Electronic Library.

———. 2018. "Pets by the Numbers." Retrieved from www.animalsheltering.org/page
/pets-by-the-numbers.

Huston, A., & Bentley, A. 2010. "Human Development in Societal Context." *Annual Review of Psychology*, *61*, 411–437.

Irvine, L. 2003. "The Problem of Unwanted Pets: A Case Study in How Institutions 'Think' About Clients' Needs." *Social Problems*, *50*(4), 550–566.

———. 2004a. *If You Tame Me: Understanding Our Connection with Animals*. Philadelphia: Temple University Press.

———. 2004b. "Pampered or Enslaved? The Moral Dilemmas of Pets." *International Journal of Sociology and Social Policy*, *24*(9), 5–17.

———. 2013. *My Dog Always Eats First: Homeless People and Their Animals*. Boulder, Colo.: Lynne Rienner.

Irvine, L., Kahl, K., & Smith, J. 2012. "Confrontations and Donations: Encounters Between Homeless Pet Owners and the Public." *Sociological Quarterly*, *53*(1), 25–43.

Jackman, J., & Rowan, A. 2007. "Free-Roaming Dogs in Developing Countries: The Benefits of Capture, Neuter, and Return Programs." In D. Salem & A. Rowan (Eds.), *The State of the Animals IV* (pp. 55–78). Washington, D.C.: Humane Society Press.

Jasper, J. 2008. *The Art of Moral Protest: Culture, Biography, and Creativity in Social Movements*. Chicago: University of Chicago Press.

Jasper, J., & Nelkin, D. 1991. *The Animal Rights Crusade. The Growth of a Moral Protest*. New York: Free Press.

Jenner, M. 1997. "The Great Dog Massacre." In W. Naphy & P. Stevens (Eds.), *Fear in the Early Modern Society* (pp. 43–61). Manchester: Manchester University Press.

Jerolmack, C. 2007. "Animal Practices, Ethnicity, and Community: The Turkish Pigeon Handlers of Berlin." *American Sociological Review*, *72*(3), 874–894.

Johnson, T., Garrity, T., & Stallones, L. 1992. "Psychometric Evaluation of the Lexington Attachment to Pets Scale (LAPS)." *Anthrozoös*, *5*, 160–175.

Johnson, Y., & Munch, S. 2009. "Fundamental Contradictions in Cultural Competence." *Social Work*, *54*(3), 220–231.

Jones, D., Zalot, A., Foster, S., Sterrett, E., & Chester, C. 2007. "A Review of Childrearing in African American Single Mother Families: The Relevance of a Coparenting Framework." *Journal of Child and Family Studies*, *16*, 671–683.

Jorgensen, D. 2015. "Participant Observation." In S. Kosslyn (Ed.), *Emerging Trends in the Social and Behavioral Sciences: An Interdisciplinary, Searchable, and Linkable Resource*. New York: John Wiley. Retrieved from https://doi.org/10.1002/9781118900772. etrds0247.

Kanter, R. 1994. "Collaborative Advantage." *Harvard Business Review*, *72*(4), 96–108.

Kartal, T., & Rowan, A. 2018. "Stray Dog Population Management." In K. Polak (Ed.), *Field Manual for Small Animal Medicine* (pp. 15–28). Hoboken, N.J.: Wiley-Blackwell.

Katcher, A. 2002. "Animals in Therapeutic Education: Guides into the Liminal State." In P. Khan & S. Kellert (Eds.), *Children and Nature: Psychological, Sociocultural, and Evolutionary Investigations* (pp.179–198). Cambridge, Mass.: MIT Press.

Katz, I., Corlyon, J., La Placa, V., & Hunter, S. 2007. *The Relationship Between Parenting and Poverty.* York: Joseph Rowntree Foundation.

Kauffman, K. 1994. "The Insider/Outsider Dilemma: Field Experience of a White Researcher 'Getting in' a Poor Black Community." *Nursing Research, 43*(3), 179–183.

Kawachi, I., & Berkman, L. (Eds.). 2003. *Neighborhoods and Health.* Oxford: Oxford University Press.

Kee, H., & Knox, R. 1970. "Conceptual and Methodological Considerations in the Study of Trust and Suspicion." *Journal of Conflict Resolution, 14*(3), 357–366.

Kellert, S. 1994. "Attitudes, Knowledge and Behaviour Toward Wildlife Among the Industrial Superpowers: The United States and Germany." In A. Manning & J. Serpell (Eds.), *Animals and Human Society* (pp. 166–187). New York: Routledge.

Kellert, S., & Berry, J. 1980. "Knowledge, Affection and Basic Attitudes Toward Animals in American Society." U.S. Department of the Interior, U.S. Fish and Wildlife Service.

Kendall, H., Lobao, L., & Sharp, J. 2006. "Public Concern with Animal Well-Being: Place, Social Structural Location, and Individual Experience." *Rural Sociology, 71*(3), 399–428.

Kent, M., Burton, J., Dank, G., Bannasch, D., & Rebhun, R. 2018. "Association of Cancer-related Mortality, Age and Gonadectomy in Golden Retriever Dogs at a Veterinary Academic Center (1989–2016)." *PLOS ONE, 13*(2), e0192578. Retrieved from https://doi.org/10.1371/journal.pone.0192578.

Kesselring, M., de Winter, M., van Yperen, T., & Lecluijze, S. 2016. "Partners in Parenting: An Overview of the Literature on Parents' and Nonparental Adults' Perspectives on Shared Responsibilities in Childrearing." *Issues in Social Science, 4*(1), 69–97.

Kidd, A., & Kidd, R. 1994. "Benefits and Liabilities of Pets for the Homeless." *Psychological Reports, 74*(3), 715–722.

Kincaid, D. 2004. "From Innovation to Social Norm: Bounded Normative Influence." *Journal of Health Communication, 9*(S1), 37–57.

Kinsler, J., Wong, M., Sayles, J., Davis, C., & Cunningham, W. 2007. "The Effect of Perceived Stigma from a Health Care Provider on Access to Care Among a Low-income HIV-Positive Population." *AIDS Patient Care and STDs, 21*(8), 584–592.

Kissane, R. 2003. "What's Need Got to Do With It—Barriers to Use of Nonprofit Social Services." *Journal of Sociology and Social Welfare, 30*(2), 127–148.

Knobel, D., Laurenson, M., Kazwala, R., Boden, L., & Cleaveland, S. 2008. "A Cross-sectional Study of Factors Associated with Dog Ownership in Tanzania." *BMC Veterinary Research, 4*(1), 5.

Knobel, D., Laurenson, K., Kazwala, R., & Cleaveland, S. 2008. "Development of an Item Scale to Assess Attitudes Towards Domestic Dogs in the United Republic of Tanzania." *Anthrozoös, 21*(3), 285–295.

Kohn, M., Scotch, N., & Glick, I. 1979. "The Effects of Social Class on Parental Values and Practices." In D. Reiss & H. Hoffman (Eds.), *The American Family: Dying or Developing* (pp. 45–77). Boston: Springer.

Kraus, M., Piff, P., & Keltner, D. 2009. "Social Class, Sense of Control, and Social Explanation." *Journal of Personality and Social Psychology, 97*(6), 992–1004.

Krause-Parello, C. 2012. "Pet Ownership and Older Women: The Relationships Among Loneliness, Pet Attachment Support, Human Social Support, and Depressed Mood." *Geriatric Nursing, 33*(3), 194–203.

Krivo, L., & Peterson, R. 1996. "Extremely Disadvantaged Neighborhoods and Urban Crime." *Social Forces, 75*(2), 619–648.

Kruse, C. 1999. "Gender, Views of Nature, and Support for Animal Rights." *Society & Animals, 7*(3), 179–198.

Kwok, Y., von Keyserlingk, M., Sprea, G., & Molento, C. 2016. "Human-Animal Interactions of Community Dogs in Campo Largo, Brazil: A Descriptive Study." *Journal of Veterinary Behavior, 13*, 27–33.

Lacour, G. 2015, September. "The Challenge of Charlotte's West Side: The Prospect of New Life for 'the Bad Part of Town.'" *Charlotte Magazine.*

Lago, D., Kafer, R., Delaney, M., & Connell, C. 1988. "Assessment of Favorable Attitudes Toward Pets: Development and Preliminary Validation of Self-report Pet Relationship Scales." *Anthrozoös, 1*, 240–254.

Lamont, M., & Lareau, A. 1988. "Cultural Capital: Allusions, Gaps and Glissandos in Recent Theoretical Developments." *Sociological Theory, 6*(2), 153–168.

Lareau, A. 2002. "Invisible Inequality: Social Class and Childrearing in Black Families and White Families." *American Sociological Review, 67*(5), 747–776.

Laurent-Simpson, A. 2017. "Considering Alternate Sources of Role Identity: Childless Parents and Their Animal 'Kids.'" *Sociological Forum, 32*(3), 610–634.

Legard, R., Keegan, J., & Ward, K. 2003. "In-Depth Interviews." *Qualitative Research Practice, 6*(1), 138–169.

Lévi-Strauss, C. 1967. *The Savage Mind.* Chicago: University of Chicago Press.

Lewin Group. 1997. *An Evaluability Assessment of Responsible Fatherhood Programs.* Fairfax, Va.: Author.

Lewis, O. 1966. *La Vida: A Puerto Rican Family in the Culture of Poverty—San Juan and New York* (Vol. 13). New York: Random House.

Lian, B., & Mathis, M. 2016. "Pet Ownership, Attitudes, and Experiences Across Income Level." *North American Journal of Psychology, 18*(3), 611–622.

Link, B., & Phelan, J. 2001. "Conceptualizing Stigma." *Annual Review of Sociology, 27*, 363–385.

Loseke, D. 2001. "Lived Realities and Formula Stories of 'Battered Women.'" In J. Gubrium & J. Holstein (Eds.), *Institutional Selves: Troubled Identities in a Postmodern World* (pp. 107–126). New York: Oxford University Press.

Lugton, J. 1997. "The Nature of Social Support as Experienced by Women Treated for Breast Cancer." *Journal of Advanced Nursing, 25*(6), 1184–1191.

Maholmes, V., & King, R. 2012. *The Oxford Handbook of Poverty and Child Development.* New York: Oxford University Press.

Major, B., & O'Brien, L. 2005. "The Social Psychology of Stigma." *Annual Review of Psychology, 56*, 393–421.

Mansour, M., Lanphear, B., & DeWitt, T. 2000. "Barriers to Asthma Care in Urban Children: Parent Perspective." *Pediatrics, 106*(3), 512–519.

Manstead, A. 2018. "The Psychology of Social Class: How Socioeconomic Status Impacts Thought, Feelings, and Behaviour." *British Journal of Social Psychology, 57*(2), 267–291.

Margetts, H., Perri 6, & Hood, C. (Eds.). 2012. *Paradoxes of Modernization: Unintended Consequences of Public Policy Reform.* Oxford: Oxford University Press.

Markovits, A., & Queen, R. 2009. "Women and the World of Dog Rescue: A Case Study of the State of Michigan." *Society & Animals, 17*(4), 325–342.

Marsa-Sambola, F., Williams, J., Muldoon, J., Lawrence, A., Connor, M., Stevens, C., Brooks, F., & Currie, C. 2016. "Sociodemographics of Pet Ownership Among Adolescents in Great Britain: Findings from the HBSC Study in England, Scotland, and Wales." *Anthrozoös, 29*(4), 559–580.

Marshall, M., & Stolle, D. 2004. "Race and the City: Neighborhood Context and the Development of Generalized Trust." *Political Behavior,* 26, 125–153.

Marsick, V., & Watkins, K. 2001. "Informal and Incidental Learning." *New Directions for Adult and Continuing Education, 2001*(89), 25–34.

Martínez, B. 2008. "Grassroots Support Organizations and Transformative Practices." *Journal of Community Practice, 16*(3), 339–358.

Marx, M., Stallones, L., Garrity, T., & Johnson, T. 1988. "Demographics of Pet Ownership Among U.S. Adults 21 to 64 Years of Age." *Anthrozoös, 2*(1), 33–37.

Masse, L. 2015. "Suburban Underdogs: Exploring the Marginalization of Youth from Deprived Urban Neighborhoods in France." Master's thesis, Utrecht University.

Matsuoka, A., & Sorenson, J. 2014. "Social Justice Beyond Human Beings: Trans-species Social Justice." In T. Ryan (Ed.), *Animals in Social Work* (pp. 64–79). London: Palgrave Macmillan.

Matthews, S. 2003. "In Defense of Civil Rights: The Paradoxical Power of Family Photographs." *Afterimage, 30*(3/4), 13–14.

Mauss, M. 1990 [1922]. *The Gift: Forms and Functions of Exchange in Archaic Societies.* London: Routledge.

Mayorga-Gallo, S. 2018. "Whose Best Friend? Dogs and Racial Boundary Maintenance in a Multiracial Neighborhood." *Sociological Forum, 33*(2), 505–528.

Mazet, J., Uhart, M., & Keyyu, J. 2014. "Stakeholders in One Health." *Review of Science and Technology, 33,* 443–452.

McCardle, P., McCune, S., Griffin, J., Esposito, L., & Freund, L. 2011. *Animals in Our Lives: Human-Animal Interaction in Family, Community, & Therapeutic Settings.* Baltimore: Brookes.

McCormick, M., Brooks-Gunn, J., Shorter, T., Wallace, C., Holmes, J., & Heagarty, M. 1987. "The Planning of Pregnancy Among Low-income Women in Central Harlem." *American Journal of Obstetrics and Gynecology, 156*(1), 145–149.

McKee, K., & Cooper, V. 2008. "The Paradox of Tenant Empowerment: Regulatory and Liberatory Possibilities." *Housing, Theory and Society, 25*(2), 132–146.

McNeur, C. 2014. *Taming Manhattan: Environmental Battles in the Antebellum City.* Cambridge, Mass.: Harvard University Press.

Menache, S. 1997. "Dogs: God's Worst Enemies?" *Society & Animals*, 5(1), 23–44.

Merton, R. 1936. "The Unanticipated Consequences of Purposive Social Action." *American Sociological Review*, 1(6), 894–904.

Miles, A. 2015. "The (Re)genesis of Values: Examining the Importance of Values for Action." *American Sociological Review*, 80(4), 680–704.

Miller, C., & Kaiser, C. 2001. "A Theoretical Perspective on Coping with Stigma." *Journal of Social Issues*, 57(1), 73–92.

Miller, S., Seib, H., & Dennie, S. 2001. "African American Perspectives on Health Care: The Voice of the Community." *Journal of Ambulatory Care Management*, 24(3), 37–44.

Miraftab, F. 1997. "Flirting with the Enemy: Challenges Faced by NGOs in Development and Empowerment." *Habitat International*, 21(4), 361–375.

Mississippi Board of Animal Health. n.d. "MS Animal Disaster Relief Fund." Retrieved from www.mbah.ms.gov/emergency_programs/animal_disaster_relief_fund.htm.

Miura, A., Bradshaw, J., & Tanida, H. 2000. "Attitudes Towards Dogs: A Study of University Students in Japan and the UK." *Anthrozoös*, 13(2), 80–88.

Mizrahi, T., & Rosenthal, B. 1996. "Building Successful Coalitions: Defining and Measuring Coalition Effectiveness." In *Annual Program Meeting of the Council on Social Work Education*. Washington, D.C.: Author.

Molento, C. 2014. "Public Health and Animal Welfare." In M. Appleby, P. Sandoe, & D. Weary (Eds.), *Dilemmas in Animal Welfare* (pp. 102–122). Boston: CABI.

Moran, C., & Lee, C. 2013. "Selling Genital Cosmetic Surgery to Healthy Women: A Multimodal Discourse Analysis of Australian Surgical Websites." *Critical Discourse Studies*, 10(4), 373–391.

Morters, M., McKinley, T., Restif, O., Conlan, A., Cleaveland, S., Hampson, K., Whay, H., Damriyasa, I., & Wood, J. 2014. "The Demography of Free-roaming Dog Populations and Applications to Disease and Population Control." *Journal of Applied Ecology*, 51(4), 1096–1106.

Muirhead, V., Levine, A., Nicolau, B., Landry, A., & Bedos, C. 2013. "Life Course Experiences and Lay Diagnosis Explain Low-Income Parents' Child Dental Decisions: A Qualitative Study." *Community Dentistry and Oral Epidemiology*, 41(1), 13–21.

Nadeem, E., Lange, J., Edge, D., Fongwa, M., Belin, T., & Miranda, J. 2007. "Does Stigma Keep Poor Young Immigrant and U.S.-Born Black and Latina Women from Seeking Mental Health Care?" *Psychiatric Services*, 58(12), 1547–1554.

Nakaya, S. 2005. *Kindred Spirit, Kindred Care: Making Health Decisions on Behalf of Our Animal Companions*. Novato, CA: New World Library.

Narayanan, Y. 2017. "Street Dogs at the Intersection of Colonialism and Informality: 'Subaltern Animism' as a Posthuman Critique of Indian Cities." *Environment and Planning D: Society and Space*, 35(3), 475–494.

Newell, S., & Swan, J. 2000. "Trust and Inter-organizational Networking." *Human Relations*, 53(10), 1287–1328.

Nichol, G., & Hunt, H. 2016. "Economic Hardship, Racialized Concentrated Poverty, and the Challenges of Low-Wage Work, Charlotte, North Carolina." Chapel Hill: North Carolina Poverty Research Fund.

Nielsen, R. 1996. *The Politics of Ethics: Methods for Acting, Learning, and Sometimes*

Fighting with Others in Addressing Ethics Problems in Organizational Life. New York: Oxford University Press.

Nolen, R. 2013, October 16. "Study Shines Spotlight on Neutering." Retrieved from www .avma.org/News/JAVMANews/Pages/131101a.aspx.

Nolo. 2019. "Getting a Dog: Legal Considerations." Retrieved from www.nolo.com /legal-encyclopedia/getting-a-dog-legal-considerations.html.

Ogbu, J. 2004. "Collective Identity and the Burden of 'Acting White' in Black History, Community, and Education." *Urban Review, 36*(1), 1–35.

Okazaki, S., Mueller, B., & Taylor, C. 2010. "Measuring Soft-sell Versus Hard-sell Advertising Appeals." *Journal of Advertising, 39*(2), 5–20.

Orellana, M. 2001. "The Work Kids Do: Mexican and Central American Immigrant Children's Contributions to Households and Schools in California." *Harvard Educational Review, 71*(3), 366–389.

Orihuela, T., & Solano, V. 1995. "Demographics of the Owned Dog Population in Miacatlan, Mor. Mexico." *Anthrozoös, 8*(3), 171–175.

Ortega-Pacheco, A., Rodriguez-Buenfil, J., Bolio-Gonzalez, M., Sauri-Arceo, C., Jiménez-Coello, M., & Forsberg, C. 2007. "A Survey of Dog Populations in Urban and Rural Areas of Yucatan, Mexico." *Anthrozoös, 20*(3), 261–274.

Osborne, A. 2013. "Costa Rica and the 'Electric Fence' Mentality: Stunting Women's Socio-economic Participation in the 21st Century." *Journal of International Women's Studies, 14*(3), 259–274.

Pariser, K. 2014. "Detailed Discussion of the Laws Regulating Rescue and Foster Care Programs for Companion Animals." East Lansing: Michigan State University College of Law, Animal Legal & Historical Center.

Park, S. 2005. "Norm Diffusion Within International Organizations: A Case Study of the World Bank." *Journal of International Relations and Development, 8*(2), 111–141.

Pearson, C. 2016. "Sniffing the Past—Dogs and History." Retrieved from https:// sniffingthepast.wordpress.com/2016/03/29/killing-stray-dogs-in-early-19th -century-new-york/.

Perin, C. 1990. *Belonging in America: Reading Between the Lines.* Madison: University of Wisconsin Press.

Perkmann, M., & Spicer, A. 2014. "How Emerging Organizations Take Form: The Role of Imprinting and Values in Organizational Bricolage." *Organization Science, 25*(6), 1785–1806.

Perri 6. 2012. "When Forethought and Outturn Part: Types of Unanticipated and Unintended Consequences." In H. Margetts, Perri 6, & C. Hood (Eds.), *Paradoxes of Modernization: Unintended Consequences of Public Policy Reform* (pp. 44–62). Oxford: Oxford University Press.

Peterson, A. 2018. "Canine Rescue as a Social Movement: The Politics of Love." *Society & Animals, 26*(4), 1–18.

Pinderhughes, E., Dodge, K., Bates, J., Pettit, G., & Zelli, A. 2000. "Discipline Responses: Influences of Parents' Socioeconomic Status, Ethnicity, Beliefs About Parenting, Stress, and Cognitive-emotional Processes." *Journal of Family Psychology, 14*(3), 380–400.

Pistorius, A., Hohn, E., & Van der Merwe, C. 1992. "A Quantitative Study of the Attitudes of Members of a Black Developing Community Towards Their Dogs and Veterinary Services." *Journal of the South African Veterinary Association, 63*(4), 166–171.

Plach, E. 2013. "Mad Dogs and Animal Protectionists: Rabies in Interwar Poland." *Canadian Slavonic Papers, 55*(3–4), 391–416.

Plemons, A. 2010. "Commodifying Fido: Pets as Status Symbols." Doctoral dissertation, Texas A&M University, College Station.

Poss, J., & Bader, J. 2007. "Attitudes Toward Companion Animals Among Hispanic Residents of a Texas Border Community." *Journal of Applied Animal Welfare Science, 10*(3), 243–253.

Pręgowski, M. (Ed.). 2016. *Companion Animals in Everyday Life: Situating Human-animal Engagement Within Cultures.* London: Palgrave Macmillan.

Putnam, R. 2000. *Bowling Alone: The Collapse and Revival of American Community.* New York: Simon & Schuster.

Ramirez, M. 2006. "'My Dog's Just Like Me': Dog Ownership as a Gender Display." *Symbolic Interaction, 29*(3), 373–391.

Randall, D., Harper, R., & Rouncefield, M. 2007. "Ethnography and How to Do It." In D. Randall, R. Harper, & M. Rouncefield (Eds.), *Fieldwork for Design* (pp. 169–197). London: Springer.

Rauktis, M., Rose, L., Chen, Q., Martone, R., & Martello, A. 2017. "'Their Pets Are Loved Members of Their Family': Animal Ownership, Food Insecurity, and the Value of Having Pet Food Available in Food Banks." *Anthrozoös, 30*(4), 581–593.

Ravenhill, M. 2016. *The Culture of Homelessness.* New York: Routledge.

Reese, J. 2005. "Dogs and Dog Control in Developing Countries." In D. Salem & A. Rowan (Eds.), *The State of the Animals III* (pp. 55–64). Washington, D.C.: Humane Society Press.

Rhoades, H., Winetrobe, H., & Rice, E. 2015. "Pet Ownership Among Homeless Youth: Associations with Mental Health, Service Utilization and Housing Status." *Child Psychiatry & Human Development, 46*(2), 237–244.

Ribton-Turner, L., & De Bruin, G. 2006. "The Unemployed Mid-career Adult: Stressors and Support." *SA Journal of Industrial Psychology, 32*(2), 31–38.

Risley-Curtiss, C., Holley, L., Cruickshank, T., Porcelli, J., Rhoads, C., Bacchus, D. N., Nyakoe, S., & Murphy, S. 2006. "'She Was Family': Women of Color and Animal-Human Connections." *Affilia, 21*(4), 433–447.

Risley-Curtiss, C., Holley, L., & Wolf, S. 2006. "The Animal-Human Bond and Ethnic Diversity." *Social Work, 51*(3), 257–268.

Rogers, E. 2010. *Diffusion of Innovations.* New York: Simon & Schuster.

Rojas, L. 1979. "Peasant Politics: Struggle in a Dominican Village." *Ciencia Y Sociedad, 4*(1), 107–111.

Rosenstock, I. 1974. "The Health Belief Model and Preventive Health Behavior." *Health Education Monographs, 2*(4), 354–386.

Rosero-Bixby, L., & Casterline, J. 1994. "Interaction Diffusion and Fertility Transition in Costa Rica." *Social Forces, 73*(2), 435–462.

Rossen, J. 2019, September 5. "Euthanasia Rates in Animal Shelters Are Plummeting—Here's Why." *New York Times*, p. 10.

Rowan, A., & Williams, J. 1987. "The Success of Companion Animal Management Programs: A Review." *Anthrozoös,, 1,* 110–122.

Rowland, M., & Isaac-Savage, E. 2014. "As I See It: A Study of African American Pastors' Views on Health and Health Education in the Black Church." *Journal of Religion and Health, 53*(4), 1091–1101.

Ruiz-Izaguirre, E., & Eilers, C. 2012. "Perceptions of Village Dogs by Villagers and Tourists in the Coastal Region of Rural Oaxaca, Mexico." *Anthrozoös, 25*(1), 75–91.

Ruiz-Izaguirre, E., Hebinck, P., & Eilers, K. 2018. "Village Dogs in Coastal Mexico: The Street as a Place to Belong." *Society & Animals, 1,* 1–21.

Ruiz-Izaguirre, E., Van Woersem, A., Eilers, K., Van Wieren, S., Bosch, G., Van der Zijpp, A., & De Boer, I. 2015. "Roaming Characteristics and Feeding Practices of Village Dogs Scavenging Sea-turtle Nests." *Animal Conservation, 18*(2), 146–156.

Rupprecht, C. 2017. "Ready for More-Than-Human? Measuring Urban Residents' Willingness to Coexist with Animals." *Fennia—International Journal of Geography, 195*(2), 142–160.

Sabatini, F. 2005. "Social Capital, Public Spending and the Quality of Economic Development." Unpublished manuscript.

Sanders, C. 1999. *Understanding Dogs: Living and Working with Canine Companions.* Philadelphia: Temple University Press.

———. 2003. "Actions Speak Louder Than Words: Close Relationships Between Humans and Nonhuman Animals." *Symbolic Interaction, 26*(3), 405–426.

Sandoval-Cervantes, I. 2016. "Semi-stray Dogs and Graduated Humanness: The Political Encounters of Dogs and Humans in Mexico." In M. Pręgowski (Ed.), *Companion Animals in Everyday Life* (pp. 169–181). New York: Palgrave Macmillan.

Saunders, J., Parast, L., Babey, S., & Miles, J. 2017. "Exploring the Differences Between Pet and Non-pet Owners: Implications for Human-animal Interaction Research and Policy." *PLOS ONE, 12*(6), e0179494.

Savvides, N. 2013. "Living with Dogs: Alternative Animal Practices in Bangkok, Thailand." *Animal Studies Journal, 2,* 28–50.

Schlenker, B., & Trudeau, J. 1990. "Impacts of Self-Presentation on Private Self-Beliefs: Effects of Prior Self-beliefs and Misattribution." *Journal of Personality and Social Psychology, 58*(1), 22–32.

Schoen, J. 2001. "Between Choice and Coercion: Women and the Politics of Sterilization in North Carolina, 1929–1975." *Journal of Women's History, 13*(1), 132–156.

Schoenfeld-Tacher, R., Kogan, L., & Wright, M. 2010. "Comparison of Strength of the Human-animal Bond Between Hispanic and Non-Hispanic Owners of Pet Dogs and Cats." *Journal of the American Veterinary Medical Association, 236*(5), 529–534.

Scott, D. 1997. "Inter-agency Conflict: An Ethnographic Study." *Child & Family Social Work, 2*(2), 73–80.

Selby, L., & Rhoades, J. 1981. "Attitudes of the Public Towards Dogs and Cats as Companion Animals." *Journal of Small Animal Practice, 22*(3), 129–137.

Serpell, J. 2004. "Factors Influencing Human Attitudes to Animals and Their Welfare." *Animal Welfare, 13,* S145–S152.

Serpell, J., & Hsu, Y. 2016. "Attitudes to Dogs in Taiwan: A Case Study." In M. Pręgowski (Ed.), *Companion Animals in Everyday Life: Situating Human-Animal Engagement* (pp. 145–165). New York: Palgrave Macmillan.

Shaw, H. 2006. "Deserts: Towards the Development of a Classification." *Geografiska Annaler: Series B, Human Geography, 88*(2), 231–247.

Sheikh, S., Pitts, J., Ryan-Wenger, N., McCoy, K., & Hayes, D. 2016. "Racial Differences in Pet Ownership in Families of Children with Asthma." *World Journal of Pediatrics, 12*(3), 343–346.

Sherry, A., Adelman, A., Farwell, L., & Linton, B. 2013. "The Impact of Social Class on Parenting and Attachment." In W. Liu (Ed.), *The Oxford Handbook of Social Class in Counseling* (pp. 275–291). New York: Oxford University Press.

Sherry, J., Jr. 1983. "Gift Giving in Anthropological Perspective." *Journal of Consumer Research, 10*(2), 157–168.

Shore, E., Douglas, D., & Riley, M. 2005. "What's in It for the Companion Animal? Pet Attachment and College Students' Behaviors Toward Pets." *Journal of Applied Animal Welfare Science, 8,* 1–11.

Shore, E., Riley, M., & Douglas, D. 2006. "Pet Owner Behaviors and Attachment to Yard Versus House Dogs." *Anthrozoös, 19*(4), 325–334.

Siddiq, A., & Habib, A. 2016. "Anthrozoology—An Emerging Robust Multidisciplinary Subfield of Anthropological Science." *Green University Review of Social Sciences, 3*(1), 45–67.

Siegel, J. 1995. "Pet Ownership and the Importance of Pets Among Adolescents." *Anthrozoös, 8*(4), 217–223.

Silver, M. 2003. "Eugenics and Compulsory Sterilization Laws: Providing Redress for the Victims of a Shameful Era in United States History." *George Washington Law Review, 72,* 862–892.

Silverstein, M., Lamberto, J., DePeau, K., & Grossman, D. 2008. "'You Get What You Get': Unexpected Findings About Low-Income Parents' Negative Experiences With Community Resources." *Pediatrics, 122*(6), e1141–e1148.

Simons, R., Lin, K., & Gordon, L. 1998. "Socialization in the Family of Origin and Male Dating Violence: A Prospective Study." *Journal of Marriage and the Family, 60*(2), 467–478.

Simpson, M., Albright, S., Wolfe, B., Searfoss, E., Street, K., Diehl, K., & Page, R. 2019. "Age at Gonadectomy and Risk of Overweight/Obesity and Orthopedic Injury in a Cohort of Golden Retrievers." *PLOS ONE, 14*(7), e0209131.

Singer, R., Hart, L., & Zasloff, R. 1995. "Dilemmas Associated With Rehousing Homeless People Who Have Companion Animals." *Psychological Reports, 77*(3), 851–857.

Snow, D. A., Rochford, E. B., Jr., Worden, S. K., & Benford, R. D. 1986. "Frame Alignment Processes, Micromobilization, and Movement Participation." *American Sociological Review, 51,* 464–481.

Song, M. 1997. "Children's Labour in Ethnic Family Businesses: The Case of Chinese Take-away Businesses in Britain." *Ethnic and Racial Studies, 20*(4), 690–716.

Sparks, J., Camacho, B., Tedeschi, P., & Morris, K. 2018. "Race and Ethnicity Are Not Primary Determinants in Utilizing Veterinary Services in Underserved Communities in the United States." *Journal of Applied Animal Welfare Science, 21*(2), 120–129.

Srinivasan, K., & Nagaraj, V. 2007. "Deconstructing the Human Gaze: Stray Dogs, Indifferent Governance and Prejudiced Reactions." *Economic and Political Weekly, 42,* 1085–1086.

Stephens, N., Markus, H., & Phillips, L. 2014. "Social Class Culture Cycles: How Three Gateway Contexts Shape Selves and Fuel Inequality." *Annual Review of Psychology, 65,* 611–634.

Stolle, D., & Hooghe, M. 2004. "The Roots of Social Capital: Attitudinal and Network Mechanisms in the Relation Between Youth and Adult Indicators of Social Capital." *Acta Politica, 39*(4), 422–441.

Strand, P. 1993. "The Pet Owner and Breeder's Perspective on Overpopulation." *Journal of the American Veterinary Medical Association, 202*(6), 921–928.

Stull, J., Shelby, J., Bonnett, B., Block, G., Budsberg, S., Dean, R., Dicks, M., Forsgren, B., Golab, G., Hamil, J., & Kass, P. 2018. "Barriers and Next Steps to Providing a Spectrum of Effective Health Care to Companion Animals." *Journal of the American Veterinary Medical Association, 253*(11), 1386–1389.

Sümegi, Z., Oláh, K., & Topál, J. 2014. "Emotional Contagion in Dogs as Measured by Change in Cognitive Task Performance." *Applied Animal Behaviour Science, 160,* 106–115.

Swidler, A. 1986. "Culture in Action: Symbols and Strategies." *American Sociological Review, 51*(2), 273–286.

Tanaka, A., Saeki, J., Hayama, S., & Kass, P. 2019. "Effect of Pets on Human Behavior and Stress in Disaster." *Frontiers in Veterinary Science, 6,* 113.

Tannen, D. 2004. "Talking the Dog: Framing Pets as Interactional Resources in Family Discourse." *Research on Language and Social Interaction, 37*(4), 399–420.

———. 2010. "Abduction and Identity in Family Interaction: Ventriloquizing as Indirectness." *Journal of Pragmatics, 42*(2), 307–316.

Tarver, E. 2014. "The Dangerous Individual('s) Dog: Race, Criminality and the 'Pit Bull.'" *Culture, Theory and Critique, 55*(3), 273–285.

Taylor, H., Williams, P., & Gray, D. 2004. "Homelessness and Dog Ownership: An Investigation into Animal Empathy, Attachment, Crime, Drug Use, Health and Public Opinion." *Anthrozoös, 17*(4), 353–368.

Taylor, J. 1997. "Niches and Practice: Extending the Ecological Perspective." In D. Saleebey (Ed.), *The Strengths Perspective in Social Work Practice* (2nd ed., pp. 217–227). New York: Longman.

Taylor, N. 2015. *The Rise of Critical Animal Studies.* London: Routledge.

TCRN. 2014, June 10. "Many of Costa Rica's Animal Shelters Are 'Off the Books.'" Retrieved from http://costaricannews.com.

Theodore, N. 2013. "Insecure Communities: Latino Perceptions of Police Involvement in Immigration Enforcement." Department of Urban Planning and Policy, University of Illinois at Chicago.

Thomas, K. 1983. *Man and the Natural World: Changing Attitudes in England, 1500–1800.* Oxford: Oxford University Press.

Tice, D. 1992. "Self-concept Change and Self-presentation: The Looking Glass Self Is Also a Magnifying Glass." *Journal of Personality and Social Psychology, 63*(3), 435–451.

Tipper, B. 2011. "Pets and Personal Life." In V. May (Ed.), *Sociology of Personal Life* (pp.85–97). Basingstoke: Palgrave.

Tissot, S. 2011. "Of Dogs and Men: The Making of Spatial Boundaries in a Gentrifying Neighborhood." *City & Community, 10*(3), 265–284.

Torres de la Riva, G., Hart, B., Farver, T., Oberbauer, A., Messam, L. L. M., Willits, N., & Hart, L. 2013. "Neutering Dogs: Effects on Joint Disorders and Cancers in Golden Retrievers." *PLOS ONE, 8*(2), e55937. Retrieved from https://doi.org/10.1371/journal. pone.0055937.

Tovares, A. 2010. "All in the Family: Small Stories and Narrative Construction of a Shared Family Identity That Includes Pets." *Narrative Inquiry, 20*(10), 1–19.

Tubbs, C., Roy, K., & Burton, L. 2005. "Family Ties Constructing Family Time in Low-income Families." *Family Process, 44*(1), 77–91.

Tudge, J., Hogan, D., Snezhkova, I., Kulakova, N., & Etz, K. 2000. "Parents' Child-rearing Values and Beliefs in the United States and Russia: The Impact of Culture and Social Class." *Infant and Child Development: An International Journal of Research and Practice, 9*(2), 105–121.

Turner, P., Berry, J., & MacDonald, S. 2012. "Animal Shelters and Animal Welfare: Raising the Bar." *Canadian Veterinary Journal, 53*(8), 893–896.

Turner, V. 1969. *The Ritual Process: Structure and Anti-structure.* New York: Routledge.

Twining, H., Arluke, A., & Patronek, G. 2000. "Managing the Stigma of Outlaw Breeds: A Case Study of Pit Bull Owners." *Society & Animals, 8*(1), 25–52.

Uddin, L. 2003. "Canine Citizenship and the Intimate Public Sphere." *Invisible Culture, 6.* Retrieved from www.rochester.edu/in_visible_culture/Issue_6/uddin/uddin.html.

Urbanik, J. 2009. "'Hooters for Neuters': Sexist or Transgressive Animal Advocacy Campaign?" *HUMaNIMALIA: Journal of Human/Animal Interface Studies, 1*(1), 40–62.

Urbanik, J., & Morgan, M. 2013. "A Tale of Tails: The Place of Dog Parks in the Urban Imaginary." *Geoforum, 44*, 292–302.

U.S. Census Bureau. 2019. "Income, Poverty, and Health Insurance Coverage in the United States." Retrieved from www.census.gov/newsroom/press-releases/2019 /income-poverty.html.

Vaaland, T., & Håkansson, H. 2003. "Exploring Interorganizational Conflict in Complex Projects." *Industrial Marketing Management, 32*(2), 127–138.

Van Gennep, A. 1909. *Les Rites de Passage.* Paris: E. Nourrey.

van Oorschot, W., Arts, W., & Gelissen, J. 2006. "Social Capital in Europe: Measurement and Social and Regional Distribution of a Multifaceted Phenomenon." *Acta Sociologica, 49*(2), 149–166.

Veevers, J. 1985. "The Social Meanings of Pets: Alternative Roles for Companion Animals." *Marriage & Family Review, 8*(3–4), 11–30.

Verbrugge, L. 1985. "Triggers of Symptoms and Health Care." *Social Science & Medicine, 20*(9), 855–876.

Vermilya, J. 2012. "Contesting Horses: Borders and Shifting Social Meanings in Veterinary Medical Education." *Society & Animals*, 20(2), 123–137.

Verzaro-Lawrence, M. 1981. "Shared Childrearing: A Challenging Alternative Lifestyle." *Alternative Lifestyles*, 4(2), 205–217.

Wakefield, M., Loken, B., & Hornik, R. 2010. "Use of Mass Media Campaigns to Change Health Behaviour." *Lancet*, 376(9748), 1261–1271.

Waldinger, R. 1995. "The 'Other Side' of Embeddedness: A Case Study of the Interplay Between Economy and Ethnicity." *Ethnic and Racial Studies*, 18, 555–580.

Walker, R., Keane, C., & Burke, J. 2010. "Disparities and Access to Healthy Food in the United States: A Review of Food Deserts Literature." *Health & Place*, 16(5), 876–884.

Wallerstein, N. 1992. "Powerlessness, Empowerment, and Health: Implications for Health Promotion Programs." *American Journal of Health Promotion*, 6(3), 197–205.

Walsh, F. 2009. "Human-animal Bonds I: The Relational Significance of Companion Animals." *Family Process*, 48(4), 462–480.

Warren, K. 2000. *Ecofeminist Philosophy: A Western Perspective on What It Is and Why It Matters*. Lanham, Md.: Rowman & Littlefield.

Weaver, H. 2013. "'Becoming in Kind': Race, Class, Gender, and Nation in Cultures of Dog Rescue and Dogfighting." *American Quarterly*, 65(3), 689–709.

Weigert, A. 1991. *Mixed Emotions: Certain Steps Toward Understanding Ambivalence*. Albany: SUNY Press.

Wessels, B., & Miedema, S. 2002. "Towards Understanding Situations of Social Exclusion." In H. Steinert & A. Pilgram (Eds.), *Welfare Policy From Below: Struggles Against Social Exclusion Europe* (pp. 61–76). Aldershot: Ashgate.

Westgarth, C., Boddy, L., Stratton, G., German, A., Gaskell, R., Coyne, K., Bundred, P., McCune, S., & Dawson, S. 2013. "Pet Ownership, Dog Types and Attachment to Pets in 9–10 Year Old Children in Liverpool, UK." *BMC Veterinary Research*, 9(1), 102–112.

Westgarth, C., Heron, J., Ness, A., Bundred, P., Gaskell, R., Coyne, K., German, A., McCune, S., & Dawson, S. 2010. "Family Pet Ownership During Childhood: Findings From a UK Birth Cohort and Implications for Public Health Research." *International Journal of Environmental Research and Public Health*, 7(10), 3704–3729.

Whay, H. 2007. "The Journey to Animal Welfare Improvement." *Animal Welfare*, 16(2), 117.

Whay, H., & Main, D. 2010. "Improving Animal Welfare: Practical Approaches for Achieving Change." In T. Grandin (Ed.), *Improving Animal Welfare: A Practical Approach* (pp. 227–251). Boston: CABI.

Whetten, K., Leserman, J., Whetten, R., Ostermann, J., Swartz, M., & Stangl, D. 2006. "Exploring Lack of Trust in Care Providers and the Government as a Barrier to Health Service Use." *American Journal of Public Health*, 96(4), 716–721.

Wilkins, A., & Pace, J. 2014. "Class, Race, and Emotions." In J. Stets & J. Turner (Eds.), *Handbook of the Sociology of Emotions* (Vol. 2, pp. 385–409). Dordrecht: Springer.

Williams, D. 2007. "Inappropriate/d Others: Or, the Difficulty of Being a Dog." *Drama Review*, 51(1), 92–118.

Wilson, H. 1974. "Parenting in Poverty." *British Journal of Social Work*, 4(3), 241–254,

Wilson, J. 1999. "Acknowledging the Expertise of Patients and Their Organisations." *British Medical Journal*, 319(7212), 771–774.

Wilson, T. D. 1998. "Weak Ties, Strong Ties: Network Principles in Mexican Migration." *Human Organization, 57,* 394–403.

Winograd, N. 2009. *Irreconcilable Differences: The Battle for the Heart & Soul of America's Animal Shelters.* CreateSpace.

Wolch, J., & Lassiter, U. 2000. "Constructing the Animal Worlds of Inner-city Los Angeles." In C. Philo & C. Wilbert (Eds.), *Animal Spaces, Beastly Places: New Geographies of Human-animal Relations* (pp.73–98). New York: Routledge.

Wolf, C., Lloyd, J., & Black, J. 2008. "An Examination of U.S. Consumer Pet-related and Veterinary Service Expenditures, 1980–2005." *Journal of the American Veterinary Medical Association, 233*(3), 404–413.

Wood, L., Giles-Corti, B., & Bulsara, M. 2005. "The Pet Connection: Pets as a Conduit for Social Capital?" *Social Science & Medicine, 61*(6), 1159–1173.

Woolcock, M. 2010. "The Rise and Routinization of Social Capital, 1988–2008." *Annual Review of Political Science, 13,* 469–487.

WSPA. 2012. "Situation of the Owned Canine Population in the Greater Metropolitan Area (GMA): A WSPA Report." Washington, D.C.: Humane Society International.

Yerby, A. 1966. "The Disadvantaged and Health Care." *American Journal of Public Health and the Nation's Health, 56*(1), 5–9.

Yoak, A., Reece, J., Gehrt, S., & Hamilton, I. 2014. "Disease Control Through Fertility Control: Secondary Benefits of Animal Birth Control in Indian Street Dogs." *Preventive Veterinary Medicine, 113*(1), 152–156.

Young, H. 2006. "Innovation Diffusion in Heterogeneous Populations." Retrieved from https://papers.ssrn.com/sol3/papers.cfm?abstract_id=1024811.

INDEX

adoption, 98, 119, 125, 128, 145, 152, 157; by animals, 33, 35, 80, 97, 186, 188; cost of, 212n2
(chap. 3); failed, 37, 41; motivation for 40,
101–102, 186; requirements of, 2, 214n6
(chap. 6); uncomfortable shelter experiences and, 101–102, 122–123, 142–143;
unwanted animals and, 1, 49, 51, 53, 55, 56,
63–66, 109, 199. *See also* animal control; El
Refugio
akita, 96, 123
Alabama Veterinary Medical Association, 195
American Kennel Club (AKC), 120
American Pit Bull Foundation (APBF), 108,
109, 111
Anderson, Elijah, 170
animal capital, 167
animal control, 13, 95, 124, 134, 163, 175, 182, 193,
215n6; adoption at, 13; approach to community cats by, 194; complaints to, 173–174;
confusion with shelter and, 132–133; euthanasia at, 13, 95, 98, 109, 110, 107, 132, 161, 199,
212n2 (chap. 4); relationship with shelter,
194, 214n2, 214n6 (chap. 5); seizure by, 98,
120; surrender to, 100, 104, 107, 108, 110, 112,
113, 205. *See also* euthanasia; Humane Society of Charlotte; overpopulation, dog and
cat; social class

animal fairs, 58
animal fostering, 47, 54, 55–56, 110, 193, 211n1
(chap. 2). *See* adoption; casa cuna; pets
animal welfare advocates: collaborative relationships among, 199–202, 216n1; distrust
among, 193–195, 201–202; intergroup differences among, 46, 48; lack of regulation
of, 211n1 (chap. 2); as moral entrepreneurs,
203, 216n7; resource competition among,
193; territorial overlap among, 47–48, 193–
194. *See also* casa cuna; El Refugio; Humane
Society of Charlotte; Nacional de Salud
Animal (SENASA); rescuers; sanctuaries;
shelter workers: outreach; shelters
animal welfare policy, 140, 141, 166–167, 197;
assumptions behind, 4–5, 201–202, 203,
206–209; problems with, 3, 13, 116–117, 134,
216n1; underlife of, 4–7
anthrozoology, 6–7, 186
attitude-behavior link, 71

Bangalore Municipal Corporation, 24
Beyond Fences, 148–149, 158, 180–181, 206,
213n10
birth control behavior, 25, 38
"border species," 27
boxers, 108, 118

breeding, 101, 140, 151–152, 165, 186, 187, 214n1;
    dog trading and, 119, 121; income from, 36,
    205; long-term, 76; pedigree and, 118, 119,
    120; shelter services and, 125, 134, 147, 161–
    162; symbolism of papers for, 119–120; types
    of, 101, 118–122, 162, 215n2; unwanted, 78.
    See also overpopulation, dog and cat; pets:
    unwanted; pit bulls; sterilization
bricolage. *See* shelter workers: outreach

casa cuna, 54–57, 62, 68, 194
cats. *See* dogs and cats
Chihuahuas, 93, 97, 157
Coalition to Unchain Dogs. *See* Beyond Fences
Colegio de Medicos Veterinarios, 53, 57–60, 61,
    68, 72, 83–86, 194–195, 200, 216n5
"community ambassadors," 153–154, 157, 158,
    162–163, 175, 197
critical incident technique, 16–17
cultural capital, 168
cultural competence: by health care and social
    service professionals, 143–144; limitations
    of, 165; shelter workers' approach to, 143–
    144, 164, 196–197

dogfighting, 120; pets as bait for, 103–104, 118;
    tension with shelter, 74, 118, 125, 129, 147–
    148, 161–162, 163, 165
dogs and cats. *See also* overpopulation, dog
    and cat; strays
—street: adoption of people by, 35; as beg-
    gars, 33; caring relations with, 27–28;
    community, 23, 27, 34, 156; as compan-
    ions, 29–30; as dirty, 24, 35, 88; "dump," 28,
    211n6; feeding of, 28, 32, 33, 34, 37, 38, 39, 98;
    "forest," 27; graduated dependence with,
    44–45; as guards, 33, 34, 44; independence
    of, 35; intolerance of, 24; liminality of, 27, 43;
    limited responsibility for, 35–39; as mas-
    cots, 31–32; "nature" of, 30, 36–39, 45; as
    neighborhood pets, 32–33, 36, 194; as nui-
    sances, pests, or threats, 33–34, 39, 194,
    211n6; problems caused by, 24, 39; roaming
    by, 38–39, 210n2; "semi-stray/feral," 23, 44;
    tourists and, 24; understanding of, 30; as
    "vacation pets," 31; "village," 23
—views of: dichotomous, 27–30; as guards, 8,
    12, 40, 88, 118; instrumental, 12, 27, 29, 35–36,
    40, 80, 88, 96–97, 102–103, 106, 108, 111, 187;
    Islamic, 24, 171; Judaic, 171; as meat, 87;

nature of, 30, 96, 117; as nuisances, 78; per-
    ceived worth, 78, 80; as threats, 39, 76, 108,
    166, 173– 174, 211n6, 215n3
Donovan, Josephine, 68

El Refugio: adjusting to local culture by, 39–43;
    adoptions at, 10, 11; background of, 10–12;
    behavior change and, 26; casa cunas and,
    54–56; community partnerships with, 198–
    199; "dumping" at, 63; euthanasia at, 62–63;
    as grassroots support organization, 49–50;
    as institutional enabler, 63; modeling by
    staff at, 212n3 (chap.3); rescue groups and,
    48–54; resource competition with, 193;
    sanctuaries and, 66–67; surrendering to,
    63–64; symbolic payments to, 212n2 (chap.
    3); veterinarians and, 57–62, 195; veterinary
    training at, 211n3 (chap. 2)
elite adopters. *See* innovations
ethic of care, 68
euthanasia, 96, 103, 108, 113, 115, 136, 156, 212n4;
    avoiding of, 104, 154, 173, 200; cost of, 104;
    disagreements over, 53, 62–63, 64, 65, 67,
    194, perspectives toward, 48; rates of, 1–2;
    reduction in, 143; shelter resentment about,
    142–143. *See also* animal control; El Refugio;
    pets: unwanted; shelter workers: outreach;
    sterilization

"failed fosters," 55–56
family: framing of, 168; military pets and, 94;
    pets as, 98, 170, 187, 215n1; photographs of,
    169; sharing of child rearing in, 190. *See also*
    pets: social roles of
feminist methods, 14
food banks and pantries, pet, 3, 106, 160, 172,
    178, 181, 182, 189; abuse of, 146–147; difficulty
    using, 105, 107, 114, 118, 127–128; require-
    ments for, 130, 145
frame disputes, 62
Freidson, Eliot, 5

Gans, Herbert, 94
gender, 18–19, 48, 91, 95; attachment to animals
    and, 30, 91; empowerment of rescuers and,
    50–52; failure to seek medical care and, 117;
    identity framing with dogs and, 168; inter-
    sectional oppression of, with animals, 91;
    shelter workers and, 129; sterilization and,
    76–77, 152–153

gentrification, 10, 111, 129, 172–173, 210n7
German shepherds, 96, 118
gift giving, 175
Gilligan, Carol, 68

Hens, Kristien, 68
hoarding: by casa cunas, 56; by "shelters" and
    sanctuaries, 63, 65, 67, 194
homelessness, 5, 9, 32, 54, 93, 111, 128, 193–194,
    198, 216n6 (chap.7). *See also* pets; social
    class; strays
Humane Society of Charlotte (HSC): back-
    ground, 12–13; collaboration with animal
    control by, 199; collaboration with private
    practice veterinarians by, 200–201; donors
    to, 150, 201; expansion plans of, 200, 216n4;
    law enforcement association with, 132, 134,
    140; Wellness Clinic at, 116, 124, 125, 146,
    159, 160, 163, 172, 175, 178, 182. *See also* adop-
    tion; animal control; breeding; "community
    ambassadors"; cultural competence; food
    banks and pantries, pet; pet owners; pets:
    responsibility for; Pets for Life; race; shelter
    workers; shelters; social class; veterinari-
    ans; veterinary care: low-cost
Humane Society of the United States (HSUS),
    143, 211n2, 214n6 (chap.6)
Hurricane Katrina, 195
Hurricane Otto, 12, 42–43

innovations, 19, 20, 117; adopters of, 25–26, 86;
    as diffusion process, 86–87; intergroup
    conflict and, 47; modernization's influence
    on, 25–26; pet-keeping practices as, 25, 70
Irvine, Leslie, 115

Jehovah's Witnesses, 129

liminality, 26. *See also* dogs and cats: street;
    pets

Mecklenburg Police Department, 124
Mississippi Veterinary Medical Association, 195
modernization, 11–12, 25, 207
moral entrepreneurship, 203, 216n7

Nacional de Salud Animal (SENASA), 40, 47, 53,
    55, 64–65, 67, 194
North Carolina Veterinary Medical Associa-
    tion, 136, 137, 138

One Health Movement, 216n1
overpopulation, dog and cat: approaches to,
    2, 48, 54, 61, 62, 67, 68; breeding and, 11, 55,
    152, 161; crisis of, 1–2; culture and, 35, 39, 69,
    72, 79, 91; problems caused by, 24; reduc-
    tion of, 4, 47, 50, 166, 202; responsibility for,
    45, 63, 73

pantries. *See* food banks and pantries, pet
pet owners: agency of, 140, 149, 150, 198; alien-
    ation from shelters by, 101, 122; assump-
    tions about, 4–5, 191; blaming of, 92, 142,
    203–204; changes in behavior of, 86–87;
    choice of breed by, 209n5; color coding of,
    162; "committed," 135, 145–146; cost of veter-
    inary care for, 134, 138; criticism of, 123, 124,
    125, 126, 140, 150, 192; as cultural straddlers,
    168; elderly, 100; emotional distress of, 98;
    eviction of, 109, 186, 189, 215n6; expecta-
    tions of, 85–86, 135–139; versus "guard-
    ians," 209n3; homeless, 111, 215n6; housing
    and, 107–113, 213n7–10; immigrant, 133–
    144; lay knowledge of, 155–158, 191, 197–198;
    lying by, 124–125; observational learning by,
    80–81; oppositional identity of, 172; "pas-
    sive," 197; problems faced by, 94–95, 99, 100;
    race "issues" of, 10; "repaying" shelter work-
    ers by, 176– 178; sacrifices by, 93–94, 98–99,
    204, 205–206, 212n1; self-concept of, 178,
    182; shame of, 126–128, 144, 145–146, 192,
    213n4 (chap. 5); social ties and networks of,
    111, 112, 178, 205; strain with shelters by, 142–
    143, 144; stress of, 81; transportation prob-
    lems of, 104–106, 111, 114, 116, 132–133, 134,
    138, 160, 165, 182, 211n1 (chap. 3), 213n1
pet resource desserts, 13, 105
pets: ambiguity of, 187–188; at-risk children
    and, 95; behavior problems of, 115; as co-
    travelers, 95, 99, 113; developing nations
    and, 12; as dirty, 105, 170–171, 181, 189; disas-
    ters and, 12, 42, 94, 195; doghouses for, 35,
    101, 158–159, 175, 177, 205, 206; empathy of,
    181; evictions of, 111; fostering of, 110; hous-
    ing restrictions on, 213n7; liminality of,
    26; microchipping of, 125, 133, 199; mis-
    fortunes of, 99–104; nature of, 96, 97–98;
    neighborhood sharing of, 97; outdoor,
    102–103, 112, 158–159, 170, 181, 189, 213n3;
    parvo in, 119, 162; as personal property, 169,
    213nn6–7; "private," 23; roaming, 97–98,

pets: (*continued*)
203; "sacrificial," 157; service, 106; social class and, 209; social isolation and, 96; training of, 102; unemployment and, 95–96. *See also* adoption; breeding; dogfighting; dogs and cats: street; family; food banks and pantries, pet; innovations; race; social class; strays
—attachment to, 165, 189–190; animal care and, 211n5 (chap. 1), assumptions about, 92; breeders and, 120–121; emotional distance and, 80; empathy and, 113; functions of, 95–96; poverty and, 96, 168; race and, 9; sources of, 94–95, 113; suppression of, 92–93, 96–98. *See also* social class
—controlling of: chaining, 38, 51, 101, 103, 109, 111, 161, 163, 170, 179, 205; fencing, 3, 102, 122, 148, 158–159, 175, 202, 206, 207, 213n10; for guard dogs, 40; improper chaining, 41, 43, 108, 159, 165, 214n6 (chap. 6); leashing, 80–81, 82, 83, 106, 166; resistance by dogs to, 180, 181–182. *See also* Beyond Fences
—feeding of, 94, 111, 181, 183, 199, 214n5 (chap. 5); cost of, 63, 116, 118, 124, 147; food desserts and, 13, 159; help with proper, 58, 159, 179, 202; human food for, 93, 160, 188; neglectful, 35, 122, 123, 161, 164, 165, 180, 203, 204. *See also* dogs and cats: street; strays
—interaction with: distancing, 170–171; dumping, 104; empathy, 179; framing identity with, 168, 169; indoor restrictions on, 23, 102, 103, 109, 112, 123, 170, 181, 187, 188, 189; investment in, 78; kissing, 82, 170, 187; naming, 171–172; ownership as conspicuous consumption, 119; petting and touching, 82; projection onto, 215n1; stability and stress reduction by, 94, 95–96; status symbols and, 210n3, 215n2; symbolism of, 168–169; walking, 180, 189
—responsibility for, 2, 24–25, 92, 99, 102, 127, 169, 189; changing, 71, 73, 78–80, 85; class, race, and, 8, 9; conceptions of, 23, 27, 48, 68, 205–207; culture and, 35, 39, 43, 44, 204; denial of, 84; encouraging, 64, 182–183, 203, 212n2 (chap. 3); indigenous, 107, 110, 112, 113–114; limited, 28, 31, 34, 36, 45, 63, 81, 205; perceptions of inadequate, 136, 140, 142, 145, 168, 174, 192, 202, 203; responsible guardianship and, 3, 122–123, 202–207; shared, 156

—social roles of: as boundary markers, 172–174; clique formation with, 173; as family members, 98, 181, 205; as guards, 35, 76, 96, 97, 158, 181, 187; as income providers, 120–121; as vacation companions, 31
—unwanted: abandonment of, 64, 66, 100, 113, 123, 186, 210n4; euthanasia and, 95, 108, 142; housing problems and, 108, 109–110, 112; limited responsibility for, 36, 63–64, 101, 113; overpopulation and, 11, 25; surrendering of, 43, 62, 100, 115, 143, 182, 205, 211n4 (chap. 2), 215n6. *See also* adoption; El Refugio
Pets for Life (PFL), 12–13, 207, 210n10; behavior change and, 202; community ambassadors and, 154; cost savings of, 118; cultural competence at, 143–144, 149, 161; demographics of, 210n8; locations of, 105, 213n3; reluctance to use, 126–127, 134; requirements to use, 130; transportation to, 106, 213n1; veterinary care at, 137
Pettidee, 171
pit bulls, 43, 64, 93, 103, 156; as boundary markers, 173–174, 215n3; breeding of, 74, 118, 120, 121, 152, 162; as guards, 96, 97; as outside dogs, 159, 180, 181, 182, 213n3; fighting of, 104; housing exclusion of, 108, 111, 112; status from, 119, 215n2. *See also* dogfighting
poverty, 68; affordable housing and, 112; assumptions about pet owners in, 29, 134, 168; definition and prevalence of, 11, 12–13, 209n2, 210n8; end-of-life care and, 104; health and social services use in, 6, 104, 126, 139, 148, 190–193, 195; illiteracy and, 214n2; isolation and, 96; parenting and, 186–190, 202; pets in, 2, 104; powerlessness in, 132, 148, 149; social networks in, 205
pulperias, 73

rabies: eradication of, 5; fear of, 24; vaccination for, 7, 130, 145, 147, 163, 203, 205
race: boundary marking with pets and, 173–174, 215n3; bridging capital and, 174; child rearing and, 190; cultural capital and, 168–172; distrust of police and, 134; distrust of veterinarians and, 130; eugenics and, 130–131; identity and, 169–170; intersectional oppression and, 91, 92, 99; medical and social service use and, 6, 104, 116, 117, 129–130, 131, 192, 196; stigma and, 128; strain with

shelters and, 130, 143. *See also* pet owners; pets: attachment to; pets: responsibility for; shelter workers: outreach

rescuers, 34, 48–54, 65–66, 68, 211n1 (chap. 2), 212n2 (chap. 3)

Rogers, Carl, 26. *See also* innovations

rottweiler, 31, 43, 108

sanctuaries, 45, 47, 63, 66, 193, 194. *See also* hoarding

Sandoval-Cervantes, Ivan, 44

shelter workers: as "animal social workers," 175; attachment to, 176; as community change agents, 196–198; contradictions of, 144, 163; distrust of, 190–195, 197–198; home visits by, 161, 175, 197–198; knowledge gap of, 155–158, 164–165, 191–192, 197; motivating owners by, 41–43; reducing authority of, 197; reducing expectations of, 39– 41, 144, 158–163, 198; "rescue brain" among, 160; seeing animals' perspective by, 41–42; socialization of, 160, 164–165; tragedies used by, 43. *See also* El Refugio; Humane Society of Charlotte

—outreach, 138–139, 153, 155, 158, 162, 164, 210n14; appearance of, 131, 132; bricolage by, 73; class and racial bias of, 123, 150, 165; dangers faced by, 74, 177; dependence on rescuers and volunteers by, 51–52; distrust of rescuers by, 53; door-to-door canvasing by, 129, 164; establishing community presence by, 73–75; euthanasia and, 212n4; humor used by, 76; modeling of and teaching by, 81–82, 179–180; norm seeding by, 70–72; rapport building by, 149–150, 162, 175–176, 197, 215nn4–5; realistic view of, 39–43, 91, 203; selling sterilization by, 148–155; veterinary competition and conflict with, 58– 61, 83, 195. *See also* gender; sterilization

shelters: ambiguous meaning of, 64–65; no-kill, 3, 65–66; perceptions of irresponsible owners by, 122; public strain with, 142–144, 164. *See also* animal control; shelter workers: outreach; social class; veterinarians

shih tzu, 109

social capital, 167, 189

social class, 174; agency and, 132; alienation and marginality by, 6; anthrozoology and, 7, 186; emotions and, 8, 113; everyday life and, 9, 18, 94; intersectionality and, 91, 99, 104, 168,

185; investigation by animal control and, 212n2 (chap. 4); "issues," 10; medical and social services use by parents and, 117, 186– 192, 196; pet attachment and, 95–97; pet care standards and, 92, 104, 169, 202, 204, 206; pet interaction and, 170–173, 183, 189, 209nn4–5, 210n3; shelters and, 122, 123, 129, 143, 165, 197; tourism and, 11. *See also* pets; shelter workers: outreach

social workers, 120, 130, 131, 144, 175

sociological "with," 30

South Carolina Veterinary Medical Association, 195

sterilization: at animal fairs, 58; benefits to animals, 4, 154, 211n9, 215n7; benefits to community, 5; cost of, 51, 58, 78–79, 211n1 (chap. 3); criticisms and limits of, 1, 3–4; deaths from, 155, 157; eugenics connection with, 130–131; euthanasia reduction by, 2, 4; fears of, 75–76, 152, 154–155, 156, 157, 193; history of, 1–2; humor and, 76, 152–153; income lost from, 117–122; lack of, in underserved communities, 2; as learning trigger, 71; machismo and, 76; normalization of, 72–77, 151–155, 196; overpopulation and, 122, 154; "personal reasons" for, 77; rates of, 117, 213n2; roaming reduction by, 25, 38; as sensitive topic, 214n3; symbolic payments for, 212n2 (chap. 3); treating medical problems during, 135–138, 201. *See also* gender; shelter workers: outreach; sterilization clinics

sterilization clinics, 146, 147; norm seeding at, 86; overestimating use of, 211n8; ownersolicited veterinary help at, 84; restrictions on, 214n6 (chap. 5); symbolism of paperwork and cost at, 78–80, 116; veterinary treatments provided at, 83–85; "wellness" at, 137

sterilization moralities: circumspect, 54–57; clashing, 62– 67; compatible, 48–54; competitive, 57–62; definition of, 148; distrust and, 69; as ethic of care, 68; responsibility for pets and, 68

stigma, 125–126, 128

strays, 152, 154, 166, 212n3 (chap. 3), 214n5 (chap. 6); befriending of, 97; feeding of, 12, 97, 127, 157; killing of, 11, 24; neighborhood pets as, 97–98, 199; normative roaming of, 1; versus pets, 29, 36; recognition of, as problem, 1–2;

strays, (*continued*)
as ruse for free veterinary care, 125;
versus street animals, 23–24, 210n2;
trap-neuter-release of, 154. *See also* dogs
and cats: street
street dogs and cats. *See* dogs and cats: street;
strays

trans-species social justice, 207
Tuskegee syphilis experiment, 192

urban fauna, 63

veterinarians, 5, 104, 155, 161, 162, 179, 205, 211n2,
212n2 (chap. 4), 214n7; access to, 11, 94, 105–
106, 114, 116, 210n9, 212n5; cost of, 13, 77, 79,
84, 125, 126, 130, 146, 211n1 (chap. 3), 216n6;
demand for, 12; intergroup competition
with, 48, 55, 57–61, 67, 83, 193, 195, 200–201,
212n5, 216n4; outreach work and, 49, 50, 51,
53, 73, 74, 75, 82, 84–86, 212n4; shelter, 14, 52,
64, 124, 127, 135–139, 195, 196, 214n6 (chap. 5),
214n8; stakeholders of, 216n2; sterilization

campaigns and, 1; training of, 65. *See also*
Colegio de Medicos Veterinarios
veterinary capital: bonding, 179–183; bridging, 174–179; definition of, 167; exclusionary,
172–174; inclusionary, 168–172
veterinary care: barriers to, 6, 13, 99–100, 105,
110, 116, 134; community animals and, 37;
community outreach for, 3; crisis of access
to, 2–3; demand for, 200, 212n5; deserts,
213n5; palliative, 104; variable standards of,
99–100, 122, 123, 144, 160–161
—low-cost: conflict among providers of, 61;
defense of, 58, 60; demand for, 161, 195; hesitancy to use, 117; misuse of, 58, 146–147, 195;
mobile vans for, 201; subsequent use of private practitioners and, 200; symbolic payments for, 212n2 (chap. 3); symbolism of,
169; as trade-off, 192–193. *See also* Pets for
Life
Vida, 61, 211n3

Washington Post, 3
World Health Organization (WHO), 2